# MADAM AMBASSADOR

# MADAM AMBASSADOR

## Three Years of Diplomacy, Dinner Parties, and Democracy in Budapest

Ambassador Eleni Tsakopoulos Kounalakis

God Bless America

**THE NEW PRESS**

NEW YORK
LONDON

The opinions and characterizations in this book are those of the author and do not
necessarily represent official positions of the United States government.

Requests for permission to reproduce selections from this book should be mailed to: Permissions
Department, The New Press, 120 Wall Street, 31st floor, New York, NY 10005.

Published in the United States by The New Press, New York, 2015
Distributed by Perseus Distribution

ISBN 978-1-62097-111-6 (hardcover)
ISBN 978-1-62097-112-3 (e-book)
CIP data available.

The New Press publishes books that promote and enrich public discussion and understanding of
the issues vital to our democracy and to a more equitable world. These books are made possible
by the enthusiasm of our readers; the support of a committed group of donors, large and small;
the collaboration of our many partners in the independent media and the not-for-profit sector;
booksellers, who often hand-sell New Press books; librarians; and above all by our authors.

www.thenewpress.com

Composition by dix!
This book was set in Adobe Caslon

Printed in the United States of America

2   4   6   8   10   9   7   5   3   1

*This book is dedicated to my family. It is also dedicated to all the families of the U.S. Foreign Service. We were honored and privileged to serve with you.*

# CONTENTS

# MADAM AMBASSADOR

# 1

# Boar Hunt

I lifted my rifle and peered through the military scope at a snow-roughened landscape, scanning the dead cornstalks and winter-stripped trees for wild boar. Crouched in the chill of a spartan wooden hunting blind, listening to helicopters patrol the nearby border of Hungary and Ukraine, I wondered if any other United States ambassador had ever been in my situation.

The phrase "Madam Ambassador" conjures an elegantly coiffed Pamela Harriman holding court in a Parisian drawing room, lifting a champagne flute and charming her fellow diplomats. As a passionate lifelong Democrat, I admired Mrs. Harriman, but I was pretty sure she had never set foot in a Central European boar blind. This rustic look-out sat about five feet off the ground, big enough for four people and bare except for a ledge running around the perimeter to serve as a prop for hunters' rifles. For company I had my hunting guide for the afternoon, Lajos Kaknics,* and our interpreter, Gréta, a young woman from

---

*In Hungary, family names are used first, followed by given names. My guide, for example, would be Kaknics Lajos. Throughout the book, I have used the English system of given names first.

a local village. The dozen other members of the hunting party were far away in blinds of their own, perched on stilts somewhere in the sprawling acres of forest and fields made available to the Hungarian Ministry of Defense and its guests, waiting for game.

Three weeks before, newly sworn in as President Barack Obama's personal representative to Hungary, I had presented my credentials to President László Sólyom. Since then I'd been making the diplomatic rounds in Budapest; I'd been busy getting to know the embassy staff and settling in with my husband and our two young sons at the ambassador's residence, where we would spend the next three-and-a-half years. This trip to Lónya, a village four hours east of the capital, was my first venture into the countryside. Truth be told, I was nervous, but not for the obvious reasons.

Hunting didn't intimidate me—I grew up in a family of hunters and had handled plenty of guns. I could take the icy weather, even though I was a Northern Californian through and through and a Greek American besides, more accustomed to bright sun and blue skies than to the mournful, monochromatic tones of Central Europe in February. And it didn't bother me that, aside from Gréta, I was the only woman on the hunting expedition—I was often the only woman working on the projects I ran for my family's land development company back in Sacramento. But I knew that for all their graciousness and friendliness, many of the men on the trip expected me to fail, and that was nettling. Sure, my own ego was at risk, but my position was more important. I was the brand-new ambassador to Hungary, entrusted with representing my president and my country, and I feared that a blunder on my part would reflect badly on all of us. It was possible that everyone else would bring in a boar but I would come back empty-handed. Every time I heard gunfire in the distance, I worried that I was inching closer to that reality.

I was still in a bit of a daze that I was in Hungary at all, because for five months I'd been training to go to Singapore, a vibrant city-state whose gangbusters economy and democratic challenges would, I knew, provide me with an action-packed few years. But that position had evaporated at almost the last moment, and although I chose Hungary from among four European countries offered to me, I feared that an ambassadorship in Central Europe would be a dull one compared with fast-moving Asia. Hungary had a complex and often tragic past: from the ill-fated Austro-Hungarian Empire through two world wars and decades of Soviet domination, the country had consistently found itself on the wrong side of twentieth-century history, and its people had suffered accordingly. But twenty years after the fall of communism, Hungary was a full-fledged member of the European Union and the NATO alliance, and its relations with the United States hummed along smoothly. The bad old days were over, I figured, and wonderful though the country was, there wouldn't be much excitement.

At forty-three, I was one of the youngest women ever to serve as U.S. ambassador, and I was full of energy. I'd leapt into work at the embassy, eagerly meeting with my staff and getting to know the diplomatic layout of the capital, paying courtesy calls on my fellow ambassadors and sitting down with Prime Minister Gordon Bajnai and other high-ranking Hungarian officials (though it already was clear that they would be swept out of power in the upcoming elections in April 2010). With my family, I'd begun to explore Budapest, an ancient city divided by the Danube River that visually combined the splendor of its imperial past with the starkness of its years in the Eastern bloc. Budapest made me think of a magnificent ball gown that through age and neglect had become faded, dusty, and torn. But how magnificent it once was!

A few days before the hunting trip, Colonel Robert Duggleby, the American embassy's defense attaché, had given a reception and dinner at his home to introduce me to members of the Hungarian Ministry of Defense, as well as the foreign attaché corps. He and his wife, Ginny, had been in Budapest for about a year; both warm southerners, they had a gift for bringing people together and making them feel at home. Ginny was an accomplished cook, and her guests, foreign and American alike, eagerly dug into the cheese grits and cornbread she placed among the catered items at their dinners. Although most of the guests at this event had brought their spouses, I was there alone. Because I was working during my sons' winter break from the American International School, my husband, Markos, had taken our two boys, seven and eight years old, on a "guys' trip" to Egypt.

Colonel Duggleby was career military, and it showed, from his ramrod posture and bemedaled chest to his cool, unflappable manner. A fluent Russian speaker and onetime defense attaché in Uzbekistan, he'd studied the former Soviet republics and would be, I knew, a valuable resource to me in Hungary. I hadn't known him long, but I liked and respected him very much, and I wanted to develop a good rapport with him. My personal experience with the military, however, was rather slim. Other than my father, who'd served in the reserves but was never called for duty, none of my relatives or close friends had been in the service.

As I sat freezing on the icy bench inside that blind in Lónya, I thought about how after one of my first briefings with the colonel, I started casting about for a common area of interest with him and hit upon hunting. I mentioned that I'd grown up in a family of bird hunters. And with that we connected, happily trading stories of our experiences and shared love of the outdoors. As we stood together enjoying the warm reception in his living room, the colonel pulled the head of the Hungarian armed forces, General László Tömböl, over to meet me. After introducing me as a Californian and a business executive, he added a final flourish: "And my ambassador can hunt."

I appreciated his attempt to make me sound tough. At five foot two, with a slight build, I am frequently the smallest person in any professional situation; to some men, I probably resemble a middle-school girl. Although General Tömböl was not a tall man, even he had to lean over to talk to me. He was a serious and imposing person, with a thick black mustache and a highly decorated uniform that stiffly crumpled as he bent down to me. As chief of defense, he was Hungary's counterpart to the head of the U.S. Joint Chiefs of Staff.

"Your Excellency, Madam Ambassador. It is my honor to meet you," he said, lifting my hand toward his mustache to kiss it, a ritual that I was quickly becoming accustomed to. "It's wonderful news that you enjoy hunting. You know, Madam Ambassador, Hungary is famous for its excellent hunting. Have you ever hunted wild boar?"

"Well," I stammered, "wild boar, no. But I've hunted many types of wild birds."

As it happened, a boar-hunting party was scheduled for that Saturday, two days later. "You must join us, Madam Ambassador."

I detected a challenge, ever so slight, in the general's invitation. I felt that he really didn't expect me to take him up on this offer. Ever since I was a schoolgirl, I'd hated being underestimated; I tended to react to any dare by, foolishly or not, jumping to accept it.

So I smiled at General Tömböl, thinking, Markos and the boys won't be back until Sunday. "Yes, I'd love to go on a boar hunt!"

He looked astonished. The fact is, ambassadors generally take pains to shield themselves from embarrassment or indignity—although I didn't exactly realize that at the time—and this excursion to a far-flung forest with a party of Hungarian military men had the potential for plenty of both.

I may have presented a game face, but I wasn't reckless. I knew I was putting myself in a vulnerable position and that I would need an entourage. So I asked not only Colonel Duggleby but also Paul O'Friel, head of the embassy's political and economic section, to accompany me to Lónya.

Paul had been in the Foreign Service for two decades. But before that, he was a Marine Corps officer; he stood nearly six and a half feet tall. He had been in Budapest only for six months, but he seemed to know everybody already, and though we'd met just a few weeks before, we had instantly clicked. Paul was a gentleman and a philosopher, an elegant tough guy, and I thought he could bridge the gap between the delegation of Hungarian military men and me—someone who was as civilian as civilian could get.

Rob, Paul, and I left Budapest before dawn, driving through the thick forests and dormant winter fields stretching across the Carpathian basin east of the capital. I was surprised to see that the landscape resembled the Sacramento area as it was when I was growing up, flat and fertile, and to learn that it produced many of the same crops, from sugar beets and corn to grapes. Of course, Sacramento didn't have the gray patina that was the hallmark of this Central European landscape. A friend of mine who took up his posting in Kiev around the same time observed, "Being in Central Europe in the winter is like stepping inside an old black-and-white film." Brand-new big-box retail outlets like Tesco, the European equivalent of Wal-Mart, occasionally appeared as we drove through the countryside, but most of the structures were old, gray concrete houses, some still roofed with straw and patched with mud. I guessed these villages hadn't changed much in generations.

When we arrived at the hunting lodge in Lónya, about a dozen military men came out to greet us. Besides our host, General Tömböl, the group included several colonels and the commander of the Hungarian Special Forces battalion. Though they had traded in their uniforms for typical hunting garb, their stature and comportment radiated an intensity that even jokes and alcohol couldn't disguise. On the one hand, they were ready to be "at ease" and enjoy a day of food, wine, and hunting. On the other hand, with me there, they were compelled to stay formal. The combination made things a bit awkward, and there was a nervous tinge to our laughter.

Experience had taught me to bundle up for a winter hunt, so I was well set with my parka, warm hat, and gloves. But poor Gréta's fashionable slacks and dainty shoes were more appropriate for an office. I'd also known to bring my hunting license, which I had managed to find in an unpacked box, though nobody checked it. My hunting guide, Lajos, was a teddy bear of a man, jovial and pink faced from the shots of brandy that he'd tossed back with the others. After he had helped Gréta and me into mud boots and the burly men of our hunting party had passed around more shots of pálinka—a strong fruit brandy—we divided into groups of three and piled into open jeeps for the journey into the snowy woods.

When I had first agreed to come, I figured I could gracefully bow out of the shooting if I was uncomfortable, telling everyone that I would "shoot" with a camera and just observe. That idea evaporated when Lajos handed me a high-caliber rifle equipped with a long-range scope. Although I'd fired a rifle before, I'd only hunted with shotguns. Fortunately, this rifle was remarkably small, scaled-down for a person my size, and it felt good in my hands. It was a far cry from some of the massive, heavy shotguns I'd been given in the past. I could shoot this gun, no problem, I realized with relief.

Hunting had been a big part of my life growing up on the banks of the Sacramento River, in a house my father had built at the edge of a wheat field, using plans he'd bought at the local grocery store. Most of our family friends were fellow members of the Greek American community, and when bird-hunting season opened, they all came to our house. This was not the refined sport of gentlemen in English riding clothes. It was more like *Duck Dynasty* with an immigrant twist. As a kid, I tagged along in the back of a pickup truck, shot targets, and plucked the birds for my mother to cook. When I came home from college, I hunted with my father as a way to spend time with him. But then work and kids intervened. It had been a long time since I'd held a gun.

It was about two o'clock in the afternoon by the time we'd climbed the frosted ladder into the blind, wrapped ourselves in warm blankets—Lajos bundling up poor Gréta as best he could—and set up for the hunt. Lajos assured me that the boars would be ambling along any minute. He had personally made sure that a large amount of dried corn was spread around the base of our blind. Looking through my scope at the landscape of bare trees, underbrush, and rattling cornstalks, waiting for game to appear, I thought of the Hapsburgs, who had once ruled Hungary. Had their extravagant hunting parties ever ventured this far east? During communist times, every single stitch of land in the country, every house, every factory, and almost every head of sheep, was owned by the central government. Even after an extensive privatization process, the government still owned tens of thousands of individual properties around Hungary. I wondered who'd had the good fortune to end up with this one—a huge swath of forest, easily hundreds of acres, and a hunter's paradise.

For an hour, my little group sat in silence. In the distance I heard occasional gunfire from the other hunters. I kept my eye to my scope, but finally, having seen nothing but birds and my own vaporized breath, I put down my gun, and Lajos, Gréta, and I began to talk, taking care to keep our voices low.

"How long does the typical hunt last?" I asked.

"We'll stay out until after the sun goes down," Lajos said in Hungarian, Gréta dutifully translating.

That meant about three more hours in the freezing cold. Listening to the far-off gunfire, I wondered if the rest of the hunting party was having success. It would be very embarrassing if everybody but me got a boar. Briefly, I considered climbing back down the ladder and looking for game myself, as I would have done with my father on bird hunts back home. But my blankets were warm, and I didn't want to run the risk of being mistaken for prey. *That* would be a terrible start for a new ambassador.

We waited, occasionally chatting, for a long time. Almost three hours later, when the late-afternoon sun had all but faded away, Lajos's eyes opened wide. Motioning me to be quiet, he pointed into the distant woods. Slowly, I propped my rifle on the ledge and peered through the scope. It took a long time to see what he had heard: a group of ten or so boars making their way through the woods, about a quarter-mile off. As soon as I spotted them, they stopped. I could most clearly make out the animal at the head of the line: shaggy, grayish brown, and at least three hundred pounds—the size of a small brown bear you might see at the zoo.

When you hunt ducks with a shotgun, you spray shot into the general area where the bird is flying, bringing your game down with a smattering of small hits. A rifle, however, shoots a single bullet, which must be precisely aimed. Earlier in the day, Lajos told me that when I took a shot at a boar, I should aim right at its ear so that the bullet would go into its brain and kill it instantly. But this boar was standing directly behind a thin, straight tree, and I could barely make out its ear, just to one side of the trunk.

When your heart is pounding and your adrenaline is rushing, time moves very slowly, but your mind moves fast. Mine was rapidly calculating: if I shot too far in one direction, I might blow off the animal's snout; if I shot too far in the other, I would strike its body. Either way, the boar might run away and suffer horribly before bleeding to death, and I could not bear the thought of causing that. So I took a breath and carefully aimed at the narrow space between the edge of the tree trunk and the boar's ear. As high as the stakes were, I would rather hit the tree and miss than fatally injure the animal for nothing.

I knew this would feel very different from any hunting I'd ever done. As I squinted through the scope, getting ready to shoot, a question formed in my mind, as clear as if someone had spoken it.

"Am I going to kill this animal?"

Yes, I decided, I would—but I would not make it suffer. I hugged the rifle to my body for better control, as my father had taught me, and I squeezed the trigger.

There was an explosion, and the boar fell dead on the snow. For a moment, I was stunned. Lajos began to holler.

"You got him! You got him! A perfect shot!" The rest of the boars made an uproar as they scattered and disappeared from my sight, and the echo of my gunshot was met with more scattered fire from my fellow hunters, who were shooting at the fleeing boars.

The sun was going down, and by now it was really cold. I was so jumpy from excitement that I happily would have returned to the lodge at that point. But Lajos insisted that because I was such a good shot, we should keep hunting. I was more than ready to go, but he was the one with the radio. "Anyway, two would be really something," I thought, imagining what my fellow hunters would be hauling back to the lodge. So we stayed. Alas, no more boar appeared. Eventually, a jeep ambled up the jagged frozen road to retrieve us. We climbed out of the blind and headed several hundred yards into the woods, to where my boar lay dead in its tracks. A trickle of blood was visible from a small hole about an inch under its ear, in almost the exact place where I'd aimed. The guide saw it too and looked at me with what might have been admiration but was more likely just amazement.

As my adrenaline rush tapered off and we bounced along on the road back to the lodge, I took a brief moment to reflect on what I'd done. I could have choked at the critical moment, intimidated by being in an unfamiliar place, among strangers. But I hadn't. I'd been able to take what I knew and use it to hit my target, calmly and without fear. I promised myself I would try to remember that moment and push back whenever I started to doubt my own capabilities, especially for the next three years.

Ours was the last group to return to the lodge. As we jumped out of the jeep, the rest of the hunters poured outside to greet us. It turned out they'd had a terrible day of hunting. Only General Tömböl had managed to get something—a piglet. Rob Duggleby had become so frustrated that he'd left his blind and wandered the fields looking for boar, his feet nearly frostbitten, somehow confident that he would not be targeted as game.

The military men had been warming themselves with shots of pálinka, and they gathered around me in a laughing circle, pushing the tray of shotglasses toward me. General Tömböl said, "Your Excellency, Madam Ambassador, I am sorry that you came so far for such a disappointing hunt, but I must commend you for staying out in the cold for so long. It must have been difficult for you."

I smiled proudly at him. "Oh, but I got one!"

For the second time that week, the general's face went loose with surprise. There was a beat of silence as the group took in my news, then the men began to laugh and cheer, and I was swept in to dinner on a wave of bonhomie. Rob Duggleby and Paul O'Friel, disappointed by their own lack of trophies to bring home, beamed with pride on my behalf.

Though the lodge was a new building, rich tradition was evident. Boar tusks and stuffed animal heads lined the wood-paneled walls, and hides covered the floors. A fire snapped and leaped in the giant stone fireplace. We sat down to dinner at a long table set with magnificent Herend china, and we loaded up on roast boar (one from a previous hunt), accompanied by wine and even more pálinka. As the drink flowed, the men got more relaxed, growing bawdier by the moment. This took me back to the frequent dilemma of my business days, when I often would be the only woman in a group of men. As a woman executive, you don't want men to think of you as a woman, but you don't want them to think of you as one of the boys, either. In this case, I made a point of drinking only the polite minimum.

Before long we stood up from the table to begin to take our leave, and I noticed that my fellow hunters were glancing at me as they talked among themselves. A few of them were grinning, but I also detected some nervousness. As we made our way toward the front door and out of the lodge, I whispered to Paul. "What's going on?"

In front of the building, the hunt master had stretched out General Tömböl's little piglet and my three-hundred-pound boar on the snow and ceremoniously surrounded them with pots of plants. The piglet was pathetically small, but with his curving tusks and dark, massive body, my boar was a magnificent animal, worthy of the reverent treatment. What a beautiful custom, I thought.

Then the hunt master timidly explained that I was obliged to participate in a ritual. In Hungary, when you shoot your first boar, you're required to kneel over it and be hit on the behind with a switch so that you can feel some of the animal's pain.

"But the animal felt no pain!" I joked.

Lajos quickly agreed. "It was a very clean shot." But rules, it seemed, were rules. The hunt master brandished a wooden switch, but he was obviously conflicted. The rest of the hunting party looked a bit embarrassed.

I turned to Rob and Paul. "Should I do this?"

"It's your call, ma'am." They were not about to tell me how to proceed.

I could have said, "Colonel Duggleby will take the hit for me." Everybody would have laughed, and Rob might even have complied.

The importance of participating in local traditions, I thought to myself, was one of the things they teach you in ambassador "charm school" at the State Department. So I walked over to the boar.

Normally, the victorious hunter gets on his hands and knees over his quarry. But this was a big boar, too big for me to do that; I had to lie directly on the animal's bristly, muddy, stinky hide. Fleas nipped at my face and hands as I looked at the encircling group of men's legs and waited for the switch. The whole process took less than a minute, and the nervous hunt master switched me very lightly. Although the whole thing started out as rather amusing, I felt a sudden rush of humiliation as I scrambled back up to my feet.

I chewed over the switching on the long drive back to Budapest, riding with Paul and Rob in our lumbering armored SUV, the trunk of which was loaded up with frozen boar meat, a trade for what I had left behind. They'd also given me the switch as a souvenir of my day. If it had just been me, Eleni, I would have laughed and been proud to have endured the old tradition. But it was different now. I would often look back on that moment and get a little red faced. And I would keep the switch in a prominent place in my office as a reminder that I wasn't "just me" anymore, I was the American ambassador, and that if I was ever asked again to do something that felt uncomfortable, like lying on top of a boar in front of a group of Hungarian military men, I would graciously decline.

The awkwardness of the switching incident could not spoil the excitement of the day. On the drive back to Budapest, still feeling the high of the hunt despite my exhaustion, I began telling Rob and Paul about some of my other adventures. Over the years my passion for extreme hiking and skiing had led to some challenging situations, like the time on a backcountry ski trip when I had to wrap my blistered feet in duct tape to keep the skin from peeling off.

Paul and Rob enjoyed hearing my stories, and as the slow, heavy car made its way through the sleeping countryside, they shared some of their own experiences. In 1989, as part of the Army's 82nd Airborne Division, with only a handful of practice jumps behind him and an eighteen-month-old baby at home, Rob had parachuted into a critter-infested swamp outside the Panama City airport, where U.S. and Panamanian troops were battling, part of America's invasion to oust the drug-trafficking dictator Manuel Noriega. The next year, as part of Operation Desert Storm, Rob went to Iraq, where he saw more violence and destruction. Paul shared some stories from his days in the marines, then went on to talk about the challenges of his recent service as a State Department officer in Iraq, where he led something called a provincial reconstruction team—a unit consisting of military officers and diplomats that worked to rebuild stable communities in war-torn areas. He was there in 2007, before President Obama won election, when there was no end in sight to the war.

This was the first time I'd heard war stories directly from the people who had lived them. Listening to Rob and Paul, I felt a bit ashamed for having tried to impress them with my own meager adventures. But beyond that, I was in awe of these two men. I'd never known soldiers, and I certainly hadn't understood that soldiers were like this: humble, quiet in their courage and patriotism.

A few days later, with Rob and fellow members of his team in my office, we started to talk about the boar hunt. They were all career military men, and I mentioned the moment when I aimed at the boar and squeezed the trigger. I told them how different it felt to use a rifle, with a single bullet to bring down a huge boar, after hunting ducks with shotguns. I told them about the voice in my head that asked if I was prepared to kill the animal. "Is that what it's like when you're in combat and you have another human being in your sights?" I asked Rob and the other men. "When you know you have a clean shot, do you ask yourself whether you are ready to do what you are about to do?"

Several of them looked down and silently nodded. We all knew that I couldn't completely understand their experiences, but I felt a sincere, deep respect for them, as well as gratitude for their sacrifices and service to our country.

Not long after, I had another experience with the military that marked me for the rest of my time in Budapest. Thirty-six Ohio National Guardsmen had been training with their Hungarian counterparts far out in the countryside in preparation for the whole group's deployment to Afghanistan. They would be deployed to a base in Northern Afghanistan where fighting recently had heated up substantially, to partner with the Hungarians on a team that would battle alongside Afghan forces they had trained. Rob Duggleby asked me to address the Ohio guardsmen in a video conference before they left Hungary. "It will be a nice send-off for them, hearing a few words from the ambassador," he said. Of course I agreed. He gave me a few talking points, and we headed to the embassy's public affairs office. I had given plenty of speeches and knew how to talk to groups, so I wasn't particularly nervous about doing this.

When the video screen lit up, I saw dozens of young men in camouflage staring back at me. They had taken off their caps, and the shock of seeing their bright, eager young faces knocked me silent. They were waiting for me to offer wisdom and meaning, to provide assurances and help them build their confidence as they headed off to fight in a harsh, strange, and notoriously dangerous place.

My mouth went dry. I prayed my face didn't betray how inadequate and overwhelmed I felt to be seeing these boys off to war. It had been hard enough listening to Paul and Rob talk about their experiences. These young men weren't much older than my sons.

I thanked them for their service and impressed upon them that Afghanistan was President Obama's number one foreign policy priority. I also asked them where they were from in the States and how they had enjoyed training in Hungary. They cheerfully answered me, respectful and polite. I'm sure they never guessed how uncomfortable I felt. But

I resolved that from that moment on, I would learn as much as I could about our military and that I would support our soldiers in every way possible.

I swore that the next time I saw young soldiers off to war, I would be worthy to do so.

# 2

# Ambassador Extraordinary and Plenipotentiary

Several weeks before my boar-hunting adventure, I'd woken up to the sight of the American flag gently waving in the wind outside my window, visible through a break in the curtains and illuminated by the outside security lighting. It was Monday, January 11, 2010, my very first day in Budapest. It was still dark outside, and although I should have been exhausted after flying in from Washington the day before, jet lag and excitement made it hard to sleep. It was going to be a big day. Not only would I be presenting my credentials to the president of Hungary, I'd be meeting the embassy staff and settling into the office where I'd be spending the next three to four years.

From pictures, I was familiar with the main embassy building, an elegant, ornate structure built at the dawn of the twentieth century. And although I'd seen photos of the residence where my family and I would be living, they had not prepared me for what the house was really like. American embassy residences around the world are renowned for their magnificence; they've inspired coffee-table books and reams of admiring prose. For U.S. ambassadors in Europe, the

15

house is supposed to be one of the best parts of the job. But the truth was, from the second I drove through the gate, the Budapest residence was a shock: darkened by encroaching trees and tangled shrubbery; filled with heavy old furniture; smelling of mold, dust, and rotten pipes. Everything creaked—the wood floors, the doors, the staircase banister, and the stairs themselves. It made me think of the Addams Family.

Fortunately, I was so excited to be in Budapest that I could look past the state of the residence. And really, nobody seemed to mind it as much as I did. Markos and our boys, eight-year-old Neo and seven-year-old Eon, had arrived more than a week before me. Because a new semester was starting at the American International School in Budapest and I had to stay in Washington for a conference at the State Department, we decided that Markos could take the boys to Hungary and get them settled. Honestly, it was a big stretch for him. I'd once joked that Markos was a great father but just a so-so mother. He was loving, devoted, and engaged, but when it came to the basics of the boys' routine—things like teeth brushing and bedtime—he could be as forgetful as they were. But Markos had mobilized impressively, checking the boys into the school, meeting their teachers, and signing them up for the bus service. Long bus rides made me carsick when I was a child, and I expected the boys to balk at taking the bus. But they loved it, as it gave them social time with kids from all grades. They loved the school too. With its expansive sports fields and brand-new facilities, the American International School of Budapest was a far cry from the concrete buildings and playgrounds of the boys' San Francisco school. In a phone call to Washington, they had excitedly reported to me, "It's bigger than Stanford, Mom. Bigger than Stanford!"

The day before, as my car drove in past the gates of the residence for the first time, I found all three guys playing in the vast front yard, covered in snow, having the time of their lives. Markos had bought the boys shovels, and they discovered that they loved to clear snow and socialize with the guards. My cousin Sofia, who lived in Athens, had flown in to stay with them until I arrived. Sofia was more like my sister than my cousin. We'd grown up together. The boys loved and trusted her, and I knew that my absence, the unfamiliarity of their new home, and the gloominess of the Central European winter would be less obvious to them with Sofia there.

Rather than flying to Budapest alone, I had persuaded my twenty-three-year-old youngest sister, Alexa, to take the trip with me. That first afternoon together, the six of us bundled up and marched out of the house, past the guard booth, and down the hill to the nearest shopping center, about two miles away. The guards must have shaken their heads as they watched us walk off, throwing snowballs, chattering in English and Greek, and literally jumping up and down in our excitement at being reunited in such a fascinating place. Although Sofia would leave in a few days, Alexa planned to stay on, and we expected a steady stream of relatives to start cycling through within weeks.

Our large, close, energetic family would surely brighten up the dank old house, I thought as I lifted myself out of bed and began to get ready for the day. I pulled a newly unpacked black pantsuit from my closet. Almost every suit I owned was black, blue, or beige, and almost every blouse I owned was white. My "uniform" approach to dressing had served me well throughout my career to minimize the time and effort it took to get ready in the morning. Since this day was special, today's black pantsuit had a shiny satin collar, and the white blouse was adorned with an elegant bow at the neck. As usual, I pulled my hair back into a neat ponytail—another time-saving trick that virtually eliminated the risk of a bad hair day.

I went into the boys' room and nudged them awake, telling them to dress quickly in the clothes I had laid out for them the night before. As I made my way downstairs to the kitchen, I took one quick turn around the large home. I paused for a moment to survey the "safe room" of the residence. The doors were steel plated, with rows of bolts, and a radio in the corner occasionally beeped and sent muffled voices from the marines' security detail into what would otherwise have been a quiet sanctuary. I couldn't help but wonder if I would ever use this room for its intended purpose. I shook off the thought and kept going.

Once in the large industrial kitchen, I opened and closed the stainless-steel cupboards in search of coffee. It was early, and none of the house staff had arrived yet. Florescent lights buzzed above and cast the room in a pale yellow light. As I opened and closed cupboards, I discovered antique bottle openers and an array of post-communist-era food processors. I was suddenly reminded of my Aunt Maria, who, after living through the lean war years in Greece, refused ever to throw anything away. It had been twenty years since the fall of the wall, but the state of our kitchen made it seem much more recent. Finally, with great relief, I found the ground coffee and French press that Markos and Sofia had procured soon after their arrival.

Before long, the rest of my family had come downstairs and we were all crowded in the kitchen, laughing and excited, pulling together breakfast. The house did not have everyday dishes, and although I made a note to get some as soon as possible, that morning we had no choice but to use the official State Department china for our breakfast. Each piece had a rich gold rim and was faintly stamped with stars and stripes, with the Great Seal of the United States elegantly hand-painted in the middle. "Who cares about the kitchen," Markos joked, "when you get to eat Cheerios out of bowls like these!"

Markos had been great about taking on more responsibility for the kids, but I knew he would not accept any home improvement assignments. I would have to deal with the house later. First, I had to get my arms around the embassy.

After saying my good-byes to Markos, Sofia, Alexa, and the boys, I headed downstairs to find a gleaming black Cadillac waiting for me, quietly idling in the frigid morning air. Zoltán, my driver, had already warmed it up. After he swiftly closed the house door behind me, he rushed around to tug open the rear passenger-side door. This took some doing. The door was built with thick bulletproof windows and was very heavy. Settling myself in the soft seat, I remembered that back in Washington a CIA officer had ribbed me about how, in any car, the right rear passenger seat would always be mine—unless Hillary Clinton was riding with me; in that case, the secretary of state would take precedence for the favored spot. As Zoltán pulled away from the house, past massive overgrown shrubbery and through the security gates to the street below, I saw that he had fastened an American flag into place on the front right side of the car.

Most people think of the "U.S. Embassy" as a building. In fact, the term "embassy" refers to the entire mission, which in Budapest included three nonresidential sites and dozens of officers' residences like mine, where we held frequent events. The building that people think of as the embassy is actually called the Chancery, and that's where my office was located, in central Budapest. To get there from the ambassador's residence, high in the Buda Hills, Zoltán had to cross over the Danube River to what was once the city of Pest. (Although Budapest's roots stretch further back than the Roman Empire, Buda and Pest were joined only in 1873.)

As we passed over the river, "The Blue Danube" started playing on the car radio. This coincidence was surprising enough, but for me the music had a special association. Back in Sacramento, when I was about twelve years old, the local PBS station had advertised a complete set of Johann Strauss waltzes. I was a first-generation American, the daughter of a Greek immigrant who had started his life in America as a farmworker. And for some reason I mailed away for the set of Viennese waltzes, playing the entrancing music on my plastic record player over and over, sometimes dancing along with it. It was strange to think of that girl in Sacramento and how she came to be here, the first Greek American woman to serve as a U.S. ambassador. Ten years since I'd first declared my interest in serving, nearly ten months of grueling vetting and training, and here I was.

But there was plenty of time to think back and examine the unlikely series of events that had unfolded, leading me to be sitting in the back of this car making its way over the Danube to the main building of the U.S. Embassy. For now, I needed to clear my head and get ready for my first day on the job.

The big black Cadillac with diplomatic plates was well known in Budapest, but the guards at the Chancery did not need to see it coming to know that we were near. As we approached our destination, Zoltán picked up his radio and announced, "Outlook One, Outlook One. This is Blue,* come in." As we turned the final corner, the guards

---

*I've changed code names.

were already mobilizing for our arrival. I watched as the massive gates moved aside to let us in.

The tradition of sending ambassadors from one country, or kingdom, to another goes back hundreds of years. The term "ambassador" is thought to date to the fourteenth century. By the sixteenth century, kings regularly sent ambassadors to live in each other's courts, serving as the points of contact for communications between monarchs. The ambassador would also gather information about the events happening at his post that he believed would interest his king.

The Congress of Vienna of 1815 formalized the system of diplomacy that we use today. At that time, ambassadors were defined as "diplomats of the highest rank, formally representing the head of state, with plenipotentiary powers." Today, an ambassador's full title is "ambassador extraordinary and plenipotentiary."* I had to look up the word "plenipotentiary" when I first heard it. It means "a person invested with the full power of independent action on behalf of their government." But this anecdote works even better than the definition: immediately after my swearing-in, one of my new colleagues whispered in my ear, "Just remember, it's always better not to declare war without first checking in with the president." In the days before a world leader could pick up a phone and speak directly to his counterpart in another country, the role was indispensable and extremely powerful. To this day, when the ambassador speaks, he or she speaks not just *for* his or her country but also *as* that country.

Most countries have embassies, and other types of missions, in the nations with which they have diplomatic relations. There are more than 190 countries in the world, and the United States has diplomatic relations with almost all of them. When we deal with countries where we don't have embassies, such as Iran and North Korea, communications happen via Washington, D.C., and often through a third party. It's important to note that not all of our missions are in other countries. We also have ambassadors to important international organizations, such as the North Atlantic Treaty Organization (NATO), the United

*See the Wikipedia entry for "ambassador": en.wikipedia.org/wiki/Ambassador.

Nations, the Association of Southeast Asian Nations (ASEAN), and others. In total, the United States has 294 diplomatic outposts around the world, all engaged in implementing foreign policy while gathering information about the world and sending it home.

A good way to understand the system is to imagine a wheel: the 294 missions form the spokes, and the hub is the State Department. The State Department's headquarters in Washington is known as Main State or, since September 2000, HST for the Harry S. Truman Building. It's also known by the name of its famous neighborhood, Foggy Bottom, and occasionally by the more descriptive term "the Mother Ship." It is a fairly nondescript government building. But once you're familiar with it, you'll start spotting it frequently in movies and on television shows.

Radiating outward from the State Department hub to all our embassies and missions are directions for the implementation and delivery of U.S. foreign policy. Some of the policy is well established, while some is fresh from the president's desk. The president of the United States creates foreign policy, but from one president to the next, policy changes far less than you might think. Although presidents come and go—and even though the White House frequently changes political parties—the vast majority of U.S. foreign policy stays the same, and so does the State Department's role in implementing it.

Radiating inward from our missions back to the State Department are information and feedback. Most of these communications are in the form of cables, which in the old days were transmitted via cable but now are sent via secure computer systems. Once the information is processed at the State Department, the president uses it to formulate foreign policy. Hillary Clinton, who was secretary of state for almost the entire time I was ambassador, helped to quantify the volume of information that makes its way into the State Department: when she was asked if she'd read a cable related to security at our mission in Benghazi, Libya, she noted that her office receives 1.43 million cables from U.S. embassies and outposts around the world each year, all addressed to her. These included thousands of cables from Embassy Budapest— which during my time as ambassador were all addressed from me.

As U.S. ambassador to Hungary, I had two main areas of

responsibility. I was the chief of mission at Embassy Budapest, with its several hundred employees and sixteen sections, ranging from public affairs to the consular section to our political and economic offices. I was also President Barack Obama's personal representative in Hungary. In this role, I would meet with the leaders of the Hungarian government—as friends and allies, we kept open lines of communication between our countries on subjects as diverse as security cooperation and educational exchanges. If these officials couldn't talk to President Obama directly, they would talk to me.

As I arrived at the Chancery on that first morning, I saw that it was even more magnificent than it appeared in photos. The six-story, cream-colored building stood regally at the edge of Szabadság (Freedom) Square, Budapest's historic heart, which since the end of the nineteenth century had witnessed protests, revolution, heartbreak, and liberation. After the U.S. embassies were bombed in Kenya and Tanzania in 1998, killing 224 people, we began building and rebuilding missions outside of city centers, in fortress-like structures. At one point, there were plans to do the same in Budapest, but the old Chancery was spared when it was determined that the security around the perimeter of the building could be upgraded sufficiently to address possible threats. As a result, it is one of the few American chancery buildings still in a city center, in a historic building. And it is beautiful.

I stepped out of the car and onto the steps leading to the bulletproof plate-glass windows of the Chancery's main entryway and was greeted by my deputy chief of mission, Jeff Levine. The deputy chief of mission is the ambassador's senior-most adviser and runs the embassy's day-to-day operations. If the ambassador is out of the country, the deputy becomes the chargé d'affaires and retains all the authority of the ambassador until he or she returns. Because the deputy chief of mission is so critical, the ambassador and his or her deputy should never be out of the country at the same time, and rarely are.

Jeff Levine had been posted in Budapest for two and a half years by the time I showed up. A fellow native Californian and a career Foreign Service officer who'd served in Egypt, Cyprus, and Bulgaria, among other places, Jeff made running an embassy look easy. He was scheduled to leave Budapest to return to a job at State Department headquarters just six months after I arrived. I didn't realize it at the time, but he was determined, before he left Budapest, to teach me as much as possible about how to run the embassy. Jeff was very protective of the staff and, as he happened to be half Hungarian American, equally protective of the U.S.-Hungarian relationship.

Several of our senior staff had also come down to greet me, and I shook their hands as they formed something of a receiving line, standing at attention with their hands by their sides. As I moved down the line, shaking hands, I heard "Good morning, ma'am, welcome to Embassy Budapest" over and over.

Jeff and I had spoken several times, and he had picked me up at the airport the day before. But I hadn't met anyone else yet. They seemed happy to see me. There had been no ambassador in Budapest for more than eight months, and although an embassy manages quite well under the leadership of a chargé d'affaires, many things are put on hold. I learned later that after our first phone call, Jeff told the desk officer that he thought I would be fun, a description that baffled the officer. "You mean you think she's going to crack a lot of jokes?" she responded incredulously.

"No, of course not. She just seems to be a fun person to work with." (This may have been prescient, because Embassy Budapest would soon be known affectionately as "My Big Fat Greek Embassy" among junior State Department personnel, a play on the wildly successful film *My Big Fat Greek Wedding.*)

After I had greeted everyone, Jeff and I passed by the marine stationed at the entry, who raised his arm to salute me. I nodded my head once in acknowledgment—the signal that allowed him to lower his hand. In the Foreign Service, ambassadors hold the equivalent rank of generals. My first desk officer at the State Department once quipped that the only difference between the Foreign Service and the armed services is that the latter wear their ranks on their sleeves. Everyone knew what level everyone else was, and junior officers paid significant deference to their superiors. For those who had become ambassador by rising through the ranks of the U.S. Foreign Service, as the vast majority do, being saluted by marines may have felt natural. But I was a political appointee, part of the 30 percent or so of ambassadors who are brought in from outside and put at the top of the chain of command. I can honestly say that I never quite got used to being saluted, even though it happened every time I walked in and out of my office or in and out of the many Hungarian government buildings protected by military guards.

Jeff and I made our way through another set of heavy bulletproof doors and into an elevator. As we came off the elevator on an upper floor where his and my offices were located, we faced two large wooden doors, locked tight, with an electric keypad beside them. As Jeff punched in his codes, he pulled out his BlackBerrys, set it in a small, lockable cubby in a box full of other BlackBerrys, and motioned for me to do the same. Even though BlackBerry have a higher standard level of encryption protection than any other smartphone (the U.S. government is the device's biggest customer), the State Department took no chances with security. Everyone, including Jeff and me, had to leave our phones outside as we entered the area where we had our offices, a highly secured part of the embassy. At a briefing back in Washington, they'd told me, "Don't think of your phone as a speaking device. Think of it as a listening device. Think of it as a way for others to listen to you without your ever knowing." Even a phone that was turned off and sitting idly on the table in front of you could be turned into a bug remotely with a very simple program available for purchase from one of the Internet's many sites for spy aficionados.

We walked into the foyer that separated Jeff's office and mine. Seated at desks in front of my office were two office management specialists— the State Department term for executive assistants. As I walked in, these two women sprang from their chairs and stood at attention. This was not just a formality for their first time meeting me; it was protocol that they and any other officer in the building must stand at attention whenever I entered the room, just as they would for the president of the United States. I didn't want to disrespect State Department protocols, but this was one I relaxed pretty quickly. How do executive assistants get things done if they are constantly jumping out of their chairs?

Other elements of the chain of command were also on full display that first day at work. Jeff had called a meeting of the senior staff in my office. My staff had arranged two sofas and half a dozen chairs in a rectangle, with two of the larger armchairs together on one end. I suppose I should have realized that those two chairs were more prominent than the other seats, but I didn't. So as everyone filed into my office, I sat down on one of the sofas and prepared to start the meeting. I noticed, however, that everyone else was standing awkwardly and looking nervously at one another, as if unsure where to sit. I didn't quite understand what the problem was. When Jeff Levine walked in, the group looked to him pleadingly. He smiled, and then gestured to the two armchairs. "Ma'am, we usually sit here," he told me.

"Oh!" I quickly changed seats. The senior staff took their usual places, smiling to themselves over my mistake, and we got started.

There were about a dozen members of our senior staff, and they made up the core of what was called the embassy's country team. They included senior counselors and section heads who were employees of the State Department. Senior staff also included attachés—senior officers from the other U.S. government agencies, such as the Department of Defense, Department of Justice, and Department of Commerce—who were attached to the embassy. For about half an hour in the morning, twice a week, we would review the main internal and external embassy issues.

As we sat down together for the first time, I could feel their anticipation about what I would say.

Secretary Clinton had started her first day on the job with a town hall meeting. State Department staff from around the world tuned in to listen to her frame her intentions and her expectations. Following her example, I would try to do the same.

"Secretary Clinton said during her first remarks at the State Department that she doesn't just welcome candid input from her team, she needs it." I asked my staff to communicate directly with me on any issue they felt was important. "I understand and will always respect how the chain of command works here. But my door is always open, and I'm asking you to come directly to me, with or without an appointment, if you ever feel that there is an issue of immediate importance to our mission and our country."

There was a great deal of excitement with Hillary Clinton in charge of the State Department. Everyone could feel it. She empowered the

Foreign Service just by having accepted the job of secretary. But her presence also brought an element of inspiration that was palpable. People were ready to do their best for her, and I wanted my staff to know that I shared the same respect and admiration for their expertise and capabilities that she did.

On that first day of work, I stayed at the embassy all morning, and there was plenty to do. But an ambassador is not official until the leader of the host country accepts his or her credentials. This can take months. In the United States, foreign ambassadors who do not want to wait to see our president will often agree to present their credentials to a lower-ranking representative. But Jeff Levine had managed to arrange for me to present mine to the president of Hungary on my very first day on the job.

That afternoon I rode in a motorcade to historic Sándor Palace, where President László Sólyom would receive me. Military guards brandished swords, holding them unsheathed high above my head, and trumpets hailed my arrival as I walked into the red-carpeted entrance and made my way up the royal staircase, escorted by members of the Hungarian honor guard and followed by Markos, Alexa, Jeff, Paul O'Friel, and an embassy officer who would serve as an interpreter.

Although the main Hapsburg palace next door had been all but destroyed by Russian bombs in World War II—only the façade remained—Sándor Palace had survived the assault, and a recent renovation had restored the two-hundred-year-old building to its original glory. Silk covered the interior walls, and finely wrought golden chandeliers hung from the wedding-cake ceilings. But I had no time to gawk. It was time to sign the visitors' book, which covered nearly the entire surface of a gold-leafed table.

A chair had been placed at the table for me, but I had to stand up and lean over the book to enter my name. For the very first time, in handwriting that I hoped would match the elegance of the page before me, I wrote "Ambassador Eleni Tsakopoulos Kounalakis, United States of America." As I tried to steady my hand, I looked up: staring down at me from her majestic portrait was Maria Theresa, Hapsburg empress, queen of Hungary, and one of the most powerful women in history.

When I finally finished my inscription, I was led toward two majestic doors. Two footmen opened them, revealing another, even more dazzling room. At the other end of a long red carpet stood President Sólyom, a tall, silver-haired man with a serious expression and a slight, welcoming smile. I carried in my hand two letters, both from President Obama. One officially recalled the preceding ambassador. The second one gave President Sólyom my credentials and asked that he accept me as President Obama's envoy.

All I had to do was walk down the carpet and hand the letters to Hungary's president. For a brief moment, daunted by the splendid surroundings and the significance of the ceremony, I wasn't sure that my legs would cooperate. But soon I was looking into the crystal blue eyes of President Sólyom and handing him the letters.

At that moment, I became Her Excellency, Ambassador Extraordinary and Plenipotentiary.

After the ceremony, President Sólyom invited me to his office for tea. Markos and Alexa stayed behind as I was ushered into yet another palatial room.

The president spoke some English, but in this ceremonial setting, he would speak Hungarian. Before leaving the State Department, I'd had only one lesson in this notoriously difficult language, which seemed to have impossible grammar, tongue-twisting pronunciation, and almost no relation to any other language in the world. Back home, I'd tried to teach myself a few words from a guidebook, with little success. During my State Department lesson, I'd asked the teacher to at least tell me how to say "hello," "please," "thank you," "excuse me," and "good-bye." As I was leaving the lesson, I suddenly remembered to ask, "What will they call me?"

"*Nagykövet asszony*," Sólyom said, as the tea was being poured. My interpreter repeated in English, "Madam Ambassador. The friendship between the United States and Hungary is very important to us." He went on to speak of our shared interests and values, our NATO cooperation, and Hungary's membership in the European Union. Then he leaned in a bit, looking at me with great intensity.

"Madam Ambassador, I understand that your Greek heritage is very important to you and that you are very proud of it. I think that because of your strong connection to your own heritage, perhaps you might be able to understand us in a way that many Americans do not."

With that, President Sólyom began to explain a contentious issue for Hungary, the loss of much of its territory after World War I, and his country's interest in preserving Hungarian culture across borders, in the sovereign lands of its neighbors. The ceremonial aspect of our meeting was over even before the tea was cool enough to drink. Five minutes into the job, I was already thrust into the complexities of diplomacy and of being a U.S. ambassador.

# 3

# "One Eye Is Smiling,
# One Eye Is Crying"

The Hungarians have a famous saying that they often use to describe their complicated history. They are apt to describe a situation by saying "one eye is smiling, and one eye is crying." I'd heard the saying before I arrived in Budapest, during one of my many briefings, and I recalled it on my very first day as ambassador, listening to Hungarian president László Sólyom explain the issue of the Hungarian diaspora.

With a smile, he said, "There are over a million Hungarians living in thousand-year-old Hungarian villages, just outside of our borders." Then with a frown, "Yet our fellow ethnic Hungarians in Slovakia are being subjected to new laws there that bar them from even speaking their native language."

I was well aware of the controversy, but I had not expected the president to raise it so soon, at our first meeting, with my husband and sister waiting outside. Though Sólyom was a constitutional scholar and had been a leading force in the transition between communism and democracy, the office of the president in Hungary was largely ceremonial. Nevertheless, I was prepared to address the issue.

Back in Washington in the fall of 2009, the desk officer who was preparing me to go to Hungary lamented that while most desks at the State Department covered one country, Hungary was one of two that were her responsibility. Slovakia was the other. The problem wasn't that two countries created too much work, she explained. It was that Hungary and Slovakia were not getting along. Slovakia had passed a law making it illegal to use any language other than Slovak for official purposes. Because 10 percent of Slovakia's population was ethnic Hungarian, this change would affect everything from school curricula to street signs in the historic Hungarian villages. People were up in arms, and back in the United States, Hungarian Americans and Slovak Americans were bombarding the desk officer with demands for U.S. involvement, at the same time asserting that she couldn't be an honest broker because she worked "for both sides." Of course, our desk officer didn't work for either side. She worked for the United States. But that was sometimes hard for her to get across to people when passions were enflamed.

Now I told President Sólyom, "Slovakia and Hungary are EU members and NATO allies, and we encourage both sides to work collaboratively to resolve any differences or disagreements. If there is a need for support during this process, the Organization for Security and Cooperation in Europe, of which both Hungary and Slovakia are members, stands ready to assist." The U.S. position, essentially, was that this was not our issue to resolve. Hungary had found its place in the EU and NATO, and it had to solve these disputes through its own diplomatic efforts. We had other challenges in the world to deal with. We hoped that Hungary and its neighbors could resolve their differences so that we could concentrate on tackling those other challenges together.

Yet I couldn't help being troubled by the fact that Hungary and its neighbors *did* have these disagreements, which furthermore didn't seem very simple to resolve.

Back in Washington, as I was preparing to go to Budapest, I kept hearing about the Treaty of Trianon. At first I was confused, wondering why people were talking about the hundred-year-old peace treaty that had ended World War I as if it had just been signed. Coming from California, a young state that was almost singularly focused on the future, I really had to recalibrate my thinking about the past and its reverberations. And I had to dig deeper into Hungarian history.

It is a long and complicated history, with high points and tragic lows. Part of what complicates Hungarian history is that while people might agree on the facts in their aggregate, there is a great deal of dispute about which facts are important and which are not. I'm not a historian, but over the years I developed an account of Hungarian history that I regularly shared with visitors. I know that there will be many who disagree with the abbreviated account I'm about to give. Indeed, it probably isn't fair to try to summarize 1,100 years of Hungarian history in a few pages. But to understand why the Treaty of Trianon was significant to the incoming American ambassador, it's necessary to take a look way back.

## A Brief History of Hungary (896–1914)

The Hungarians pinpoint their arrival in the Carpathian Basin to 896 AD. They were led from the steppes of Asia by Grand Prince Árpád, bringing with them Magyar, a language that is now the most widely spoken non-Indo-European language in Europe. Some say that another group broke off along the way and went north to settle in what is now Finland and Estonia. Hungarian, Finnish, and Estonian belong to a very small language group called Finno-Ugric, even though they have only a very few words in common with one another. They have even fewer words in common with any other language. There are even some Koreans who say they too have ethnic and linguistic ties with Hungarians, though the claim has been largely debunked.

In the year 1000, Árpád's great-great-grandson King Stephen brought Christianity to the Hungarian tribes. In 1222, the Hungarians adopted the Golden Bull—widely recognized as the first constitution in mainland Europe. These advances were short-lived, however. The Mongols swept into the region in the thirteenth century, brutally killing almost half of Hungary's two million people. The Mongol expansion westward eventually subsided and their power dissipated. After they left the territories, the remaining Hungarians invited settlers from around the region in an effort to repopulate the devastated country.

In the sixteenth century, the Hungarians again succumbed to invaders when the Ottoman Empire defeated the Kingdom of Hungary at the Battle of Mohács in 1526. To this day, when things get tough, Hungarians will say that no matter how bad things seem, "more was lost at Mohács"—thousands upon thousands of Hungarian soldiers were brutally slaughtered. A large part of Hungary remained within the Ottoman Empire until the beginning of the 1700s, when Hapsburg armies drove the Turks back down the Danube to Belgrade. Though the Turks were gone, the Hapsburgs stayed and counted Hungary as part of their empire for the next two hundred years.

In 1848, Hungarians staged a major revolt against the Hapsburgs, who were able to crush the uprising only after they had called in the Russians for help. When revolutionary leader Lajos Kossuth visited America in 1852, the U.S. government declared our solidarity with Hungarians in their demand for independence from Austria.* Though their revolution failed, Hungarians continued their struggle for independence, and in 1867 the Hapsburgs and the Hungarians negotiated a power-sharing agreement, giving birth to the Austro-Hungarian Empire and a golden age for Hungary.

By virtue of both its rich farmland and its location on the border of the Ottoman Empire, on the spice route from Asia to Europe, Hungary was fast becoming an important economic center. The Danube was an artery of trade. Hungary's fertile basin produced abundant crops, allowing it to take advantage of its location by trading farm products for the vast riches of the East.

By the end of the nineteenth century, Hungary was a place of innovation and economic opportunity. New technologies advanced the industrialization of farm products, and commodities like flour were processed in huge quantities, packaged, and shipped around the world. The largest commodities exchange in the world was located in Budapest. The soaring Hungarian Parliament building—the largest in continental Europe—and hundreds of other magnificent structures were

---

*P.C. Headley, *The Life of Governor Louis Kossuth with His Public Speeches in the United States and a Brief History of the Hungarian War of Independence* (1852; Budapest: Osiris Publisher, 2001), 158.

erected during this period. The first subway system on the European continent was built in Budapest. As 1896—Hungary's thousand-year anniversary—approached. Budapest was one of the most prosperous, diverse, and fastest growing cities in the world.*

## A Brief History of Hungary (1914–1945)

When you look out over the dramatic skyline of Budapest, you see the shadow of what Hungary was like during the glory days of the Austro-Hungarian Empire. But from the early twentieth century forward, Hungarian history took a dramatic turn for the worse. Very often, friends of mine would visit Budapest, find themselves awed by its lingering grandeur, and wonder, "Where am I?" Struck by the shabbiness of the city's once-imperial boulevards, they would then wonder, "What happened?" The short answer is that for most of the twentieth century, Hungary was on the wrong side of history. During that century—World War I, World War II, and the Cold War—Hungary was ground zero for all three great conflicts and on the losing side each time.

The losing streak started in 1914, at the height of the Austro-Hungarian Empire, when Archduke Franz Ferdinand was shot and killed in Sarajevo by Gavrilo Princip, a Serb nationalist rebelling against Austro-Hungarian expansion into Bosnia Herzegovina. This, as you might recall from your high school history, was the first shot of World War I. The Great War raged for four years, killing ten million soldiers and ending with the dissolution of *three* empires—the Russian, the Austro-Hungarian, and the Ottoman—and the remapping of the world.

For Hungary, the consequences of losing World War I were enormous. Along with Germany, Hungary had been part of the alliance that started the war. In 1919, the Treaty of Versailles was signed, formalizing peace between the Great Powers and Germany. The Treaty of Trianon was a separate agreement: imposed on Hungary by the Great Powers in 1920, the treaty redrew Hungary's boundaries so that it lost more than two-thirds of its prewar territory and more than half of its prewar population.

*John Lukacs, *Budapest 1900: A Historical Portrait of a City and Its Culture* (New York: Weidenfeld & Nicolson, 1988).

From the signing of the Treaty of Trianon in 1920 up until 1938, when Hungary joined with Hitler's Germany as an Axis power, the Hungarians lowered their flags on June 4, the day Trianon was signed. Their top foreign policy priority was to win back the lost lands—a determination driven by the fact that millions of ethnic Hungarians, without ever having moved, now lived in villages outside of the borders of Hungary.

The interwar period in Hungary was chaotic. Refugees from former territories flooded across the newly contracted borders. Many of these refugees were Hungarian Jews, who were strongly patriotic, and many had been heroes in the failed war. With Hungary's historical legal protections for minority populations, Jews preferred to leave their homes outside the borders to continue to live in Hungary. It is estimated that Jews made up nearly 25 percent of Budapest's population in the 1920s, contributing greatly to the cultural and economic life of the city, as they had for generations.

But discontent was rampant in post–World War I Hungary, and people craved a scapegoat. Jews came to be commonly blamed for everything that had been lost, and the national demagoguery made them responsible for the hardships of the Great Depression. Hungary's leader at the time, Admiral Miklós Horthy, supported the passage of laws that systematically limited the number of Jews in the professions and in universities to reflect their percentage of the population.* If one of your grandparents had been born Jewish, you were required to register as a Jew. All of this happened in Hungary under the leadership of Admiral Horthy nearly a decade before Hitler instituted the same type of policies in Germany.

When Hungary joined the Axis, a driving factor may have been its goal of reuniting with its lost territories. But public enthusiasm and government support for Hitler's larger agenda are also well documented.

World War II raged through the early 1940s, but the Allies eventually began to turn the tide. By 1944, the Russians had invaded southern

---

* "Horthy, Miklos," Shoah Resource Center, Yad Vashem, yadvashem.org/odot_pdf /Microsoft%20Word%20-%206429.pdf.

Hungary and were making their way to Budapest. Horthy began secret negotiations with the Russians for a peace agreement. When Hitler found out, he sent German forces into Hungary. The occupying force didn't remove Horthy as the governor, but installed the Hungarian Nazis—the Arrow Cross party—in power, and in March 1944, when the war was almost over, the deportation of Hungarian Jews began. The effort was coordinated with the active participation of the Hungarian civil service and started in the countryside, where resistance was believed to be weaker than in Budapest. In just a few short months between March and July 1944, an estimated 440,000 Jewish men, women, and children were deported to work camps, where most of them would die. Most were sent to Auschwitz-Birkenau, which prepared for the Hungarian prisoners by extending the rail line inside the main gates to prevent escapes. One out of every three Jews killed at the Auschwitz camps was Hungarian, most of them in the last few months of the war.

One of the last great battles of World War II was over Budapest. Russian and Allied bombs rained down on the city. On Christmas Eve 1944, the retreating Germans blew up all the bridges over the Danube, leaving the river uncrossable for the first time in nearly a century. On one of the bridges, the charge exploded early, sending a tramcar full of passengers into the water below. Yet even in the midst of this chaos, the Hungarian Arrow Cross persisted in persecuting the Jews. That late in the war, the deportations from the countryside were complete, but most of Budapest's Jews remained. So the Arrow Cross marched thousands of them, their own fellow citizens, to the banks of the Danube, ordered them to remove their shoes, and tied men, women, and children together in groups of three. They then shot one person in each group and pushed them all into the river to their deaths.

At the Yalta Conference in February 1945, when Roosevelt, Churchill, and Stalin divided up the postwar continent, Hungary went to Stalin. With Budapest still smoldering, the Soviet Army began its occupation. A few months later, in 1946, Winston Churchill declared, "an iron curtain has descended across the Continent." With the exception of a brief, heroic, and deadly uprising in 1956, the Iron Curtain would remain firmly in place for forty-three years.

If there was any single reason my husband and I told the White House that we wanted to go to Hungary rather than to the other European countries we'd been offered, it was because, years before, Markos spent one of the most important periods of his life there. In the late 1980s, he was a journalist, working for *Newsweek* in the Rome bureau. He often mused that if the Iron Curtain had not collapsed, he would still be in Rome, drinking espresso and going to parties with beautiful Italian women. But in 1989, his world turned upside down.

Like Markos, I was in Europe at the time, in Greece. I too was amazed by the first images of East Germans pouring into Hungary, which as a fellow Soviet satellite didn't require a special passport. The Hungarians had signaled to the Soviets that they would no longer keep the East Germans from crossing their border on their way west, and thousands left Hungary for Austria. On June 27, 1989, Hungarian foreign minister Gyula Horn met Austrian foreign minister Alois Mock at the barbed-wire fence between their countries, brandishing a large pair of wire cutters. Together, they pulled down the first part of the Iron Curtain.

While I saw it on Greek television, Markos witnessed this historic era on the ground, living in Prague and covering the revolution there as well as the uprisings in Romania and Yugoslavia. He marched with the Hungarian demonstrators in the March 15, 1989, protests—the first free demonstrations since the Hungarians had risen up against the Soviets in 1956 (a revolution that was brutally crushed by tanks and machine guns).

During the March 15 protests, Markos made his way to the edge of the crowd as it gathered in Freedom Square and positioned himself in front of the doors of the U.S. Embassy. There were 200,000 Soviet troops stationed in Hungary, and quite a few of them were poised at the edges of the demonstration. If they started to fire as they had in 1956, Markos figured he would be able to rush into the embassy for cover.

Later, Markos would tell me about the Hungarians' bravery and sophistication. His experiences covering these events inspired him in a way that he never forgot. When I moved into my office in Budapest, Markos gave me a photo he had taken of the massive crowds on March 15, 1989. Shot from just in front of the embassy, the photo was almost the exact view that I had from my window, with one glaring change: above the crowds in Markos's picture, you could see a red Soviet star firmly planted in the pediment of a building in the background.

Markos once noted that he and I are part of the "fall of the wall" generation. Technically, he's a baby boomer and I'm a Gen X-er. But we know that the most significant historic event of our young adulthoods was the fall of communism and the end of the Cold War. When we had a chance to live in Hungary twenty years later, Markos was eager to see how things had worked out.

By the time we arrived in Budapest, Hungary had made great strides toward becoming a modern European nation. In just two decades, The country had transformed itself from a totalitarian regime with a centralized economy to a democracy with a free-market economy. It joined NATO in 1999 and became a member of the European Union in 2004.

Once I had presented my credentials to President Sólyom, my next step was to make dozens of courtesy calls on officials around Budapest. Protocol dictated that I pay my first courtesy call on the dean of the diplomatic corps. In the case of Hungary, that person was the papal nuncio, the Vatican's equivalent of an ambassador. He was old and frail, and he had been in Hungary for quite some time. For our meeting, he wore his clerical robes and a skullcap that clung firmly to his nearly hairless head.

The nuncio, like all envoys, had a list of priorities in his bilateral relationship with Hungary. In his case, it was largely focused on the challenges faced by the Catholic Church in the post-Soviet era. One concerned marriage. Even if couples wanted to be married in a church, the law required that they have a separate civil service as well. As a result, he explained to me, most people simply opted for the civil service; rarely would you see a church wedding in this country that has a church on every corner. In general, church attendance had dwindled to one of the lowest rates anywhere: although going to church had not been illegal under communism, anyone who attended was denied a high-level job, and their children often were not offered spaces in the universities. Although church attendance rebounded in Poland after the fall of communism, the nuncio lamented, it had not yet begun to recover in Hungary.

My courtesy calls also included members of the Hungarian government. Just a few days after my arrival in Budapest, I paid a visit to the prime minister, Gordon Bajnai.

There are few buildings in the world that can claim to match the beauty of the Hungarian Parliament. Built at the turn of the twentieth century on the east bank of the Danube, the massive Gothic Revival structure was intended to symbolize the union of the ancient cities of Buda and Pest. Along with St. Stephen's Basilica, it is one of the two tallest buildings in the capital; in a nod to the founding of Hungary in 896 AD, both were built ninety-six meters (315 feet) high. Parliament was itself a sort of secular cathedral, with soaring columns, intricately painted vaulted ceilings, and graceful arches.

On the day of my visit to the prime minister, the Hungarian guards saluted me as I walked through the grand hallways. Gordon Bajnai met me in a splendid chamber, and we posed for a photograph together with our countries' flags on either side of us. The forty-one-year-old leader was impressive and disarmingly young, with a polished manner and perfect command of English. Our meeting was polite and friendly, as were the meetings I went on to have with his ministers of foreign affairs, defense, economy, and justice, along with a handful of key deputy ministers. But it was clear that the upcoming elections were dominating the climate and that these leaders of the Socialist Party knew their days in office were numbered.

Almost more informative to me than the meetings' fairly predictable substance was their structure. There is a distinct ceremonial nature to diplomatic meetings. First and foremost they are formal, reserved, and polite. They often start with a photo of the two principals shaking hands, usually with their countries' flags behind them. I learned a new word as I made my way around Budapest: interlocutor. When the meetings were being planned, our staff would decide in advance how many people I would bring, and my interlocutor, or counterpart, would usually match us with the same number.

In the land development business, meetings had generally been free-for-alls, with everyone jumping in and interrupting one another to make their point. The rigid planning and format of diplomatic meetings was quite a contrast for me. The parties would sit on opposite sides of a long table, flanked by an equal number of staff. No matter how many people attended these sessions, no one ever—ever—spoke except my interlocutor and me unless we asked him or her to do so. The highest-ranking officer, usually deputy chief of mission Jeff Levine, would listen, eyeballing his counterpart across the table, with whom he would usually have a follow-up meeting soon afterward. The next highest-ranking officer, usually Paul O'Friel, would serve as the note taker, though he too did his share of eyeballing his counterpart. After these high-level meetings, Jeff and Paul would engage with their interlocutors on a day-to-day basis. The note taker, by the way, was also tasked with writing up the classified cables that often followed the meetings.

There were rarely surprises, because my staff would write up my talking points and give them to me for review and approval before the meetings, and they often let their interlocutors know in advance what I was going to talk about. I quickly sensed that opportunities were missed when no one else was able to pipe up. So over time I developed a ritual of my own. After I'd exhausted my list of talking points, I would turn to my staff and ask, "Is there anything else?" For more junior officers, the rule was that if I hadn't raised one of my talking points, it wasn't because I forgot, so they shouldn't bring it up. The other rule was that they shouldn't root around for something to say just to say something. But I never felt that my authority was threatened if it was revealed that someone on my staff knew more about an issue than I did, and my new ritual created an opportunity for us to make the most of our meetings. It was also my way of signaling to my staff, as well as to our interlocutors, that I respected and exercised the expertise of the embassy's Foreign Service professionals.

All of this was good practice for what was to come. National elections would be held on April 11 and 25, 2010, in a two-round system that was baffling in its complexity. All indications were that the Socialist Party was collapsing and that Viktor Orbán and his conservative Fidesz Party would sweep the elections. There was no question that Fidesz would win; the only unknown was how big their victory would be. If Fidesz won two-thirds of the seats in Parliament, they would be able to change laws that under Hungarian law required a two-thirds vote of legislators to modify. Orbán had been campaigning on this, blaming problems with Hungarian governance on the inability to change these laws. Without specifying exactly what he would change, he insisted that if he won a supermajority, he would be able to fix all that ailed the country, which was suffering on many levels from the global, European, and Hungarian economic crises.

Protocol required that, in addition to meeting seated government officials, I pay calls on leaders of the opposition. But no one at the embassy was certain if Viktor Orbán would accept our meeting request. Under normal circumstances, the opposition leader in a country like Hungary would eagerly have sat down with the American ambassador, but Jeff Levine was skeptical. During the nearly nine months before my arrival, when Jeff had served as chargé d'affaires, Orbán had not met with him. Complicating the situation was the fact that Orbán saw his political party in kinship with the Republican Party in the United States. Ronald Reagan and George H. W. Bush were both heroes in Hungary. Herbert Walker, a cousin of George Bush Sr., was one of my predecessors in Hungary and had been well loved there.

But even if I had been a Republican appointee, I would not have been assured a robust working relationship with the unpredictable Viktor Orbán. Ambassador Nancy Brinker had been appointed to lead Embassy Budapest by George W. Bush and was an extraordinarily accomplished woman. She created Susan G. Komen for the Cure in honor of her late sister and was a recipient of the Presidential Medal of Honor. Soon after Nancy's arrival in Hungary, in September 2001, she expressed the United States' concerns about the rise of anti-Semitism in the country. Orbán was prime minister at that time, and he was so offended by Nancy's public comments—well grounded and measured though they were—that he refused to meet with her more than a token amount for the rest of her time in Hungary.

Another event from the past contributed to our concern over the unpredictable nature of Viktor Orbán. One of the most significant acts of Orbán's first term as prime minister, from 1998 to 2002, was the decision to supply the Hungarian military with fighter planes.

This was a very expensive purchase for a small country. The story was that, after examining the options long and hard, the Ministry of Defense had come to a consensus to buy a fleet of U.S.-made and U.S.-military-compatible F-16s. But at the eleventh hour, Orbán overruled the decision of his cabinet members and their ministries and announced that Hungary would lease Swedish Gripen aircraft instead. No one ever figured out exactly what had happened. Some said the decision was driven by backroom payoffs, but there was no real evidence of that. Others said it was a testament to Orbán's mercurial nature—a message to his ministers that he, and he alone, would make the big decisions.

So my team was somewhat taken aback, but also very pleased, when the Fidesz leader swiftly accepted the request and invited me to his office in the Parliament building. We had heard rumors that Orbán regretted not working with the United States in a more collaborative way during his first stint as prime minister. We had even heard that he regretted the F-16–Gripen decision, which by then had overwhelmed the budget of the Hungarian Defense Forces. Maybe his eagerness to meet meant that he was ready for a fresh start.

On a cold day in late January, Jeff Levine, Paul O'Friel, and I made our way to the Parliament building. As we hurried up the stairs to the appointment—with me, as always, craning my neck to take in more of the building's exquisite details—I assumed that whatever our differences with the Fidesz leader, this would be an outwardly civil gathering.

Orbán's office was small and cramped compared with the prime minister's rooms. The opposition leader was not meeting with us alone. János Martonyi, who had previously served as Orbán's foreign minister, and several other of his top foreign policy advisers were with him. We all shook hands, though Orbán's greeting was not exactly warm, and sat down in a small, tight cluster of chairs and sofas. The forty-six-year-old Fidesz leader clearly had no intention of trying to charm me. But he made a powerful impression, from his unruly thatch of hair to his stubborn, square chin and doleful eyes. He'd been born in a small village west of Budapest, but his résumé was anything but humble: after earning a law degree in Budapest, Orbán had participated in a Central and Eastern European study group financed by the Soros Foundation, then studied political philosophy at Oxford.

We sat down to our meeting.

"Mr. Orbán," I said, "I am very happy to be here in Hungary representing my country. Hungary is an important and reliable friend and ally of the United States."

Orbán shrugged. "Well, we like it here," he chuckled, gesturing emptily with his hand. With his red-rimmed eyes, he looked tired, no doubt from endless days of campaigning and traveling throughout the countryside.

I went on. "My husband lived in Prague in 1989 and covered the collapse of the Soviet Union for *Newsweek*. He told me how passionately Hungarians embraced their liberation. He was deeply moved to experience it."

Orbán had earned notoriety as part of those demonstrations, boldly declaring "Russians, go home!" to a cheering crowd. A businessman who had been there later told me, "I thought to myself, that young man is going to jail." He said that even though he didn't support Orbán as a politician, he couldn't deny his bravery in standing up to the Soviet regime.

"This is one thing that we can say about ourselves: we are freedom fighters," Orbán said, laughing loudly this time, looking at his colleagues for reassurance.

Figuring that I had finally broken the ice, I launched into the substance of my talking points.

"Over the last few months," I noted, "Hungary has handled a dramatic economic crisis with great skill. Hungary took quick action, stabilized the situation, and prevented it from becoming worse."

Rather than taking my point as a compliment to the people of Hungary for their resilience during their economic crisis, Orbán took it as a tribute to the Socialist Party, which he blamed for the crisis. He began to describe, with intermittent jabs at Socialists, how painful the economic crisis was, and would continue to be, for the Hungarian people. Piece by piece, he laid out the need to rebuild the economy so that the young people of Hungary would have opportunities, jobs, and the ability to move up. Orbán's speech reminded me of the vision

President Clinton years before had articulated for our country: "If you work hard and play by the rules, you can build a better life for yourself and your family."

I listened carefully, but wanted to steer the conversation away from domestic politics and back to the elements of our bilateral cooperation. I quickly thought of something to say that he would surely agree with. "Still," I offered, thinking of all the incredible strides forward that Hungary had made over the previous twenty years, "Hungary has come a long way from 1989."

Practically jumping out of his seat, the former prime minister snapped, "But this is the problem! Your country thinks that everything has gone very well since the changes." Hungarians commonly referred to the collapse of the Soviet bloc as "the changes" or "the political changes." He continued, "But it has not gone well. It has been a disaster!"

Clearly, my effort to get back to common ground had misfired. Orbán proceeded to launch a stream of insults against the Socialists. They had created the crisis, he said, bringing Hungary to the brink of bankruptcy. He outlined the policies and practices that in his view had destroyed the economy: mismanagement of the privatization process, mismanagement of government, and massive corruption on all levels.

Instead of a polite courtesy call, our meeting had devolved into a full-blown podium speech, with Orbán animated and gesticulating as if he were whipping up a crowd at a campaign rally.

"They stole everything! They are all communist millionaires! No, they are *Bolshevik billionaires!*"

When he was finally finished, he leaned back in his chair. For a split second, we all just looked at one another. Even Orbán seemed to suddenly realize that this was not the way to greet the new American ambassador. I was stunned. I still had several items left on my list of talking points, but how could I go on after that? His demeanor had been so inappropriate, so unexpected, that I really didn't know what to say in return. So I did the only thing I could: I stood up. Everyone nearly jumped up out of his seat in response. I could see Orbán's advisers looking at one another with concerned faces. Jeff and Paul scrambled to put their pens and notepads away, and Jeff whispered in my ear, "Afghanistan."

I extended my hand to Orbán and said, "I want to thank you for your party's votes in Parliament supporting Hungary's contributions to the Afghanistan coalition. It is my president's number one foreign policy priority, and Hungary's contributions are important and appreciated."

Orbán smiled tentatively at this and, awkwardly shaking my hand, said, "You see, maybe we can agree on something."

That night I tossed in my bed, unable to sleep. I was going to be in Hungary for another three to four years, and Viktor Orbán was likely to be prime minister for the entire time. One of my main responsibilities was to keep an open line of communication between Washington and Budapest. What if Orbán kept his door closed to me, as he too often had to Nancy Brinker? As the dark hours ground on, I tried to figure out a way to fix the situation, and when I woke up, I had a plan. I would try to extend an olive branch to the touchy opposition leader, a message that I wanted to try to work with him in spite of our rough start.

When I gave an interview to the respected weekly magazine *Heti Világgazdaság* (World Economy Weekly), or *HVG*, a few days later, the reporter asked me if I'd met Orbán and, if so, what I thought of him. I responded that I had met him and said that the way he talked about his people reminded me of a "young Bill Clinton." I knew the reporter would use my quote in the piece, but I didn't realize that my words would be irresistible to every news outlet in town.

A U.S. ambassador must stay far away from domestic politics in his or her host country. So when my quote started to go viral, my team stepped in and worked swiftly to kill the story, arguing—sometimes pleading—that my comment should not be used as a campaign weapon by either side. Fortunately, our press attaché at the time, Jan Krc, was well liked and very well respected in Budapest. He entreated his contacts to cut the new ambassador some slack and not make a bigger deal of the quote than it deserved. In the meantime, Jeff and Paul reached out to Orbán's associates and insisted that my comment not be used as a campaign slogan. These efforts worked and a potentially big problem was minimized.

In the meantime, we'd heard back from the Orbán aides who had been in the meeting. They conveyed that Orbán too wished it had gone better. Risky though it was, my public comment had been accepted as an olive branch. I was relieved and satisfied that there was at least a chance for me to try again to get on a good footing with Hungary's next prime minister. But by now, I had begun to realize that when it came to Viktor Orbán, nothing would be simple or easy.

I had also begun to realize—while sitting with President Sólyom amid the antique silk and gold leaf of Sándor Palace, then with Viktor Orbán in the cramped offices of the opposition leader—that the wounds of Hungarian history would continue to fester. The following months would show just how much hurt and resentment remained from Hungary's troubled past, with disturbing implications for its future—and for America's relationship with our friend and ally.

# 4

# A Long Way from Home

Living amid layer upon layer of history, and having that history so present in my everyday work, was a new experience for me. I have always been a student of the past, but it had been outside my everyday life, as it is for most Americans. In Hungary, as in many other places in Europe and the rest of the world, history and the present are fused together. As I worked to reorient myself to this reality and sort out the implications, I could not help but think of my own family history.

It did not escape me that I had become a U.S. ambassador after a long string of improbable events. During my small swearing-in ceremony in Secretary Clinton's office, I said at one point, almost just realizing it, "You know, Hillary, my grandmother never learned to read or write. It was her dream in life to travel from her village to see Athens, but she died of a stroke before ever making the trip. Can you imagine what she would have thought if somehow she could have known I'd be standing here today?"

My friend Susie Tompkins Buell, one of the few guests at my swearing-in and a close friend of Hillary's, had given me a beautiful portrait of the secretary of state for my office in Budapest. Putting an arm around me, Hillary said, "Eleni, when you hang that portrait in your office, please put it next to the one of your grandmother."

My father, Angelo Tsakopoulos, left Rizes, his village in the province of Arcadia, in central Greece, in 1951, when he was fourteen years old, largely at the urging of his mother, Ekaterina, who insisted that my grandfather "let the boy go!" Those who knew her have told me that she was a smart woman, full of energy and ambition for her children. The stories of how she survived and kept her family safe during World War II and the Greek civil war, with her husband away fighting, are largely lost. Among the few details I ever learned about her was that she had the reputation of being one of the most generous women in her village, but she would react fiercely if anyone tried to steal from her.

Back then, in postwar Greece, it was reasonable to believe that if you sent your fourteen-year-old son off to America, you might never see him again. In fact, Ekaterina saw my father only once more, about twelve years later, when she was sick and dying. Throughout those years, this brilliant but illiterate woman made up songs about him that she sang as she went about her daily chores. One survived:

> In the mountains of California
> I have—and it's mine,
> A pot with a basil plant
> Which must be watered often.
>
> If only the mountains could lower.
> If only the spruce trees could bend.
> I would see my little child
> With my own eyes.
>
> Στης Καλιφόρνιας τα βουνά
> έχω και 'γω και ορίζω
> μια γλάστρα με βασιλικό
> συχνά να την ποτίζω.

Να χαμηλώναν τα βουνά
Να γέρναν τα ελάτια
Να βλέπα το παιδάκι μου
με τα δικά μου μάτια.

Far from home, Angelo was seeking his fortune in the United States, where he would live the American dream. He had two uncles to receive him, one in Chicago and one in a small town in Northern California called Lodi. I have one picture of him from his first days in America: he's stretched out on a green lawn, smiling like the Cheshire cat, with a round little belly protruding from his small, thin body.

Lodi was, and still is, a farming community between Sacramento and Stockton. My father lived with his uncle Angelo in a one-room plywood garage that his uncle had converted to a home. During the week, he went to school, where he was two years older than his fellow students. After school and on weekends, he labored in the fields with the other, mostly Mexican, immigrants.

My father eventually made his way to Sacramento, where he registered as a student at Sacramento State University. He later married my mother, Elaine Demson, a first-generation Greek American from Yakima, Washington. Her mother, Helen, was a first-generation Greek American, but her father was a Greek immigrant. So my mother, her mother, and I are all at least in part first-generation Americans, as all of our fathers were Greek immigrants. We are all also named some version of Eleni.

I was born in 1966, named Eleni Chicos—the Americanized version of our last name, which my father's uncles had adopted. Around 1968, when I was a toddler, my father changed our name back to Tsakopoulos. At that time, we were living in a part of Sacramento called Meadowview. Today, Meadowview has fallen on hard times in terms of crime and economic hardship. But back then, it was a pretty little neighborhood, where my father was known as "the Mexican with the funny accent." By this time, he was working as a real estate agent and my mother was teaching elementary school.

I should say that while I know my life was shaped by my father's extraordinary story, my mother taught me many of my most fundamental values. Though she was a first-generation American, she was an all-American girl, right down to being homecoming queen at her junior college. She taught me how to cook, sew, and clean house. But far more important to me, she passed on her 1950s American values of hard work, honesty, and fairness.

My dad not only shared those values, he possessed charisma and ambition that led him to build a very successful real estate business. When I was about six, he was able to build us a house near the Sacramento River, in the middle of wheat fields. His new company, AKT Development (after Angelo K. Tsakopoulos), replaced Chicos Realty; we used the old Chicos Realty "for sale" signs to hold up the mattresses on our beds. It was an idyllic childhood—for a long time, I thought everyone grew up catching snakes and mice, eating fish that they'd caught in their backyards, and occasionally picking barbed wire out of their ankles.

In the late 1970s, my father's business started to soar, and he began to bring our family on summer trips to Europe. We were a funny crew: my parents, my grandmother Helen, us four kids. My father insisted on staying in the finest hotels, which drove my frugal mother nearly batty—we would walk into glorious establishments wearing inexpensive hand-me-downs she had tailored by hand. Between the late 1970s and the early '80s, we took three trips to Europe, visiting museums and monuments in England, France, Spain, Italy, Germany, Switzerland, and, of course, Greece.

I think my father was, in a way, pursuing his own educational goals. He had studied business in college. Now, as a grown man, he had an unquenchable thirst for knowledge of the past, particularly concerning ancient Greece. I remember the massive tomes sitting by his bedside: all eleven volumes of *The Story of Civilization* by Will and Ariel Durant (Volume II, *The Life of Greece*, was heavily worn with his reading and rereading) and the little green volumes of the Loeb Classical Library. The latter included important works that had survived from ancient Greece. They were printed with ancient Greek on the left page and the English translation on the right. Not only did my father memorize the key names, dates, figures, and events of ancient Greece, he taught himself the ancient Greek language in the process.

Our motley family from Sacramento would spend hours at a time touring museums. While my siblings squabbled over who got to sit on the cushioned poufs in the endless galleries, I would stand with my father until my legs hurt, never admitting how confused I was by the tour guides' lectures.

When I was about thirteen, we took a trip that really stood out from the others. Although my father was young enough to have only hazy memories of the curfews and hunger in Greece during World War II, he vividly remembered the carnage of the Greek civil war, which immediately followed the global conflict. The communists, funded by the Soviet Union, had tried to pull Greece behind the Iron Curtain, but the royalists, financed in part by the Americans, succeeded in stopping them. My grandfather had a picture of King Constantine II by his bedside until the day he died (something I later had the privilege of telling King Constantine). But though he was a fiercely patriotic American, my father had always been curious about communism. The communists of Russia and China had overthrown the aristocrats with a vision of empowering ordinary people. Angelo wanted to see for himself how it had worked out.

So in the summer of 1979, he packed us all up and took us to Eastern Europe. We rode a train through East Germany to Berlin. On the train, officers demanded to see our papers, confiscated all of our passports, disappeared for what seemed to my mother like hours, and returned the documents only after my father made a substantial cash payment. It was a wonder that my mother and grandmother survived their anxiety. They thought my father was half crazy for taking us to a communist country for our summer holiday.

I remember going through Checkpoint Charlie into East Berlin as if it were yesterday. We walked from prosperous West Berlin into a gray, lifeless, walled city still filled with rubble from World War II's bombs. There were almost no cars on the streets, except for a few shabby Trabants with mismatched doors. We went to an empty restaurant with a very fancy menu and eagerly ordered, but nothing we wanted was available. We settled for the soup and bread offered to us. As we left the restaurant, my father took the East German marks we'd been required to buy at the border and stuffed them into the waitress's hands. There was nothing to buy in East Berlin, so I'm not sure they were of much use to her either. Walking the sad streets, we saw that communism was, at best, a failed attempt at utopia.

As we made our way back through Checkpoint Charlie, there was a long delay as the Soviet officers examined and reexamined our passports, asking and re-asking my father the same questions. I had plenty of time to survey the scene beyond the windows of the small border station. I was mesmerized by the Berlin Wall, where armed guards stood in the watchtowers, scanning the ground below them, ready to shoot if anyone made a run for freedom. Thirty years later, in Budapest, I would draw on those chilling memories of East Berlin when I tried to imagine what life in Hungary had been like during the country's decades behind the Iron Curtain.

East Berlin had been oppressive and even frightening, but our European trips made a big positive impression on me, and I longed to return to the Continent. When I was fifteen, I found the address of a Swiss boarding school and mailed in an application. This process took about three months—overseas mail was pretty slow in 1981. Only when I got my acceptance did I tell my parents about the school and ask if I could go.

Sometimes my mother and father looked at me as if I were an alien, and this was one of those times. My father said I was too young, but I argued that he had been even younger when he came to America, alone and penniless. After much discussion, they let me go. Before they dropped me off in Lugano, my family took a final trip together. Once back home, my parents started what would be a lengthy, painful, and disruptive divorce. Eventually, things got better. But in many ways, my year in boarding school was the beginning of my adulthood. I was responsible for myself from that point forward.

After high school, I enrolled in Dartmouth College, in New Hampshire. Dartmouth was a conservative, preppy bastion and probably not the right fit for me, a first-generation American from the wheat fields of Sacramento. But I always joked that if I'd been remotely more successful in my social life in college, I never would have spent four years studying in Baker Library. And without my liberal arts education from Dartmouth, I'm sure I wouldn't be who I am. After graduation, I moved to Greece; I spent a year and a half there and in France. I worked as a teacher, as an editor at the *Athens News*, and on an archaeological site, gaining fluency in Greek and improving my French.

Back in Sacramento, my father's land development company had been growing tremendously, and I started to think that I should know more about business. So I came home from Europe and enrolled at the UC Berkeley School of Business. With its liberal vibe and diverse student body, Berkeley proved to be the perfect school for me. My plan was to get my master's in business administration, put it in my pocket in case I ever needed to help my dad, and then head out of the country for another adventure. But once I graduated from business school, my life took a different turn.

When I was in high school and college, I was very interested and active in politics. As a teenager, I interned in the state capital for state senator Nick Petris (an extraordinary man, and the one who had given my father the books about ancient Greece) and in the Washington office of my district congressman, Bob Matsui. While in high school, I painted signs for Walter Mondale, and in college four years later I worked in a New Hampshire phone bank for Michael Dukakis. So as the 1992 presidential campaign heated up, it was no surprise that I was drawn in. I signed up to work for the California Democratic Party. By then, my father was one of California's biggest political contributors, and the state party chair was Phil Angelides, who at one time had been president of our family business. But my connection to Phil didn't mean I got an easy berth—quite the contrary. To show that I was just staff and not his friend's daughter, he gave me extra responsibilities and fewer perks. He set a high bar, and when he later served as California state treasurer and his staff complained about what a tough boss he was, I was very sympathetic. But Phil, whether he meant to be or not, was my first real mentor. No one worked harder, and no one fought harder, to advance his strong values and lofty goals than Phil did.

It was an incredible time to be working at the California Democratic Party. The 1992 election would be called "the year of the woman": the state elected Dianne Feinstein and Barbara Boxer as its first and second women senators. As I write this twenty-one years later, they are still serving. I met them both back then, and they made a strong impression on me. I also met the woman who would be the greatest role model and mentor of my life: Congresswoman Nancy Pelosi. The future Speaker of the U.S. House of Representatives gradually pulled me under her wing, giving me priceless advice and encouragement.

Although my love of politics kept me very involved in the Democratic Party, I decided that I was ready to put my MBA to use. I went to work for another of my father's friends and fellow Greek American George Marcus, who had a home-building company in Palo Alto, called Summer Hill Homes. Soon after I started, George saw my dad at a party and told him what a great job I was doing. Although I was living in San Francisco and would have been happy to stay there forever, it didn't take long for my father to lure me back to Sacramento to work for his company. "George only has you as an assistant project manager," I remember him saying. "If you come here, I'll make you a project manager!"

So in 1993, I moved back to my hometown. It was a little hard at first. Why, I asked myself, had I gone to all that trouble to learn French if I was just going to end up back in Sacramento? But I found a new outlet for my energy and enthusiasm in the city's vibrant sports culture, taking up mountain biking, swimming, and running, and completing three marathons and several triathlons.

For the next fifteen years, I worked side by side with my father as a land developer, managing a wide variety of projects, some involving raw land, others centered on agricultural and commercial properties. The years I worked at AKT represented the greatest expansion of our business since the time my father founded it. There's no doubt that the economic boom between 1993 and 2008 was a major driver of our success. But I also know there was a special chemistry between my father and me that allowed us to take advantage of the strong business climate. He was the visionary and could see where we wanted to go. I drew up the road maps and managed the teams to get things done.

Land development in California is a very tough business. Because land is a highly regulated commodity—maybe the most highly regulated commodity—you have to satisfy everyone from local activist groups to city and county municipalities to state and federal authorities. And it's an all-or-nothing business. You are either able eventually to develop your property or it continues to sit vacant. With each project running up millions of dollars in engineering, design, legal, and advocacy costs, a loss can be pretty gruesome. Many people give up, unable to cope with the process, but if you make it to the finish line, it can be extremely profitable and satisfying work.

I believe there were several keys to the business success my father and I shared. First, we always proposed developments that were, as he liked to say, "good for our community, our state, and our nation." We knew that if you couldn't pass the straight-face test when you looked people in the eye and tried to convince them that your project was worth supporting, you would be finished before you began. Second, when we did well, we gave back—advocating for light-rail lines, donating land for hospitals, supporting educational opportunities for low-income kids.

My disclosure report to the U.S. Senate before my confirmation hearing included a list of sixty-two different organizations with which I was associated. Even longer was my list of political contributions. In the five years before my nomination alone, I had supported more than one hundred individual candidates who were running for public office.

My involvement with Democratic politics and my passion for the issues facing my community often led people to ask when I planned to run for political office. Even though I'd always thought that one day I would like to serve, I couldn't help feeling that the hyper-contentious nature of land use, regardless of how much success I'd had or respect I'd gained along the way, would cause problems. I've made an informal survey based on my own movie-watching experience and concluded that the most common categories of villains are psychopaths, terrorists, communists, and land developers. When Phil Angelides ran for governor of California against Arnold Schwarzenegger, his eight successful years as state treasurer could not help him overcome the fact that he was once a developer. Phil's projects had won awards for being models of sustainable development. If he could be attacked so easily, anyone could be. So although I loved politics and community activism, I felt sure that I would participate in American democracy as a citizen and businesswoman.

———

At age thirty-three, I was still single, devoted to my work and political interests. My family joked that I was too stubborn to get married, but I knew it was because I hadn't met the right person. All that changed in December 1999.

Gregory Maniatis, a friend of mine who was living at the time in Athens, asked me to host a small dinner in honor of a Greek diplomat, Ambassador Stavros Lambrinidis. Stavros would be visiting San Francisco and wanted to meet some local members of the Greek American community. I arranged for the dinner to be held at Allegro Romano, a restaurant in the Russian Hill neighborhood, and invited a handful of friends. Gregory invited Markos Kounalakis, a journalist who had recently published his second nonfiction book.

Markos and I sat next to each other at dinner, and we couldn't stop talking. He had traveled the world as a foreign correspondent, and he saw things through the lens of a guy who only needed a notebook, a pen, and a good story to be happy. We spent about a month chatting by phone, me in Sacramento and him wherever he was at the moment, from San Francisco to London. But soon we were dating. On about the fifth date, we were sitting in a park at the top of Nob Hill, where a very large wedding party was having pictures taken. It was just after the millennium, and weddings were happening everywhere. For this one, there must have been a dozen bridesmaids, all in pink. "Why do people have such fancy weddings?" Markos asked.

"I don't know," I answered. "But if I ever get married, it will be in Istanbul."

"Really? Why Istanbul—other than because it's a great city?" At forty-three, Markos had never been married. He'd always felt that his choice of career was too dangerous for him to have a family waiting far away.

"A few years ago, Patriarch Bartholomew was in San Francisco," I explained. "My father introduced me as his daughter, and the patriarch asked if I was the daughter with the four children. My father said, 'No, that's my older daughter. I can't convince this one to get married.' The patriarch smiled at me and said to come to Constantinople when I was ready. He said he would have a beautiful wedding for me."

Sitting there in the park, I didn't realize how appealing this prospect sounded to Markos. But a few days later, he asked me to marry him. On February 11, 2000, just eight weeks after our dinner at Allegro, we were secretly married in City Hall in San Francisco. He wore a blue blazer and khaki-colored cargo pants. I wore a light beige work suit and held flowers that Markos had surprised me with that morning. He'd gone to the florist without my knowing, and the lady at the shop arranged a bouquet. We hadn't told anyone about City Hall because we were planning a church wedding in Istanbul, at the Greek Orthodox Ecumenical Patriarchate, just a few weeks later.

On the evening of our civil wedding, we went back to Allegro for dinner, just the two of us. I'd been introduced to Allegro by the Pelosi family, who dined there regularly, so I wasn't all that surprised that Nancy and her husband, Paul Pelosi, were there that night. As they were leaving, they came over to say hello. I'd already brought Markos to dinner with them, and I knew they liked him. This evening they could see from our smiles that something was going on.

"Did you just get engaged?" Nancy asked excitedly.

I couldn't keep the secret any longer. "Nancy, we just got married!" First, she looked shocked, and then her eyes filled with tears. I was not as close to my own mother as I should have been, and Nancy's maternal reaction overwhelmed me. My eyes teared up too.

It is incredibly romantic to marry someone you hardly know. It's also pretty risky. Markos and I barely knew each other when we got married, but we have always treated each other with the respect of people who both feel lucky, every day, to be together. I began to tell my two little sisters that the most important thing to look for in deciding to marry someone is that your world becomes bigger, not smaller, because you are together—and that your husband feels the same way.

If he knew little else about me back then, Markos knew that although I loved my work in land development, my real passion was policy and politics. But he also recognized that even though people, including Nancy Pelosi, encouraged me to run for office, my career as a land developer could be used against me. We were discussing this one evening when he made an observation that changed everything.

"You know, Eleni, you don't have to be elected to serve. You could be appointed. You could be an ambassador."

# 5

# How Do You Become a
# U.S. Ambassador?

There is a very simple answer to the question "How do you become a U.S. ambassador?" The fact is, if you want to be an ambassador, you should join the Foreign Service. At any given time, about seven out of ten American ambassadors are career Foreign Service officers who have worked their way up the chain of command at the State Department through many years—sometimes decades—of hard work and proven capability. They are most often found running the largest embassies, the most dangerous ones, and those where the bilateral relationship is the trickiest and most nuanced.

In most other countries, only professional diplomats like these serve as ambassadors. But the United States has a tradition of allowing the president also to nominate people who are not professional diplomats. Of the three out of ten or so of these "politically appointed" ambassadors, many are university professors or foreign policy experts from the nation's think tanks. Others are onetime members of Congress, such as former senator Walter Mondale, who serves as U.S. ambassador to Japan.

The political appointee group also includes businesspeople. They are usually individuals the president knows well—people who have been active in their communities and likely supported the president's political party, and the president himself, in campaigns. This was the category that Markos believed I could fall into when he suggested that I could aspire to serve my country as U.S. ambassador.

A few months after that conversation with Markos, in May 2000, we held a fund-raiser for another of my most inspiring role models: First Lady Hillary Rodham Clinton. Markos and I had been married for less than three months. Though over the next ten years we would welcome Hillary to our home in Sacramento and our apartment in San Francisco many times, this party was at my father and stepmother Sofia's house. Just as I had done over years of fund-raising for Democratic candidates, I called all of our business partners and colleagues, and every consultant I knew, to ask them to come and support Hillary's bid for a seat in the U.S. Senate representing New York State. "Bring your daughters," I urged them.

As I prepared my speech to welcome our guests and introduce Hillary, I told Markos that I would make the point that there had never been a first lady as influential. Much to my surprise, he laughed at me.

"Eleni, you need to read Lou Cannon's book about first ladies. There were many who were extremely powerful. It's just that Hillary doesn't see why the public shouldn't know it—that's the difference!" True, I conceded. And that's why her Senate race was so important. If she won, it would be the first time in history that a U.S. first lady was elected as a leader in her own right.

After the party was over and the guests had all left, my father, Sofia, Markos, and I sat down in the living room with Hillary. She asked me about my political future. "Are you still thinking about running for Congress, Eleni?"

I looked at Markos, straightened my spine, and told her that I hoped to be a U.S. ambassador one day. It was the first time I'd said it out loud.

But Hillary didn't react as if I'd said something outrageous. "Well, then, we'd better get a Democrat elected president after Bill! Where would you want to serve? Greece?"

Markos and I told her we would go anywhere.

For the next eight years, I continued to work in the family business and I continued to support Democratic candidates. Al Gore famously did not win the 2000 election. John Kerry less famously did not win election in 2004. I worked hard on both of those campaigns. I'd been a delegate to the Democratic National Convention for Bill Clinton and went on to serve as a delegate for Gore and Kerry. To become a delegate, I ran in local district elections, which reaffirmed for me the importance of grassroots politics and how much I enjoyed the democratic process. Dianne Feinstein had appointed me to the California Democratic Party Central Committee, and I loved the colorful characters and diverse ideas and backgrounds of those who made up my party.

Along the way, Markos and I began to spend more time in San Francisco. We wasted no time in starting a family, and by our third anniversary we were the proud parents of two baby boys, Neo, born in 2001, and Eon, born in 2002. Both of our boys were born in Sacramento, but when it was time for them to go to school, my polyglot husband insisted that they go to a foreign language immersion school. We settled on the Chinese American International School in San Francisco, one of the best Mandarin schools in the country.

For me, working in Sacramento while living in San Francisco posed an enormous challenge. This was the busiest time of my life, complicated by the fact that Markos and I didn't want to rely on nannies to raise our boys. Instead, we used a combination of school, after-school care, grandparents, and babysitters. We wanted our boys to have a lot of people in their lives, but we wanted to provide their primary care. I always made the boys breakfast, even if it was usually cold cereal, and when they were little either Markos or I almost always managed to give them their baths and read to them before bed. They were often among the last kids picked up from the extended day program after school, but one of us was always there to get them.

My days were crammed with meetings: meetings with our in-office development team, with architects and engineers, with environmental attorneys and government agencies. Between meetings I made phone calls to raise money for candidates and causes. My evenings were often spent at city council meetings, board of supervisor hearings, and fund-raisers. When Hillary ran for reelection to the Senate in 2006, I had three hundred people for a lunch fund-raiser at our house in Sacramento. When it was over, we jumped in the car and raced to San Francisco, where we were hosting a cocktail party for Hillary at our apartment that same evening; we arrived just a few minutes before the guest of honor.

The *San Francisco Chronicle* once described our midrise San Francisco apartment building as the "Tower of Power." Of the twelve families in the building, three, including mine, were very active in national politics. The biggest power was a founder of the Esprit clothing company, Susie Tompkins Buell, who lived with her husband on the top floor. After we moved in, I told Susie that any time she wanted to expand one of her standard high-dollar, thirty-person sit-down dinners to include a lower-dollar cocktail party, I was in. And so our progressive-progressive parties were born. Susie's fund-raising infrastructure managed everything for the San Francisco events. My own base was mainly Sacramento and the construction industry. But our combination had chemistry. The parties were fun and exciting, and people flocked to the events. We hosted dozens of fund-raisers for Democratic candidates and progressive causes. Twice in 2006, our guest of honor was a rising star in the Democratic Party: Illinois senator Barack Obama.

But from the very beginning, Susie and I were both strong supporters of Bill and Hillary Clinton. Coincidentally, Susie first met President Clinton in the early nineties at a fund-raiser my father and Phil Angelides threw for him in Sacramento. A plaque on the wall of the clubhouse in our Laguna West project notes that then-Governor Bill Clinton inaugurated its opening.

Susie and I were overjoyed to join forces for Hillary's presidential campaign. But I greatly admired and respected Barack Obama, who called me many times to ask if I would switch over and work for his campaign. I made it clear that I was devoted to Hillary's candidacy, but I assured Senator Obama that he would never hear a negative word from me and that when the primary was over, I would back the winner with all my might. In a December 24, 2006, article in the *San Francisco Chronicle*, I commented that my dream ticket would have Hillary at the top and that "I would love to see Barack Obama as the vice presidential candidate."

We all know what happened next. After a grueling and competitive race, Senator Obama emerged as the Democratic candidate. Inside I was crushed. But true to my word, I snapped into gear to help. Two days after Hillary ended her campaign, I told *USA Today* that one dream was over, but now there was a *new* dream, and we needed to move quickly to win back the White House for the Democrats. Senator Obama called me right away and asked me to serve as a member of his national finance council. I said yes, of course, and worked hard to encourage my Hillary-supporting friends to help him win. At the convention in Denver, in what was a bittersweet moment for me, I cast my delegate vote for Senator Obama.

Our first African American president was elected on November 8, 2008. On inauguration day, Markos and I sat on the podium, just a few rows behind the U.S. Senate and a few feet from Obama as he took the oath of office. I had all the respect in the world for President Obama. He was the first of my generation to become president, but even more important, I had identified with him as a first-generation American and as someone who also believed strongly in the Constitution and rule of law. Truly, witnessing his inauguration was one of the most extraordinary experiences of our lives. We were seated with a whole slew of Californians, including Magic Johnson, Leonardo DiCaprio, and Steven Spielberg—all of us guests of Dianne Feinstein, who as chair of the Senate Rules Committee also chaired the inauguration.

Since we were high up and facing the crowds, we could see more than one million people watching in perfect silence as the president took his oath of office. During his inaugural speech, when President Obama talked about his immigrant father, Markos and I both teared up. Our fathers too had come to America with little more than their dreams, and their dreams for their children. My thoughts turned to my grandmother. When she sent her son off into the unknown, aware that she might never see him again, but with faith in this place called America, could she have imagined the opportunities that her granddaughter would one day have?

As proud as I was to have helped support President Obama, I did not expect to be part of his administration. I had worked hard on his behalf because I believed in his leadership and that it was important to my country and my children's future that he be elected. The few, coveted ambassadorships surely would go to those who had been with him from the beginning. I knew quite well that in every presidential administration you wore your sign-up date on your sleeve as a badge of honor.

The day before the inauguration, I visited Nancy Pelosi in the Speaker's office in the Capitol. Nancy had mentored, trained, and guided me since I was a twenty-something staffer for the California Democratic Party. I had been in her office several times during the previous two years. But it was still a thrill to visit the historic rooms, which had been occupied by some of our country's greatest leaders—and I firmly believe that Nancy is one of them. Now, as we sat down, she asked if I still wanted to become an ambassador.

My heart skipped a beat.

If I did, she said, she would recommend me to the president.

I couldn't help but respond, "Nancy, are you sure that I'm qualified to do this?" We both knew that I didn't doubt my capabilities in management and leadership. I was regularly recognized as an important leader in the Sacramento community—as a successful businesswoman and influential community activist. It had been nearly ten years since I first told her, along with Hillary Clinton and Dianne Feinstein, that I wanted to serve my country as an ambassador. During that time I involved myself in several important international efforts, as part of the Greek American community, as a member of the California World Trade Commission, and as a trustee of the World Council of Religions for Peace. But even after all of that, it still seemed somewhat incongruous to me that a Sacramento land developer could become a U.S. ambassador.

She smiled. "Eleni, I've known many people who have served as ambassadors. Some of them do not come with vast diplomatic experience. What they bring is an outside perspective, business savvy, and leadership skills. But let me just say, even in a crowded field of talented people, Eleni, you stand out." As if she recognized the kind of self-doubt that was all too common in even the most qualified women, she grabbed my hand, the one with my wedding ring. Leaning in close, she said, "Never forget, you are like this golden ring."

Nancy always had a mother's faith in my abilities. I promised myself that no matter what happened with the ambassadorship, I would never let her down.

A few weeks later, at the end of February 2009, I received a phone call from Hillary Clinton, who was just weeks into her new job as secretary of state under President Obama.

"Eleni, I am calling because the president has authorized me to ask if you would serve as his ambassador to Singapore."

Because I'd been so passionately involved in Hillary's presidential campaign, this was not the scenario that either of us had envisioned. But clearly she had moved on and was ready to serve our country. So was I.

"This is the greatest honor of my life, Hillary. Thank you for your faith in me and the president's faith in me." It wasn't a time to think or talk about what might have been. It was time to think about the future.

"You'll do a great job, Eleni. I know you've been preparing for a long time."

I promised to work hard and be ready for my Senate confirmation, and I promised I would do my best to make her proud.

"Get ready," Hillary said before the call was over. "There is a mountain of paperwork!"

She did not exaggerate. Between the day I got Hillary's call and early May 2009, when I arrived at the State Department for training, my home office became a war room as I prepared for the three-part vetting process. The State Department was required to conduct a microscopic background check in order to grant me top secret clearance, the White House needed to know what felt like my entire life story, and the U.S. Senate had to confirm me.

For the State Department clearance, I had to provide, among other things, a list of all the locations where I'd lived over the previous ten years, as well as the names of three people who knew me in each place. State wanted to know where I attended school, from high school on, and the names of three people who knew me at each school. They also wanted the names of people I'd worked with. And names weren't enough. I had to provide contact information for all these people.

A few weeks after submitting the information, I got a visit from a retired FBI agent working for the State Department. We sat down in my office, and he asked lots of questions about my professional and personal lives, including whether I had ever cheated on my husband.

"Have you seen my husband?" Markos is a particularly handsome guy. But the agent didn't laugh at my joke, so I quickly changed my answer to no. Sometimes he asked things twice to see if I would change my story. The last question really floored me. He asked, "Have you ever conspired to overthrow the government of the United States of America?"

By that point I knew better than to joke. I uttered a clear no and waited to see where that particular line of questioning was going. But that was it. As the agent left, he told me that he would be visiting some of my friends.

"If they call you to find out what it's all about, just tell them they should tell the truth," he advised.

This agent, along with two others, interviewed the people I'd identified in my paperwork. When the agents met with my contacts, they asked for more names and numbers. All told, the agents interviewed thirty-two people that I knew of, but I'm sure there were more.

It turns out that the agents asked everyone if I'd ever conspired to overthrow the government. This was a standard question, but it horrified one of my friends. Steve Mavromihalis—a professor of ancient Greek history, a successful San Francisco businessman, and a fellow first-generation American—gave the agent a long, impassioned explanation of the patriotism that he and I shared as children of Greek immigrants. Afterward, he called to tell me that he'd been asked this outrageous question and to assure me that he'd made it very clear that I did not pose a risk for treasonous activity. Much as I appreciated Steve's strong defense, it was a little stressful to imagine what people were saying to the agent and to wonder whether there would be anything problematic.

As the process unfolded, I began to understand the actual purpose of the questioning. For instance, infidelity in a couple's relationship is not a deal breaker for top secret clearance—unless one of the people in the relationship *doesn't know about it*. The State Department isn't looking to see if you've ever made mistakes in your life, but it does want to know if anyone could use those mistakes to compromise you or, to put it bluntly, blackmail you.

The State Department clearance process required me to list all the countries I'd visited in the previous ten years, as well as where I stayed and whom I met. Another form asked me to list any non–U.S. citizen I had a relationship with, along with the approximate date of the person's birth and the nature of our relationship. For me, this was a bit complicated. I'd traveled the globe on behalf of the World Council of Religions for Peace, and I still had family in Greece. Because not to reveal someone would be perjury, I listed about thirty people. When I got to the relatives in our family village in Greece, though, I was exhausted and got a little sloppy. As the process dragged on, I was terrified that I hadn't put enough of my cousins down.

In the end, though, after several months of waiting, I got my top secret clearance.

As rigorous as the State Department process was, it didn't come close to the clearance required by the White House Ethics Office. Just for starters, the paperwork required a list of all my assets, copies of the last ten years of my federal and state tax returns, a list of all the political contributions made by me and my immediate family for the preceding ten years, and a list of all the organizations that I'd been affiliated with since I was eighteen years old, including any positions held within those organizations. There were notes on each of the forms reminding me to answer honestly, under the penalty of perjury.

A lot of this information would be required for the Senate confirmation process, but the White House wanted to see the answers before the ambassadorial nominees got that far. And the White House had its own questions—not only if I had been unfaithful to my spouse but if I'd been involved in lawsuits or accused of criminal activities. I began to understand that the White House already knew if you'd done something illegal. Now it was looking to see if its nominees had ever behaved in ways that could be construed as unethical. An extreme, and public, example of this came in 2013, when the president's candidate for ambassador to France was revealed to have a hobby of playing high-stakes poker. Some of the people he'd played with were under investigation for being part of a Russian money-laundering scheme. The prospective nominee had committed no crime, but he was disqualified nonetheless.

I didn't play high-stakes poker. But when you have to prove you're an ethical person, you start to question everything about yourself. Answering the White House questions was a challenge; some were sweeping, while others were very narrow. Here's one: "Have you ever sent an e-mail, which, if it became public, would embarrass you or the President?" Fortunately for me, I had always been suspicious of e-mail, assuming that anyone could read it. But my sister Katina used to forward some rather tasteless (though also pretty funny) jokes from time to time. Should I send them to the Ethics Office?

Part of the reason the White House vetting process was so stressful was the attitude of some of the staffers. Early on, I received my first call from the White House lawyer who had been assigned to me. He introduced himself as my sherpa—my guide through the vetting.

"Great!" I said.

"Don't sound so happy," he replied. "I just got finished working at the Treasury Department, vetting potential nominees over there, and they called me the Angel of Death."

This gave me a chill. Another "angel of death," Josef Mengele, was a notorious Nazi war criminal, and I didn't think people should joke about it. Another White House staff person told me that although he was part of the appointments office, they really should call it the disappointments office because so few people made it through the vetting process.

My tension ratcheted upward. Later, a fellow Hillary supporter who had just endured a very difficult process at the State Department, told me, "Eleni, you have a scarlet H on your dress. The president may love you and want you to serve, but some staffers are very resentful of any Hillary person getting any position in the administration. Many of them think that Hillary shouldn't be here either."

As it turned out, I was the only Hillary campaign cochair who became an ambassador in President Obama's first term. I know of two others, both excellent people, who were tapped by the president but never made it through the vetting process.

Honestly, I don't think I'll ever know if I was put under special scrutiny during the vetting process because of my friendship with Hillary Clinton. Almost every prospective nominee I met, including those who'd been Obama supporters from the start, also looked pretty red-eyed and overwhelmed by the vetting process.

Here's one of the things in my life that drew scrutiny: at the time of my nomination, I was serving as a member of the California First Five Commission. Back in 2000, the actor, director, and activist Rob Reiner championed an initiative to collect one dollar on each pack of cigarettes and use the money to fund preschool programs in the state. Over the years, the First Five Commission would take positions on legislation being considered in Sacramento. Because I knew a lot of the members, I agreed to chair the legislative subcommittee. When we took positions, I was the one who would communicate with them, via e-mail. The question was, did this make me a lobbyist? I wrote a letter clarifying my role, and the issue was eventually resolved.

At the time, Norman Eisen was the head of the White House Ethics Office and one of the architects of the vetting process. Years later, when he was serving as the U.S. ambassador to the Czech Republic, we had lunch at his residence in Prague. He noted that President Obama's vetting process had been the most aggressive in history, and as a result scandals in the appointment process were virtually eliminated. He also told me that he remembered when my file came through his office. "Eleni," he recalled, "you were a piece of cake. I can't remember a single issue that came up."

I wish I'd known that when I was waiting on edge in San Francisco, checking for hair loss.

With my top secret clearance and my White House vetting complete, two-thirds of the approval process was over. My Senate confirmation hearing wouldn't come until summer of 2009 at the earliest. In the meantime, I needed to learn how to be an ambassador.

Markos and I flew to Washington for our training in May 2009, in the first ambassadorial seminar following President Obama's inauguration. When we walked into the designated meeting room at the State Department, there was a sign on the table in front of each seat, with our names and the flag of our soon-to-be host country. Markos and I sat behind the flag of Singapore. Our group included several career diplomats, but most of us were political appointees.

The two-week-long ambassadorial seminar was also affectionately called charm school—an ironic name for a very intense, substantive training program. The ten or so of us who were in the class were given daily briefings by high-level government officials—not just from the State Department but from other agencies as well. There was an individualized process that was going on simultaneously and included dozens of specialized briefings, again from people inside and outside the State Department, about issues and programs specific to our embassies. For many of us, these briefings had already been going on for two to three months and would continue until we left for our posts.

The combination of the individual briefings and charm school was designed to ensure that when you got to your post you were ready to serve. It was often said during this time that nominees were being asked to take sips out of a fire hose, and that wasn't much of an exaggeration. They were long, long days, packed with information. The two former ambassadors who ran the seminar gave us organizational charts to help us understand the management structure of our posts and how they related back to the department. We received long lectures in U.S. foreign policy by key officials. We heard from generals, undersecretaries, and assistant secretaries from across the government. The flood of information was rapid and endless, but one key message was drilled in: you are in charge.

Throughout all of our briefings, the State Department made it clear that there is a chain of command, with the ambassador at the top. At one point, we heard from a State Department official who gave us detailed directions on how to deal with a particular, complicated management issue. As everyone tried to make sense of it all, scribbling away on our notepads, Lou Susman, who was on his way to serve as the U.S. ambassador to the United Kingdom, put up his hand.

"These are some pretty specific instructions you're giving us. If we have to deal with the scenario you're talking about, there are others at the embassy, including our deputy chiefs of mission, who will know these procedures and advise us on the appropriate course of action—right?"

"Yes, of course you will be advised." The officer looked a little sheepish, as if he had been caught trying to show us up. Then he collected himself and delivered his bigger point. "But the ultimate decision, and the ultimate responsibility for making the right decision, is yours."

Lou was a high-powered, brilliant Chicago lawyer nicknamed "the vacuum cleaner" for his fund-raising prowess, both political and philanthropic. I'd known him since John Kerry's presidential campaign. Now he leaned toward me in his chair, eyes twinkling. "This is a real job!" he said, half teasing. But I knew exactly what he meant. We all did.

A few days later, our group got a briefing from the State Department's Bureau of Diplomatic Security. They divided us into subgroups and gave us a scenario: Diplomatic Security approaches you with a concern about possible unlawful activities happening within your embassy. They tell you to keep the information to yourself and not to tell your deputy chief of mission. What do you do?

My group started to agree that we should follow the directions from Diplomatic Security. But I disagreed.

"Guys, they've been telling us for weeks that we're the ones who make the decisions. So if we think that for whatever reason our deputy should be told, it's up to us to make that call."

I was alone in my opinion, but when the trainer asked us to voice our conclusions, I ended up being right.

Another indelible message I took from charm school was that I would need to keep many of my personal opinions in a box. For the next four years, I would be speaking as a representative of the administration, tasked with clearly and effectively communicating the policies of the United States of America. I have never been shy about joining a debate and giving my point of view, but I relished this challenge and was determined not to fail. If a discussion in my host country turned to a different part of the world, I needed to be prepared to effectively articulate the U.S. position. I also understood that if I ever personally disagreed with the president's foreign policy, I could either keep those opinions private or resign from his administration.

During charm school and through the summer of 2009, I was still designated to go to Singapore. The Asian city-state had been my first choice, for the same reason Markos and I had sent our boys to Chinese school: living in San Francisco, on the Pacific Rim, I had a heightened understanding of Asia's importance. There were a lot of people on the East Coast who were experts on Europe; I believed there should be as many on the West Coast who were experts on Asia. Singapore's ambassadors traditionally had been political appointees, and with my business background, I felt sure it was the right place for me.

In the midst of all the paperwork connected to the vetting process, I had been immersed in the East Asian and Pacific Affairs Bureau of the State Department, building a solid understanding of the region's developing diplomatic architecture and the important issues on the table. I'd read all of the speeches delivered by the previous ambassador. And I was working my way through the thousand-page first volume of the autobiography of the founder of modern Singapore, Lee Kuan Yew.

When charm school was over, the White House began announcing the names of my fellow ambassadors. They went before the U.S. Senate for their hearings and shipped off to their posts. But I'd heard nothing about my own post. I began to wonder why it was taking so long for the White House to make its announcement. Whenever I asked this question, I was told to sit tight, that it was coming. Finally, in late July 2009, as I was playing golf with Markos at the Presidio Golf Course in San Francisco, the White House called.

It was a lower-level staffer calling to tell me that Singapore was a "nonstarter."

"But I'm preparing for confirmation," I said, dumbfounded. "The government of Singapore has already sent a cable approving me!"

He went on to say that he could offer me one of four other European countries, including Hungary.

I managed to hide my distress until the call was over.

For six months, since Hillary's call at the start of the year, I'd worried every day that my nomination would be derailed. I was exhausted, and my hair had begun to fall out in clumps. Now I turned to Markos on the ninth hole of the golf course.

"We're not going to Singapore. It's gone," I tearfully told him. "We will have to start the process all over again, from the beginning. Markos, are we sure we still want to do this?"

Markos gave me a look that made it clear how ridiculous I sounded. He leaned on his driver, smiling. "Eleni, they've offered us Budapest. That would be amazing!"

Markos was delighted at the prospect of returning to the place where he'd covered historic events, but I was disappointed beyond belief not to get the Singapore post, and I didn't give up right away. I appealed to Nancy Pelosi to see if there was any way to get the White House to change its mind. As we sat on the sofa in her Pacific Heights living room, looking out over San Francisco Bay, I remembered all the times I'd sat in the same spot, listening to Nancy as she shared with me her own journey of overcoming challenges to become the highest-ranking woman in the history of the United States. Now here she was, Speaker of the House of Representatives, wearing her bedroom slippers, giving me counsel. Yet if I was expecting much sympathy, I was mistaken.

"Dear, you'll be going to an important post in Europe," she pointed out. "Most people would consider this a step up." We talked for an hour, but the conclusion was the same. These things happen with the White House. It is an unpredictable process, and they are known to change their minds.

I walked down the street from Nancy's house to my apartment and packed up my boxes of information about Singapore, along with my name tag from charm school with the Lion City's flag. Over the following days, I said my good-byes to everyone at East Asian and Pacific Affairs and made my way over to the Bureau of European and Eurasian Affairs. I stripped off the brown paper wrapper I'd used to cover the outside of Lee Kuan Yew's book to conceal my impending appointment and transferred it to a volume about Hungarian history that I'd found in a San Francisco bookstore.

I was going to Hungary.

Four months later, in October 2009, I went before the European subcommittee of the Senate Foreign Relations Committee for my hearing. The committee allows you to be introduced by a U.S. senator from your state, but you're lucky to get a senator to speak on your behalf. In my case, three senators—Dianne Feinstein, Barbara Boxer, and my friend Olympia Snowe, a Republican from Maine and a longtime friend and a fellow Greek American—all testified. In what was a highly unusual act for a Speaker, Nancy attended the hearing. She only planned to watch, but the presence of the Speaker of the House sent the Senate staff into a flutter. The committee chair asked Nancy if she would also speak, so she made her way to the podium and testified on my behalf. Dianne, Barbara, Olympia, and Nancy clearly knew something about the importance of women helping women. I was nearing the finish line, and they wanted to be there to see that I made it over. It was an important lesson for me, and one I will never forget, to make sure that I help other qualified women whenever I have the opportunity to do so.

A few hours after the hearing concluded, the *Sacramento Bee* declared, "Confirmation Is a Breeze for Tsakopoulos Kounalakis." If they had only known all of the difficult work it took to make it look so simple. I had passed my first major public hurdle as a diplomat. Nancy's daughter Christine Pelosi quipped, "You proved one of the Pelosi adages. 'Proper preparation prevents poor performance.'"

I often think about how hard it was for me to get through the process to become a U.S. ambassador. It took ten months, two countries, a lot of hard work, and many sleepless nights. But never, not for one moment, do I look back and think it wasn't worth it.

# 6

# Viktor Orbán's Revolution Begins

Every U.S. ambassador arrives at post with a list of priorities. When I was preparing to go to Singapore, the list had been long and exciting, ranging from East-West trade to military training. Though Singapore is geographically little more than a large port city, it had become one of the United States' largest trading partners and was growing strategically in global importance every day. With President Obama's pivot—or rebalancing—toward Asia, Singapore was right in the heart of the new frontier for U.S. diplomacy.

Twenty years before, Central Europe had been the new frontier. After the collapse of the Soviet Union, Hungary had been a key strategic ally in the rebuilding of Central Europe after more than forty years of communism. During most of the 1990s, the United States was very busy in Budapest, helping the country construct a democratic system out of the autocratic, oppressive one that preceded it. We were instrumental in helping the Hungarians establish a system of rule of law, law enforcement, and a new free-market economy.

Hungary now was a full-fledged member of NATO and the European Union, and in some ways Washington considered Central Europe to be "mission accomplished." Critical as that was for Hungary and the world, I couldn't help lamenting that this made my list of priorities, or goals, rather thin. Nonetheless, my State Department briefings made it clear that there was still a lot of work to be done at Embassy Budapest. Hungary might not have been as dynamic as Asia, but we had hundreds of U.S. government employees located there, and it was up to me to lead the embassy forward and make progress on our goals.

I've already mentioned that Afghanistan was, at the time of my arrival in Budapest, President Obama's most important foreign policy priority. But there were many other issues more specific to Hungary. First, energy: Hungary sat on the main gas and oil routes from Russia to the rest of Europe. Europe gets the majority of its energy from Russia, a fact that has long troubled the United States. President Obama appointed Richard Morningstar special envoy for Eurasian energy, and he would come to Hungary several times over the years I was in Budapest—he once quipped that he had been accused of caring more about European energy security than the Europeans did. Part of his job was to urge the Europeans to find new sources and routes for oil and gas into the Continent. Azerbaijan was developing new gas fields, and the United States strongly supported the effort to get that gas to Europe in the cheapest, fastest, most efficient way possible.

Another priority in my portfolio: advancing what the European Union termed the "Eastern Partnership." With the expansion of NATO to include the former Soviet satellite states, a new line had been created between Russia and the West. The Baltic States, Poland, the Czech Republic, Slovakia, Romania, and Hungary—all countries that had been part of or allied with the Soviet empire—were now part of the most important Western alliance, NATO. Russia chafed at this, but other countries, like Ukraine, which abutted Hungary's eastern border, saw the value of becoming closer to the West. We weren't proposing that Ukraine join NATO, only that we find innovative ways to expand our cooperation. The Hungarians shared this objective, so they were natural partners in advancing the effort.

The United States and Hungary also worked together to promote the Eastern Partnership by training police officers from all over Eurasia at the International Law Enforcement Academy, located in Budapest. In 2010, with Dmitry Medvedev serving as president of Russia and

Vladimir Putin running the show from behind the scenes, the Eastern Partnership was more of an insurance policy than a top strategic priority for the United States. (It would come sharply into focus over the next few years, especially once Putin reclaimed the presidency and relations with Russia started to fray.)

Far-right extremism and intolerance were on the rise in Hungary, and another one of my priorities was to redouble our efforts to help Hungarians combat it. Around the world, the United States vigorously advocates for tolerance. This is a critical part of our foreign policy regardless of which party sits in the White House; it stands for who we are as a country. In any healthy democracy, the majority rules, but minority rights are protected. To most American ears, this sounds simple, maybe even frivolous—our country is made up largely of immigrants, and we get along pretty well. All around the globe you will find countries with political, religious, and ethnic majorities that are accustomed to controlling the power base and setting the rules for everyone. As the United States advocates for tolerance and minority rights, we argue that countries are better off economically, socially, and culturally when all their citizens enjoy the same rights and opportunities.

As I headed to Budapest, I knew my priorities inside and out. They had been outlined for me for months by the State Department. My briefings had been oriented around them, and State Department officers had helped me carefully craft a statement to the Senate Foreign Relations Committee to reflect them. But important though they were, I still couldn't shake the feeling that the wheel that advanced these priorities turned slowly. That's why a few weeks after I arrived in Budapest, when my courtesy calls were over and the pace had slowed, I began looking for other ways to advance U.S. interests and increase U.S.-Hungarian cooperation.

It didn't take long for me to find a project I could sink my teeth into. By an incredible coincidence, it turned out that Embassy Budapest had a real estate portfolio that was an absolute mess. As was evident from my first morning at the Chancery, we were in the midst of a major construction project. I soon found out that it was over budget, behind schedule, and mired in problems. "Eureka!" I thought. I shocked the management staff by jumping headlong into the details of our project to rebuild the security gates and guard posts around the perimeter of the Chancery. Gleefully, I reviewed the construction documents, sorted out the glitches, and made the kinds of executive decisions that would move the project forward. Who else, I thought, had the experience to demand that a contractor buy commercial-grade cement rather than agree to their plan to manufacture their own at a communist-era factory?

My deputy chief of mission, Jeff Levine, was thrilled to see me roll up my sleeves and jump into the details of the perimeter security project. He actively supported my hands-on engagement and was eager to see me take up an even bigger real estate challenge facing the embassy: a long-stalled property swap with the Hungarian government.

Nearly every embassy has a Marine House, home to the marine security guard detachment and the location of frequent and popular parties for the U.S. embassy community. But our Marine House was special. Many said it was the most beautiful of its kind anywhere in the world. It was perched high above the Danube, inside the gates of the Buda Castle, the medieval part of Budapest. It was one of the largest single properties in the Castle District, and its expansive outdoor space, with breathtaking views of the whole city, was unparalleled.

The United States acquired the property after World War II from the Hungarian government, and the Hungarians had wanted to get it back for many years. It had significant symbolic importance: in addition to the stately nineteenth-century buildings on the property, there was also a very old prison, which during Hungary's turbulent past had held some of the most important individuals in the country's history, including freedom fighter Lajos Kossuth; statesman Miklós Wesselényi; the country's first prime minister, Lajos Batthyány; and the writer and political activist Mihály Táncsics. The prison was located on a street named after Táncsics, so as a result, the property was referred to as Táncsics Mihály.

Back in 2006, the Hungarian government asked the U.S. government if we would give the property back. The two sides structured a simple land-swap deal, formalized by a very short, vague, nonbinding agreement. The deal went like this: the Hungarian government owned the building immediately adjacent to our Chancery. It agreed to remodel that building to U.S. government standards and give it to us when it was completed. In return, we would give Hungary the Táncsics Mihály compound and a twelve-unit apartment building that we had once used to house embassy staff. We also would give Hungary funds for the cost of the security upgrades needed in the adjacent building, estimated to be less than $2 million.

Most people in Hungary believed the Táncsics Mihály compound had been handed over to their country back when the agreement was signed, but that was not the case. In fact, in the three years before my arrival, the swap had turned into a very complicated and expensive mess. It wasn't just that the agreement was moribund; somebody needed to pay millions of dollars in unpaid engineering and design fees for studies that had been done for the annex building next to the Chancery. It was even worse. When I looked at the plans, it was clear that the work that had racked up all those unpaid bills was completely worthless. I could see that the Hungarians had been going in circles—there was no way to renovate the building to meet our security standards. It was obvious to me that the Hungarians would have to demolish everything but the building's historic façade and rebuild it from the inside out and from the basement up. That would cost far more than the Hungarian government had budgeted.

Every politically appointed ambassador thinks about the particular expertise he or she brings to the table, and I was excited to have a complicated project that was squarely in my wheelhouse. I also saw that I really couldn't lose. If the United States went forward with the deal, we would consolidate nearly all of our embassy staff in one location, improving efficiency and security, while realizing a huge savings on the rent we had been paying for office space around Budapest. If the deal didn't happen, that would be okay too. We would keep the magnificent Táncsics Mihály property. The only way we would lose would be if nothing happened and the situation remained stagnant.

The apartment building involved in the swap was perched right on the Danube, almost next door to the Parliament building. The views were magnificent, but because the apartment house had only one entry and exit and failed to meet U.S. safety standards, we'd been forced to stop using it for embassy personnel a few years before, and the valuable property was standing vacant. Now, if there's one thing that gets under the skin of a real estate developer, it's an empty building. At a minimum, I was determined either to move forward with the property swap or let it die, so that I could deal with the empty apartment complex. One way or another, I would put our real estate portfolio into proper shape before my tour of duty ended.

Settling into embassy work consumed my first few months in Budapest. But busy as it was, we were also waiting—for the April elections and what would almost surely be a change in the party that controlled Parliament and the government.

There had been just five parliamentary elections in Hungary since the fall of the Iron Curtain in 1989. Though the country had made tremendous progress in the installation of a democratic system, it had a very complex election process. Not only did elections span two separate days of voting about two weeks apart, members of Parliament were elected two ways. First, voters in each district picked the candidate they wanted as their direct representative. Next, they voted for "party lists," lists of names put forward by each political party running; whatever percentage of the vote each party won would determine the percentage of people on the list who got seats in Parliament. The leader of the party that won the most seats through these two methods combined became prime minister and was able to form a government.

A big part of what American embassies do around the world is observe and try to understand all the important things going on in the host county. With well-trained U.S. officers and knowledgeable, locally employed staff, we have tremendous resources to do this. During the elections, we deployed officers to communities throughout Hungary to interview voters and candidates and to watch the process unfold. Along with our trained American staff, our highly capable Hungarian political analysts Máté Hegedűs, Linda Mézes, and Tamás Zemplén traveled extensively and played a major role in our election coverage.

While our political and economic officers were in the field, other officers back at the embassy surveyed and analyzed the landscape. During the 2010 Hungarian elections, Jeff Lodinsky was one of the most important of these officers. The State Department often says consular officers are on the front lines of host-country engagement, because their section is where foreign citizens go if they need a visa to travel to the United States. American citizens tend to find the consular section if they are traveling and something goes wrong, like a lost passport—or worse. American expats also are usually aware of an embassy's consular office, as that's where they go to register a new baby as a U.S. citizen or figure out how to vote in elections back home.

Technically, it was not Jeff's job to evaluate the Hungarian political scene, but it was very fortunate for us that he did. As it happened, his wife, Judit, was Hungarian. They had met in the mid-eighties as students in Budapest, where Jeff was on a scholarship, determined to get a peek behind the Iron Curtain. After they were married, he joined the Foreign Service. He, Judit, and their family had been posted all over the world. As they traveled from post to post, they waited hopefully for the opportunity to serve in Hungary. Foreign Service officers are known and in large part hired for their facility with languages; in addition to the handful of languages that Jeff had learned for his other postings, he spoke fluent Hungarian.

In our country team meetings, Jeff reported on what was going on in the consular affairs section. But in our smaller meetings of senior staff, he provided another service, telling us what he was hearing on the radio, seeing on television, and picking up by talking to relatives or just people around town. He provided a perspective other than what Paul O'Friel and his political and economic section were hearing. Jeff also would tell us how my interviews and our embassy statements were resonating with the public. With an engaging personality and deep knowledge of Hungary, Jeff was well loved at Embassy Budapest. A few years later, while posted in Afghanistan, Jeff would be critically injured in the line of duty, and we would all take the news very hard.

Throughout the spring of 2010, the embassy watched the political campaigns electrify the country. In April, Viktor Orbán's center-right political party, Fidesz, and its coalition partner, KDNP, scored a huge victory, sweeping both district seats and party list votes, for a total of 263 out of 386 seats in Parliament. The Socialists had all but collapsed, coming in second but with a meager 59 seats.

Some cried foul that Orbán won a two-thirds majority when only

53 percent of the country had voted for his party. Orbán retorted that if there had been no party list but just district votes, as is done in the U.K., 95 percent of Parliament's seats would have gone to Fidesz or its coalition partner; the candidates he backed won in all but three of Hungary's 176 districts.

It was a landslide.

Of course, we had been watching closely to see whether Orbán would win a two-thirds majority or just a simple majority. We knew it was an important difference. But Hungary's brief history as a modern democracy indicated that there were checks and balances in place to control Orbán's power, even with a supermajority. Back in the 1990s, the Socialists and Liberals had held a supermajority, and though they had been able to make many more legislative changes than with a simple majority, there had been no overreaching that had caught the attention of the United States or the international community. The media, judiciary, and business sector appeared to be sufficiently independent to ensure that even with a supermajority, Orbán would have to work within the limits of the Hungarian legal system and respect the checks and balances put in place since 1989.

It was also important to remember that this was an internal political issue for Hungary. Domestic politics in countries that are democracies, friends, and allies are generally left outside of the purview of our bilateral engagement. Even when there are highly partisan arguments in our country over controversial issues like abortion rights, immigration, or same-sex marriage, our leaders generally do not wade into these arguments overseas. We generally don't tell our NATO allies how to run their democracies.

Though Hungary's domestic politics were largely out of bounds for us, political extremism was not. For months, we had been laser focused on the rise of a relatively new political party in Hungary called Jobbik, the Movement for a Better Hungary (Jobbik Magyarországért Mozgalom). During my confirmation hearing a few months before, I testified that radical anti-Roma and anti-Semitic sentiment in Hungary was confined to a small, vocal minority. But Jobbik, an extreme-right, ultranationalist, anti-Roma, and anti-Semitic party, was gaining political popularity at an alarming rate. Most troubling to me was where the support was coming from. It is generally believed that the best way to expand tolerance for minority groups is through education. But we were learning that university campuses across Hungary were becoming hotbeds of support for this radical new party. Jobbik had appeared on the scene in 2009's elections for the European Parliament, winning 14 percent of the Hungarian vote and three seats. In a June 18, 2009, article titled "A Nasty Party," *The Economist* described one of Jobbik's leaders thus: "Jobbik's public face is Krisztina Morvai, a blonde, telegenic law professor, noted for both her forthright feminism and her vituperative attacks on Israel. A message posted under her name on an Internet forum demanded that Hungarian Jews should play with their 'tiny circumcised tails' instead of attacking her. Ms. Morvai declines to discuss the matter. Jobbik says it will not comment on private correspondence."

Jobbik's nastiness was not confined to its rhetoric. It was closely connected to a large, aggressive militia called the Magyar Gárda (Hungarian Guard). The Magyar Gárda wore uniforms designed to echo those of the Arrow Cross, the Hungarian Nazis of World War II. They marched in areas with large Roma populations, with the clear intention of spreading fear and intimidation. Both the Socialists and Fidesz advanced policies to disband the Magyar Gárda and legally constrain its ability to demonstrate in a way that would incite violence. But in public forums, Jobbik continued to shout its slogan, "Hungary belongs to Hungarians."

Before the 2010 elections, Jobbik held no seats in Parliament. On the night of April 11, the first round of elections, Jobbik won 17 percent of the vote, two points shy of the Socialists' 19 percent. Close to a million Hungarians had voted for Jobbik, and its election success was deeply troubling to the United States. It was estimated that nearly 25 percent of the party's votes came from young people aged eighteen to twenty-nine.* I had been invited to all of the different parties' election-night celebrations. Although I went to the gatherings held by Fidesz; the

*Paul Hockenos, "Inside Hungary's Anti-Semitic Right-Wing," *Global Post*, June 1, 2010.

Socialists; and the newly created Hungarian green party, Lehet Más a Politika (LMP), I skipped Jobbik's festivities. When our talented press attaché, Jan Krc, was asked by the media why I hadn't celebrated with the ultranationalists, he noted dryly, "The United States does not consider Jobbik to be a democratic party." This prompted an angry open letter from Krisztina Morvai to me in which she stated that I had offended the Hungarians who voted for Jobbik. "Let me point out to you that your ideas concerning democracy are rather peculiar," she wrote to me. Morvai was arguing that because Jobbik was elected through the democratic process, it was by definition a democratic party. We strongly disagreed.

When they told me about the letter, Jeff Levine, Paul O'Friel, and especially Jan Krc were concerned that I would be upset about the public volley in the media. But I was just fine with it. "I know what Krisztina Morvai stands for, and I know what we stand for," I told them. "Jan simply made the point that Jobbik does not stand for values the United States defines as the core principles and values of democracy. We've said it before. Her reaction ensures that more Hungarians will hear that this is the U.S. position, so we've achieved something."

At the end of April—after the elections, but before Viktor Orbán was sworn in—I went to see the prime minister–elect in his transition offices. This encounter turned out to be much easier than our first, awkward meeting. With the election behind him, he was relaxed, rested, and basking in the glow of victory. His transition offices were filled with clean-cut, sharply dressed, confident young staffers, busily moving around with efficiency and purpose. Orbán and his political family had been in power from 1998 to 2002, and they were reportedly caught off guard when voters declined to grant the prime minister a second term. They knew how government worked and were eagerly preparing for their resumption of power now, nearly a decade later.

Going into this meeting, I had decided to keep my list of talking points very short.

"I'm sure," I began, "that by the time we see each other next and you have been sworn in as prime minister, you won't recall much of this conversation." He laughed, and I inwardly marveled at the change in his demeanor from our last meeting. "So let me just raise a few things that I think are timely. First, my old friend Justice Anthony Kennedy, a member of the United States Supreme Court, will be coming to visit Budapest in June. I hope you will be able to receive him."

Orbán immediately responded that he knew who Kennedy was and would do his best to be available. He glanced over at a staffer, who nodded vigorously and proceeded to scribble down the dates.

I continued. "Second, our national day of celebration is coming up soon. We've sent you a letter asking that you be our guest of honor and that you say a few words at the reception."

Orbán didn't appear to know that he had been invited to our Fourth of July event. He promised to look into it and get back to me.

Although protocol dictated that I invite the incoming prime minister as guest of honor to our Fourth of July celebration, I had an additional reason for wanting him there. In recent years, the embassy's reception was held at the ambassador's residence, which had a big lawn and space to accommodate the thousand or so people who typically attended. But in keeping with my plans to sort out the embassy's real estate portfolio, I decided that this year we would hold the celebration at the Marine House.

In my first salvo to resolve the entrenched property swap mess, I told Viktor Orbán that even though I was having Fourth of July at Táncsics Mihály, I was not reneging on the land swap deal. "But the property is so beautiful and the views are so breathtaking, I feel it will be a much better location for the party than up at my residence."

He looked perplexed and said he thought that the property had already been transferred, or at least promised to be transferred, to the Hungarian people.

I clarified that the deal was far from completed. But, I said, if he wanted to move forward with it, I would honor the terms of the outdated agreements. "However," I said, "I've drawn up a timeline, and we will have to hit the targets. I can't leave Budapest without having moved forward, one way or another."

Orbán was very clear on how he felt about the deal. "We are going to do it," he said emphatically. "Whatever it takes, I will do what needs to be done to make sure that property comes back into the hands of the Hungarians."

I mentioned that there were a lot of problems that would need to be sorted out, and he used this as another opportunity to bash the previous government, though in a more reserved way. Knowing what I did about the property swap mess, this time I had to take his point.

Just like the U.S. Congress, the Hungarian Parliament sets aside a gallery for the ambassadorial corps to come and observe proceedings. On May 29, 2010, the day Viktor Orbán was sworn in as prime minister, I was there. What I saw dramatically illustrated the shift in power in my host country.

The seats in Parliament were arranged like a horseshoe, and on the left I could see the remnants of the Socialist Party. Next to them were the proud but few members of the green party, LMP, who won sixteen seats. To the right were Jobbik's radical nationalists, many of them clad in the traditional Hungarian jackets they'd co-opted as one of their symbols. They were often referred to as Hungary's neo-Nazis, using rhetoric and taking positions reminiscent of the evildoers of the past. How sad, I thought, that on top of everything else, those who associated themselves with Hungary's Nazi history had managed to co-opt the country's traditional costumes.

In the middle of the horseshoe, spanning more than two-thirds of the seats, was a sea of Fidesz/KDNP members. Looking at them, I realized that none of us at the embassy or back in Washington had fully comprehended the party's massive victory. We'd been primarily focused on Jobbik, but now I could see that the Jobbik members, intimidating though they tried to appear in their black vests, were a minuscule group next to Fidesz.

While I was watching Fidesz take their oaths that day, visualizing their confidence and unity, the importance and implications of the supermajority came into focus for me. This, I thought, was why Orbán had been so nervous and excitable when I met him back in January. He knew his party would win and that he would be prime minister again, but he had been anxious about whether the Hungarian people would hand him this kind of power. I had worked among powerful men in my life, and I already knew enough about Viktor Orbán to understand that this was a man who knew how to wield power.

When I returned to the embassy, I called in Jeff Levine and Paul O'Friel.

"Guys, I think we've had it wrong," I told them. "The biggest story in this election isn't Jobbik, it's Fidesz. There may not be much to hold them back."

In all fairness, I should note that for weeks anti-Orbán pundits had been declaring that in handing him a supermajority the Hungarian people had signed a death warrant for Hungarian democracy. While these pundits included well-respected and well-informed Hungarian American scholars, they were almost all people who had a personal history with Orbán.

Pundits are certainly entitled to their predictions. Open debate is a critical part of how democracies function. But even with my own concerns about what might lay in store, it was the duty of the U.S. Embassy, and my duty as the ambassador, to view the Fidesz victory without prejudices or preconceived notions of what the party's supermajority would bring. As a friend, partner, and NATO ally, we owed Hungary that. It was our job to build bridges with the new government and take every opportunity to strengthen our cooperation and our relationship. We would watch very carefully what Viktor Orbán did with his power. But we would evaluate his policies as they were formulated, without political bias.

We didn't know it at the time, but the first salvos of Orbán's two-thirds revolution were about to be launched. In the new Parliament's very first vote, lawmakers passed a two-thirds law establishing the Day of National Unity in Hungary. It was to be celebrated on June 4, the anniversary of the signing of the Treaty of Trianon. This Day of National Unity called for all members of the "Hungarian nation"—including Hungarians living outside the country's borders—to come together in commemoration.

A few weeks later, Parliament passed another piece of watershed legislation, allowing ethnic Hungarians from former territories to apply for citizenship in Hungary and eventually vote in Hungarian elections. Such a measure had been debated for years. Now it was a reality, and to my mind a potentially troubling one. I alerted Washington, asking whether this was something we should be concerned about. The answer was no; many countries, including the United States, offered dual citizenship, and we couldn't tell Hungary who could and could not become a citizen of the country.

I pointed out that the United States had just granted Hungary entry into the Visa Waiver Program, allowing Hungarians with valid passports to register online and bypass long lines at the embassy to get tourist visas. If hundreds of thousands of new Hungarian citizens living in neighboring countries not in the Visa Waiver Program, such as Serbia, Romania, and Ukraine, were eligible for Hungarian passports, didn't that create a potential problem? But again, the answer from Washington was no, this is an internal Hungarian domestic policy issue. Do not engage.

On June 4, 2010, Hungary celebrated its first Day of National Unity. It was the first time since the end of World War II that Hungary would officially commemorate the anniversary of the signing of the Treaty of Trianon, the day Hungary lost two-thirds of its territory and more than half of its population. Ethnic Hungarians who were born and lived in historically Hungarian villages in Romania, Serbia, Slovakia, Austria, the Czech Republic, Ukraine, and Croatia were now eligible to become Hungarian citizens through a simple procedure for the first time in nearly one hundred years. A part of the job of ambassador includes attending the host country's celebrations. We were still a long way from comprehending the full implications of these first new laws adopted in Viktor Orbán's two-thirds revolution, but there was something slightly ominous about the reemergence of the Trianon Day commemorations—and we knew enough to stay away. After checking with us, many other embassies also declined to attend. We weren't the only ones who were getting nervous.

# 7

# Family Life

The ambassador's residence—so daunting on my first morning in Hungary—was slowly becoming a home. Some of the change was purely physical. The heavy darkness lifted when we hired a landscape architect to prune back the overgrown shrubbery and trees that surrounded the house. The light made everything better.

We knew we couldn't change some things, like the wood parquet floors, which, though beautiful to look at, creaked so badly that when we had dinner parties we had to wait until the waiters had set all the plates on the table and left the room before we could resume our conversations. But other problems were more serious. The wiring, for example, was old and unreliable. I was told that the Hungarian inventor who built the house in the 1920s had invented a system of copper wiring whose prototype still thrummed sporadically behind the walls. Whatever the reason, the house's power failed at least twice a week, the Internet went out twice a day, and the phones barely worked at all.

Jeff Levine had arranged a densely packed series of welcome parties at the residence for the first few weeks after my arrival. Though I was eager to meet the A-list of the embassy's Hungarian contacts, I worried about entertaining in the house. Not only was there a long list of repairs to be made, but its walls were still bare.

Every new ambassador is responsible for selecting a collection of art to be exhibited in his or her residence, working with the State Department's Art in Embassies program. Before I left Washington, the Art in Embassies staff asked me what kind of art I wanted. I told them I wanted anything by Andy Warhol, for the simple reason that the first time I'd ever been in an American embassy residence—in Greece, on a visit with my father back in 1990—the home was filled with fabulous midcentury modern art, including a giant Warhol portrait of Elizabeth Taylor. From that point forward, it defined my sense of American representational art.

The Art in Embassies staff had a stable of galleries and museums around the United States that would lend the art until the ambassador's tour ended. Eventually, I would have a house full of vibrant Warhol lithographs, all from his Endangered Species series, to liven up the dour-looking residence. But when I arrived in Budapest, there was nothing on the walls; the artwork that had come with my predecessor's Art in Embassies package had departed when she did, and it would be many months before the Warhol lithographs arrived.

Looking at the empty walls in that dark, creaky house, I was beginning to despair about the looming entertainment schedule. So I called in my secret weapon: Kerry Valine. Kerry had worked for me in Sacramento and San Francisco for nearly as long as Markos and I had been married. A master of organization and detail, he had skillfully helped plan and manage nearly every event we hosted, big and small, from political fund-raisers to baby showers.

Before leaving for Budapest, I'd asked Kerry to relocate with us, but his soon-to-be husband wasn't willing to give him up that long. Now, seeing what I was up against with the welcoming events, I asked him to give me a few weeks. "The walls in the entertaining rooms are all bare, and the chef wants to serve whole chicken legs as cocktail hors d'oeuvres. They're delicious but very, very drippy. Please, Kerry, get on a plane!"

He arrived two days later. Eon and Neo were even more thrilled to see him than I was. While I worked long days at the embassy, Kerry gave the boys an extra helping of love and care and took control of the events Jeff had arranged at the residence. To compensate for the stale decor and naked walls, he filled the house with wall-to-wall flowers, making it beautiful in a way I could not have imagined on my own.

Kerry's keen eye saved me in those early weeks. So did the help of another friend. Eleni Korani, a Greek Hungarian, and her husband, Ernst Wastl, owned one of Budapest's most respected art galleries. It hadn't taken Eleni and I long to find each other—we shared a name and an ethnicity, and we were about the same age. Eleni showed up at the residence one morning with a truckload of art from her gallery to hang on the walls until the Warhols arrived from the United States.

Eleni was one of the most energetic and enthusiastic people in all of Budapest. Blessed with glamorous good looks and a dynamic personality, she lit up every room. She told me, "Foreigners say to me, 'Hungarians are known for being a little gloomy. But Eleni, you are always so happy, why?' I tell them, 'I am not Hungarian, I am Greek!'"

But until she was about nine years old, Eleni had actually been a stateless person, without citizenship in any country. Having fled Greece in the early 1950s after the end of the civil war, her communist grandparents (Greek partisans) and their young children arrived in Hungary as refugees, seeking the promised utopia. I thought I had met diaspora Greeks of every conceivable background, but I'd never met communist refugees. Eleni and I became close friends, bound by our common ethnic heritage. It was irrelevant to us that our families had been on opposite sides during the Greek civil war.

In general, friends are a tricky business when you work for the U.S. government and have a high-level security clearance. You are required to provide the name, citizenship, and approximate birthdate of anyone close to you who is not a U.S. citizen. That doesn't mean you can't have friends, and it doesn't mean they are subject to any particular scrutiny. It just means you have to let the government know about those relationships. Because of this sensitivity, you start thinking about friends in a very different way. It also tends to bring embassy families very close, and we made some wonderful friends in the Foreign Service, as well as a small but dear group of Hungarian friends along the way.

With our large family and my political passions, Markos and I had

90## Madam Ambassador

always done a lot of entertaining, but our business and social calendars really filled up once we got to Hungary. It would have been easy to go out every night, but I set a limit of three evenings per week that I was willing to host or attend events. We preferred events at the house because then the boys knew we were home. Back in California, Markos and I had a deal with Eon and Neo: we would always invite a few kids when we entertained, but it was their job to host the kids' party while we hosted the adults. "But it won't work if kids are running into our party crying," I told them. "You have to make sure they're happy. Give them first pick of the toys, and share everything."

Though they were only about five and four years old when we gave them these responsibilities, Neo and Eon took their duties seriously. When we began to entertain at our house in Budapest, I wanted to continue our tradition of inviting guests for the boys, so I would ask the embassy's senior staff if they would bring their kids to each event. At first, no one volunteered. The officers themselves were on their best behavior at the ambassador's residence. Rising through the ranks as career Foreign Service officers, they were trained to never eat too much from the hors d'oeuvres table and to be sure to mingle with guests rather than chat with one another. No one wanted to have to keep an eye on their kids at the same time.

Eventually, however, I had a few takers whose children always arrived dressed in their prettiest dresses and nicest outfits. Eon and Neo shared their toys with their young guests, and by the time the party was over, a parade of kids had usually marched down to the bar for some nonalcoholic champagne—a breather from the Nerf-gun battles taking place upstairs, shoes off and hair bows flying.

The house may have presented some challenges, but one thing was clear: Neo and Eon had settled enthusiastically into life in Budapest. They loved the big ice-skating rink in the center of town, the nineteenth-century thermal baths, and the old-fashioned circus. They especially enjoyed their classes and classmates at the American International School of Budapest. But the boys were less enthusiastic about the activity we'd arranged for their weekends.

Back in San Francisco, from the time each was three years old, Neo and Eon had attended the Chinese American International School. One reason Markos and I had considered Singapore the ideal embassy post was that the boys would have been able to attend a local public school that mandated Chinese as part of the curriculum. When we were handed Hungary, one of my biggest concerns was that they would lose their grasp of Mandarin. But Markos investigated Budapest's Chinese community and found that, astonishingly, we would be living amid the largest Chinese population in continental Europe.

It turned out that in 1988, Hungary, hoping to reduce its international isolation, had signed a treaty with the People's Republic of China that allowed for visa-free travel between their two countries. For almost five years, Chinese nationals traveled to Hungary with the official intention of tourism, but many of them stepped off the plane in Budapest and never returned. As the community grew, it established a weekend Chinese-language school in Budapest. Every Saturday and Sunday, from nine in the morning until three in the afternoon, about two hundred ethnic Chinese kids, many with Hungarian names like Judit and Imre, gathered at a building that during the week was a Hungarian elementary school. Even though they were native Mandarin speakers, they attended the weekend school to learn to read and write in Chinese (an intense and difficult process, given that you need to be able to recognize at least three thousand symbols just to read a Chinese newspaper with any proficiency).

The curriculum at the boys' Chinese school in San Francisco had hewed pretty close to the Western model. But at the Kínai Nyelviskola (Hungarian for "Chinese Language School"), Neo and Eon used the same books that children in the People's Republic of China used. The other kids at the school were all PRC nationals, many of them from northern China.

As Eon and Neo already were enrolled in weekday classes at the American International School, they were not very happy about spending Saturdays and Sundays at the Kínai Nyelviskola. And the school itself presented some challenges. Back in San Francisco, the mainly Taiwanese teachers were taught how to nurture the children American-style—something that's not built in to the Chinese education system, to say the least. After the boys had attended the Kínai

Nyelviskola for a few weeks, they came home with a complaint. Not only did the teacher never hug them, smile, or speak sweetly—as my then second- and third-graders were accustomed to—she used a tennis racket to discipline misbehaving students. Markos and I knew how much the boys didn't want to spend their weekends at Chinese school, so we figured they were exaggerating. But a few weeks later, when I picked them up from school and asked them about their day, Neo said, "Here's some good news: the teacher doesn't hit kids with a tennis racket anymore. Now she uses a bamboo stick."

I realized my kids had been telling the truth about the tennis racket. First off, I advised them not to do anything that would cause the teacher to hit them. Then I called Ed Loo.

Ed, the embassy's public affairs counselor, was part of my senior staff. He and I had bonded early—he had been born in Hong Kong and raised from infancy in San Francisco, and it hadn't taken us long to figure out that his brother up in Marin County was my aunt's doctor. Ed was press attaché Jan Krc's boss and skillfully led one of the embassy's most important sections. He also spoke perfect Mandarin and had volunteered to speak to the Kínai Nyelviskola, as no one there spoke a lick of English. Tactfully, Ed let the director of the school know that the teachers couldn't hit the American ambassador's children. The director responded that the teachers didn't actually hit the children with the sticks. They just used them to scare the kids, encouraging better behavior.

For Neo and Eon, the Kínai Nyelviskola's playground provided no respite from the classroom. The teachers didn't monitor recess, so there was a bit of a *Lord of the Flies* situation. The big kids ran the show. If you were little and you had money or a device to play computer games, they took it. Once, one of the big kids left school on his own to go to McDonald's, and Eon told the teacher. Neo had to step in and negotiate to pay the kid 2,000 forints (about ten dollars) not to beat up his younger brother.

Markos and I were secretly, if a bit nervously, pleased that the boys were facing these kinds of real-world situations. We knew that the fact that they had to get along using only Mandarin was especially good for them and would serve them well.

Still, the boys tried to get out of the Kínai Nyelviskola with every tool at their disposal. One method was to try to find sympathy outside the family. One of their jobs was to greet our guests at residence parties when they arrived. When asked the inevitable question "Where do you go to school?" they would explain, "We go to the American School during the week, but on Saturday and Sunday we go to Chinese school. So our parents make us go to school *seven* days a week. And the teachers hit us with bamboo sticks." One day I overheard them talking in their room. Neo was telling Eon, "Forget it. She's never going to change her mind. We might as well just accept that we're going to have to go." Friends told me my boys would thank me one day for insisting they go to Chinese school. I really hope they are right.

The transformation of the Budapest residence into a happy home was driven in part by visits from a virtual parade of parents, siblings, cousins, and friends. Some traveled to Hungary from the United States; others came from Greece. Together, they turned the old house into a warm place filled with laughter and love. My cousin Sofia took time off from her job as a television reporter in Athens to take care of the boys every time Markos and I had to travel together, which was often. My niece Marisa came from Sacramento near the end of our tour and attended a whole semester of high school in Budapest. Of my four sisters, Athena, Chrysa, and Katina all visited (Katina twice), and Alexa, the youngest, lived with us for nearly half of our tour.

My father had remarried when I was in college, and my two youngest sisters were his daughters with my stepmother, Sofia. Now, at twenty-three years old, Alexa was more of a daughter to me than a sister. Kind and clever, she'd always had the key to my heart. After my swearing-in ceremony, when Markos and the boys were already in Budapest and it was clear that I would have to fly to Hungary by myself, I asked her to make the trip with me. She was eager to do it. After two weeks with us, she asked if she could stay indefinitely. We were delighted. Markos introduced her to Central European University, where she was accepted into the master's program for human rights law. From a logistics standpoint, having my young sister living with us might have been more work for me than it was help. I had to remind her to keep her room clean, and on nights we could have used a babysitter, she often had her own plans. But I could see Alexa growing responsible and mature in the context of our family unit, and I was proud and happy to be able to give her up-close mentoring at an important time in her life.

One unexpected benefit of having Alexa as an official "member of household" was that she was able to keep me in the loop about what was happening in parts of the embassy that I was less likely to hear about. While her weeks were filled with studies, on the weekends she went to parties and socialized with some of the embassy's junior officers. Her stories helped me stay informed about goings-on throughout the embassy community. It was actually pretty useful. But far more important than anything else, Alexa's presence with us provided the boys with abundant love and familiarity, and I instinctively knew how critical that was. When I had busy days or busy weeks and felt like I was physically and mentally absent from my children, I knew they were in the warm embrace of their aunt Alexa and so many other aunts, uncles, cousins, and family members who came and stayed.

Though our home was always full of extended family, my father only visited me in Budapest once. The Great Recession of 2008 had hit Sacramento hard and land developers extra hard. There were moments when I felt tremendously guilty that he was weathering the storm without me to help him. I did what I could from afar, and I knew that my ambassadorship was bringing honor and prestige to him and our family. I also knew that it had been time for me to strike out on my own. I'd been given the rare opportunity, even if it was for just a few years, to do something entirely unrelated to the business that had been more his dream than mine. Still, I had loved working with him over so many years—nearly two decades. I missed talking to him every day and worried about him constantly. Although he would manage to get through the economic tsunami, as he called it, without me, part of me always felt like I should have been there to help.

Though my father could only visit once, my stepmother, Sofia, came five times. Most of those visits were to see Alexa while she was living with us, but she also was very close to Neo and Eon. Even though she isn't my mother, Sofia Tsakopoulos is every bit my boys' grandmother. When Markos and I traveled to Washington for the ambassadorial seminar, she moved into our San Francisco apartment and took care of them. "This job isn't about overseeing a nanny," I warned her. "You'll have to be the nanny, okay?"

Sofia had always had a lot of help with Chrysa and Alexa when they were small, so the kind of heavy lifting involved during those two weeks was new to her. Back then, Kerry helped out with grocery shopping and driving, so Sofia wasn't entirely on her own, but my step-mother fed the boys, dressed them, bathed them, read to them, settled disputes, and put them to bed every night. And the way she took care of Neo and Eon, the love that she showered on them, powerfully en-deared her to them. Her visits to Budapest were very important to the boys, reminding them that they were well loved and that their Califor-nia home was waiting for them when their tour of duty was over.

As I immersed myself in the daily work of running an embassy and grappling with the rapid changes unfolding in Hungary, I could see that my husband was struggling to find his own footing.

From the very beginning, Markos and I had jumped into the ambas-sadorship as a team. When we first started talking to Hillary Clinton and Nancy Pelosi about it years before, we said that "we" wanted a post. At one point, Nancy looked at us, confused, and said, "Which one of you would actually be the ambassador?" Everyone knew how compat-ible we were—that we finished each other's sentences, complemented each other's expertise, and enjoyed doing things together whenever we could. Again and again, friends and family referred to us as "two for one" in terms of what Hungary would get.

But the edges of this unity quickly started to fray. When we arrived at the State Department for charm school, we started out in the same briefings, but after a few days they separated us. While the future am-bassadors went off to classified briefings, spouses received instruction in how to run a residence. Markos had no interest, to put it mildly, in table settings and name tags.

After a day we'd spent in very different ways—I'd been in meetings with the commander of U.S. Special Forces, and he'd been with the spouses getting a lesson on protocol—we took a walk on Washing-ton's Mall, and Markos told me he was worried by something one of the women, married to a former politician, had said. She told Markos, "When my husband ran for election, *we* were running, and then *we* won. But then he disappeared to go do the job, and I rarely saw him or even knew what he was doing all day." She confessed that she was worried that the same thing would happen when he was an ambassador. Markos relayed this to me, concerned it was about to happen to us.

We both sensed that our roles, long entwined, were about to break apart. And there was another issue that we had to discuss: my name.

Eleni Tsakopoulos-Kounalakis was not going to work. Although we had legally hyphenated our names when we got married, it was too unwieldy even for us, and we never used the whole thing. At the boys' school in San Francisco, we were known as the Kounalakis family, but professionally I was always Eleni Tsakopoulos. For protocol reasons, the officers in the East Asian and Pacific Affairs Bureau (at that point, I was still planning on Singapore) were practicing the whole long name.

"It's too much to ask of people to say both names," I told Markos. "Even one will be a problem for the Singaporeans—can you imagine both of them? I'm going to have to pick one."

If we had discussed this even just a few weeks before, it would have been obvious that I should use my professional maiden name. But an uncharacteristic bit of insecurity had crept in during those first days of charm school, and Markos took a clear position.

"Have I got a name for you!" He said it like he was joking, but I knew he wasn't.

He wanted me to be Ambassador Kounalakis. I was shocked. How could he ask me to suddenly take a name that I'd never used before? Markos explained that he believed it would be better for our family, all four of us, if we had the same name.

As my husband and I stood together on the Mall, my instincts told me not to push back on this issue. Marriage is, after all, about give and take. Markos had never before asked me for anything that was really hard for me to give. Yet I knew he was giving in a way that was already very difficult. It was my turn to bring things back into balance. So Ambassador Kounalakis it would be.

When we arrived in Budapest, the split in our roles cracked wide open. I was whisked off to the embassy each morning, while he was left at home in the dark old house, trying to get the Internet working. Every time it crashed, everyone would look to him to fix it, and I would see the hairs on the back of his neck stand up.

I should explain that before we were tapped, Markos was publishing the *Washington Monthly*, a venerable and well-circulated magazine based in the nation's capital. Without a doubt, he was the foreign policy expert in our family; all along the way, he had coached me, helping me prepare for my Senate confirmation hearing. But as we packed up for Budapest, he and editor Paul Glastris found a partner for the *Monthly* to take over the fund-raising responsibilities. Markos became the magazine's publisher emeritus and prepared himself to help me in Hungary. But he found little to do. It turned out that of all the American Foreign Service officers working at the embassy, only two spouses were not eligible for a job at the embassy—those of the deputy chief of mission and the ambassador.

I'd never known Markos to be deflated, but I saw it starting to happen, and I grew worried. This was exacerbated by the fact that because I was busier than ever, the demands of parenthood, for the first time, fell disproportionately on my husband. Markos had always been a very engaged father, but he was suddenly thrust into the role of stay-at-home dad. He had to take the boys to the doctor, get their immunizations, meet their teachers at school, arrange for the school bus, figure out lunch, and make sure they were doing their homework. I didn't meet the boys' teachers until we'd lived in Budapest for three months. If there was one upside to my packed schedule, it was that it gave Markos and the boys valuable time together. Over the next three-and-a-half years, they took "guy" trips to Egypt, the Czech Republic, Slovakia, Germany, Austria, Italy, and other places. Although I would have loved to have joined them, I was happy to see my husband and sons growing so close.

Between meetings at the school and trips to the kids' doctors, Markos started to figure out a plan. First, he called his friends Ellen Hume and John Shattuck. Ellen and Markos had served together on the board of Internews, a global NGO, primarily funded by the U.S. government, that helped communities around the world train journalists and set up independent media. John and Markos sat together on the board of

Common Cause, the influential "good governance" organization. Only after we found out that we would be coming to Budapest did Markos learn that Ellen and John were married to each other. Even better, they had moved to Budapest just a few months before us, when John became the rector of Central European University, which George Soros founded in 1991. Ellen was working at CEU's Center for Media and Communication, and she immediately offered Markos a perch there.

The position at the media center was a godsend for my husband, but it wasn't enough to keep him completely busy. So Markos started to devise projects that would allow him to get out into the community and satisfy his journalistic drive. Each project, however, had to be vetted and approved by the State Department, and that proved problematic. An HBO documentary on Budapest's Chinese community was shot down for being too political. A job with a start-up technology company was considered a conflict of interest. A proposal for an apolitical television series called *Ambassador's Kitchen* might have made money for someone, so it would have been an exploitation of Markos's position. He couldn't win, and he was growing more and more frustrated.

I tried my best to make it easier on him. By then, we knew several other couples posted in Europe who were going through the same thing, so at least Markos wasn't alone. Trying to make the best of the situation, he joined the local diplomatic spouses' club, where he befriended Claus, the husband of Aliza Bin-Noun, the Israeli ambassador to Hungary. Claus and Markos decided to attend their first spouses' club tea together. They had no idea that their presence would cause a scandal, with the wives of several diplomats from Islamic countries leaving the tea and refusing to return. It was improper for men to attend the event, they said.

It helped that the embassy staff understood that Markos was a foreign policy pro. At every opportunity, Paul O'Friel pulled him aside to get his take on things going on in the world. He could see that Markos had a gift for recognizing trends in world affairs, and Markos appreciated someone noticing.

Eventually, my husband found his place. With the encouragement of his colleagues at CEU, he decided to go back to school. At fifty-four years old, he enrolled in CEU's doctoral program in political science.

He was studying and working with students half his age, but he loved every minute of it. And while I would be Ambassador Kounalakis for the rest of my life, he would earn a title in Hungary too: Doctor Kounalakis.

Markos's parents, who were in their late eighties, came to visit after we had been in Budapest for just a few weeks, and they stayed for three months. Though Markos's mother, Vasiliki, suffered from Alzheimer's disease, she was still cognizant enough to know who we all were. The stimulation of the family and the bustle of the embassy residence were good for her. But even though Vasiliki still knew who we were, she didn't exactly know where she was and repeatedly asked her husband to tell her. My father-in-law Tony's hearing was weak, and I had to wonder what the Hungarian staff thought when Markos's parents were yelling at each other and we were yelling at them, all in Greek.

"Tony, where are we?" Vasiliki would shout at him.

"We're in Sacramento," Tony would reply, hoping that would ring a bell, knowing that "Budapest" would not.

"Oh, Sacramento," she would respond. "When are we going home?"

"A few days, don't worry," my father-in-law would yell back.

"Okay." But after a pause, it would start all over again. "Tony, where are we?" And so on. It wasn't always easy, but I was determined not to squelch my family's voices. I didn't want Neo and Eon ever to feel they had to hide their family just because it wasn't always picture-perfect.

Once again, my dear friend Eleni stepped in to help. Her children had a Greek nanny but didn't need her when they were in school. So Eleni sent the nanny to my house to take Vasiliki on long walks through the nearby tree-lined boulevards, giving my elderly mother-in-law much joy.

My father-in-law loved being with his grandsons and making sure they were learning everything that young Cretan Americans should know about life. And Tony knew a lot, because he had seen a lot. When he was a teenager, he witnessed the Nazi invasion of Crete. His father, Markos, had gone to fight the Italians up north, along the Albanian border (my grandfather Kyriakos was there too). Although Tony and his three brothers were too young to deploy with the Greek army to

Albania, they were plenty able and very willing to take up the fight at home. They joined the resistance, fighting in the Battle of Crete, when everyone who hadn't left to fight elsewhere—the young, the old, and the women—attacked the Nazi paratroopers as they attempted to take the island by an air invasion. The Germans assumed the invasion would be a quick and simple matter, but more than three thousand Nazi soldiers were killed. Though they had already invaded much of Europe, including Poland, Czechoslovakia, and France, the invasion of Crete was the first time they encountered mass resistance from the civilian population. As a direct result, the Nazis abandoned their strategy of using large numbers of paratroopers to take new territory.

Critical to the underground resistance movement's efforts was the dissemination of information to counter the powerful German propaganda. The Nazis had confiscated all radios and told the people that there was no use resisting; Crete's future would be in German hands, so they might as well cooperate. The resistance printed flyers that kept Cretans informed on the war's progress and let them know that all was not lost. They printed the information on thin cigarette paper; Tony and his brothers would deflate the tires of Tony's truck, stash the papers between the tube and the tire, and then re-inflate them. Tony was still a boy, not even eighteen, and he had the dangerous job of moving the papers from village to village, passing Nazi checkpoints, and casually standing by while his truck was searched. (The first time I heard this story, I looked at Markos and said, "You know, you did the same thing. That's what war corresponding is all about, right?")

Tony gave me one of my proudest moments during my time in Hungary. Admiral Eric T. Olson, who commanded U.S. Special Forces—*all* Special Forces, including the Green Berets and Navy Seals—came to Budapest to check on the American effort to help the Hungarians develop their own Special Forces capabilities. One night, I had the admiral and his team over for dinner with his Hungarian counterparts. Admiral Olson walked into the house surrounded by a dozen of his staff, all in uniform. I introduced them to my tall, silver-haired father-in-law, who stood leaning delicately on his cane. When they learned that Tony had fought in the Battle of Crete and served in the underground resistance, they were astonished. They had studied the famous battle during their training and couldn't believe they were meeting a veteran of that conflict—one who could speak English "pretty good" and still held himself with the casual confidence of the young man who had calmly stood by as his propaganda-laden truck was searched again and again.

In the eyes of my embassy staff, my ambassadorship was in many ways characterized by the steady stream of visitors who came through. Not just cousins and extended family—many of Markos's and my friends visited as well. It was no accident. Rather than push back against the flood of requests to visit, Markos and I would strongly insist that people come. "Please, just get on a plane," I remember writing in e-mails again and again. Sometimes I would even threaten, telling them they would have a hard time over the next fifty years explaining what good friends we were if they hadn't managed to visit when I was an ambassador!

It wasn't easy to manage so many visitors. Very often, I would only get to see our guests once or twice during their stay. But the most important moment for everyone, the moment that they all remembered, was the visit to my office. I should point out that my "office call" policy wasn't limited to people I knew. In fact, during my three-and-a-half years in Budapest, I had literally thousands of visitors from the United States come see me in my office. Family and friends, yes, but also friends of friends, students, sports teams, religious groups, business leaders, cultural groups, and others. Many of them I knew; most of them I didn't. My policy was that I would agree to see just about anyone from the United States who contacted my office and asked for a visit. It wasn't because I had nothing else to do, and it certainly wasn't expected of me. My assistant, a highly capable Foreign Service professional named Sheila Jefferson, couldn't quite believe I was willing to open my door this way. While she dutifully handled all the paperwork and logistics that came with so many visitors, Sheila would tell me in her British-American accent, with some exasperation, "Ambassador, some of these people think the embassy is a travel agency!"

Once people were sitting on my sofa, wearing everything from suits and ties (appropriate) to shorts and T-shirts (not so much), they all, even the best educated and most experienced among them, asked the same questions: "What does an ambassador do? What does the embassy do? How do you *become* an ambassador? How did *you* become an ambassador?" and so on. As a representative of the American people, I felt obligated to answer these questions as completely as I could (though I also enjoyed doing so).

One of the first things I showed people in my office at Embassy Budapest was that I had two computers on my desk. One was plastered with red stickers warning "Secret." Because the computer was turned off and the screen was black, it was impossible for anyone to really imagine what they would see if I flipped the switch. I always wished that I could turn it on and let them experience this new dimension—without, of course, compromising our important system of private diplomatic communications.

The fact is, many Americans really don't know what our embassies do or what our ambassadors do. And although I was legally and morally bound not to disclose classified information, I knew that while I had people in my office, I could help them begin to understand the critical work our embassies perform. I would try to explain to them how, through our embassies, the United States shares our democratic values with the world and protects our families back at home. What we do, no other country does. People sometimes say that America can't be the world's police officer. But I would say, "Imagine for a moment a world without police."

Welcoming fellow Americans in for office calls was one of the most fulfilling parts of my ambassadorship. As I answered my visitors' questions, I would see their faces, old and young alike, start to change as they caught a glimpse of what so many members of the U.S. foreign and military services who serve our country overseas witness every day: even with all of our imperfections and the many mistakes that we have made along the way, the United States remains the greatest force for good in the world.

# 8

# The Curse of Turán and the Fourth of July

Growing up on the sunny banks of the Sacramento River, in our middle-class immigrant household, one of the first words I ever learned was "optimism." My father regularly declared that he was an optimist, and we kids should always do our best to be optimistic too. "Accentuate the positive, eliminate the negative!" I remember the old Bing Crosby song blaring over the radio with the whole family singing along. "See the glass half full, not half empty," I can still envision my dad telling us all at the dinner table, holding up a glass of water to demonstrate.

Upon arriving in Budapest it didn't take long for me, by this time a resolutely optimistic person, to see that pessimism was practically written into Hungary's history through something called the Curse of Turán. A poem written in 1832 by the nineteenth-century Romantic poet Mihály Vörösmarty explains its origin.

THE CURSE
"Men!" announced the baneful god of Pannon memory,
"I give to you a joyous land; yours to fight for, if necessary."

So great, brave nations fought determinedly for her
Until the Magyar [Hungarians] finally emerged as the bloody victor.
Oh, but discord remained in the souls of the nations: the land
Can never know happiness, under this curse's hand.


*"Férfiak!" így szólott Pannon vészistene hajdan,*
*"Boldog földet adok, víjatok érte, ha kell."*
*S víttanak elszántan nagy bátor nemzetek érte,*
*S véresen a diadalt végre kivítta magyar.*
*Ah de viszály maradott a népek lelkein: a föld*
*Boldoggá nem tud lenni ez átok alatt.*


Hungary's national anthem continued the lament: "Fate, who for so long did'st frown / Bring them happy times and ways." I heard the song played everywhere, seemingly constantly, its doleful melody contrasting sharply with Greece's hard-charging anthem or our own stirring "Star-Spangled Banner." How many times I listened as Hungarians joined in the singing, reminding themselves of their national misfortune.

One of Hungary's best-known songs, "Gloomy Sunday," written in 1933 by Rezső Seress, is popularly known as "The Hungarian Suicide Song." A romantic ode to death, "Gloomy Sunday" is simultaneously enticing and chilling. The song was made famous by Billie Holiday in the 1940s, but because Seress never had a copyright on it, he gained neither fame nor royalties. In response to his bad luck, the story goes, he jumped out of the window of his apartment. His wife killed herself not long after.

All morbid legends aside, Hungarian pessimism has very serious implications. Hungary's suicide rate has ranked the sixth highest in the world, and it's reliably in the top ten. During my time in Hungary, tragic reports regularly peppered the news: two girls in a car poisoning themselves with exhaust, a Roma leader hanging himself, a business leader with cancer overdosing on sleeping pills.

So it is important to recognize how significant it was that the new Orbán government, in those early days after the election, had sparked a genuine sense of optimism in the country. I'm not suggesting that everyone in Hungary was behind them—certainly, the opposition and many of its supporters were quite unhappy about the situation. But people across all walks of life felt that a new day had arrived in Hungary and that, at a minimum, it was only fair to give Orbán a chance.

As I began to make my way around Budapest to visit the new cabinet members appointed by Orbán, I found tremendous support for continuing the strong cooperation that characterized our bilateral relationship with Hungary. Most of the ministers recognized that the partnership with the United States was as important, or more important, for them as it was for us. Hungary benefited tremendously from the United States in terms of security, trade, and investment. My staff and I moved quickly to build strong relationships with Orbán's ministers, particularly those in charge of defense, foreign affairs, justice, and the interior. I already had my concerns about the mercurial Orbán and reasoned that if he was ever tempted to throw a grenade into the U.S.-Hungarian relationship, as he had tried to do with Ambassador Brinker, his own ministers might be motivated enough to hold him back.

The prime minister had managed to attract some of conservative Hungary's best and brightest to work in his government. Many officials were not just the top experts in their fields but also had impressive records showing a strong commitment to transatlantic cooperation. They were energized to have won the two-thirds majority, and most of them told us, with humility, that they realized great power carried tremendous responsibility.

All this was very encouraging. Still, as I made my rounds, I couldn't help but feel I was racing the clock. The stronger the linkages between the embassy and the ministries, the less we would have to rely on the prime minister's temperament to ensure that cooperation between the United States and Hungary, and our bilateral relationship, remained strong in the coming years.

Though the swirl of the elections had immersed Hungary in political discourse, economic problems still threatened to pull the country under. The global crisis of 2008 hadn't hit only the United States hard.

There is a saying: "When the United States sneezes, the world catches a cold." Imagine what happens when the United States has a crippling flu. Europe was suffering so badly that there were doubts about whether the Eurozone could survive intact.

The economic crisis that had clobbered so much of Europe and the United States had come to a head in Hungary in 2008. The amount of debt the country had racked up under the Socialist government was staggering. If not for a $25.1 billion bailout package, Hungary would have defaulted on its sovereign bonds, sending the economy into a downward spiral. As a condition of the bailout, Hungary was required to reduce its deficit to less than 3 percent of GDP. The usual way for a bailed-out country to do this is to dramatically reduce government spending—a tactic known as austerity. When he was prime minister, Gordon Bajnai had made drastic, painful cuts and implemented many of the emergency austerity measures required under the bailout. But a significant deficit remained, and as it took office in the summer of 2010 the Orbán government had precious little time to close the gap. The International Monetary Fund was calling for structural changes to the budget that would further reduce government spending. But with its two-thirds supermajority in Parliament, the government had other ideas, and it began to implement what it called "unorthodox measures."

These measures aimed at closing the budget gap not with additional cuts in government spending but through increased revenue. Where would Hungary get the money? Orbán's first move was to tax the banks. In most countries, best practices call for taxes to be implemented over time, giving businesses a chance to adjust, but almost overnight Hungary adopted a tax on banks calculated as 0.5 percent of the value of their assets. That was more than three times what had been proposed in any other European country, and because the tax was levied based on asset values rather than profits, many banks saw that year's earnings immediately wiped out.

Rumors then began to circulate that the government was going to nationalize the pension system. Government contributions to private pension funds counted as government expenditures, adding to the deficit, unlike public pensions, where the expenditure only occurs once pensions are paid out. In Hungary at that time, about $13 billion of citizens' pension money was managed by private investment groups. The word going around was that the government planned to snatch all that pension money from the private firms and put it back into the country's coffers so it could invest in its own projects and plug the year's deficit with one swift action.

As rumors about Orbán's unorthodox measures swirled in Budapest, I was invited to attend a luncheon before the 2010 graduation ceremony at Central European University. I sat next to CEU's founder, George Soros, the multibillionaire finance mogul and probably the most famous living Hungarian American. Soros and his family had narrowly survived the Holocaust by hiding out in Budapest in 1944, and they helped others survive as well. Years later, Soros was involved behind the scenes in nudging forward the collapse of the Soviet Union, and many Central Europeans considered him a hero. His philanthropy in the region, from charitable assistance for the Roma to his pro-democracy Open Society Institute, was unmatched. But of all of these efforts, Soros was clearly most proud of the establishment of CEU. Every year, he attended the graduation ceremony, personally handing diplomas to hundreds of graduates.

As we sat together in the dining room of the lavish Hungarian Academy of Sciences, I asked him what he thought about Orbán's "unorthodox measures" to close the budget gap. "Of course, most of what they're doing is certainly bad policy," he told me. "But Orbán has to fill the gap somehow, and he doesn't have many options, does he?" Was the legendary financier defending Orbán's unorthodox measures? It certainly sounded like it. But he went on. "Here's the problem: there are people in Budapest who are scared. And in Hungary, when people are scared, it is a very bad thing."

Given Soros's experiences in the Holocaust, his words chilled me. We had been talking about politics and economics. Of course, these are hotly debated issues around the world and in our country too. But what did Soros mean? Exactly what were people afraid of? Were the stakes still so high in Hungary that people could be "scared" when it came to politics and economics? George Soros seemed to be saying so.

———

National day celebrations are a staple of diplomatic life. As ambassador, you attend those of other countries and host yours when the time comes. For some countries, like the United Kingdom, the national day is the queen's birthday. For others, like France, which celebrates on Bastille Day, the day is in commemoration of the start of a revolution. For the United States, of course, it's the Fourth of July, celebrating the Declaration of Independence.

The year 2010 was our nation's 234th birthday, and for Embassy Budapest, the Fourth of July 2010 was a spectacle. When I first told my staff that I wanted to have our party at the Marine House, they strongly resisted. It wasn't set up to accommodate such a large event, they said. But I pushed back against the pushback and laid out my arguments as to why we needed to hold the party at the Táncsics Mihály compound. My plan was to make our Fourth of July party so fantastic that Viktor Orbán and all the government officials in attendance would remember why they wanted the Marine House property so badly.

The event drew nearly a thousand guests, and the property was splendidly decked out with red, white, and blue bunting, tents, and stages. Food stations overflowed with American specialties: hamburgers, cupcakes, and—recently arrived in Budapest—Starbucks coffee. We had invited the Hungarian media to cover the event, and they were there in full force, drawn by the news that Viktor Orbán would attend the party, along with most of his cabinet. Reporters and cameras packed the risers to get the best possible shots of the stage.

As I escorted the prime minister onto the property, I could see that he was impressed by the overflowing crowd, the boisterous Hungarian Defense Forces military band, and the general festivity. We stopped for an espresso at one of the Starbucks stands, then made our way down a long stone staircase to the second tier of the party, where the guests had gathered for the presentation of the colors by the marines. The band struck up a march, and Orbán and I passed through the crowd to the bunting-draped stage. As we did, he told me, seriously, "This is an important property for us. We are going to get it back."

I beamed at him and said I would work very hard to make sure that happened.

At the podium, I welcomed our guests, then I asked the prime minister to take the stage. As he did, he raised my hand, bowed, and kissed it. Our protocol office had asked Orbán's office whether he would perform this traditional Hungarian greeting, and the answer had been a clear no. Standing onstage, I was so surprised by his gesture that I broke out laughing.

When Orbán addressed the crowd, he spoke of the greatness of America and of democracy. It was a wonderful way to remind the Hungarian people of our countries' enduring friendship. I remembered my comment comparing him to a young Bill Clinton. Though it had been a diplomatic gaffe, it had probably led to his being on the stage that day. Maybe, I hoped, it was the kind of gesture that could lead to a relationship of trust and cooperation with Hungary's powerful new prime minister.

I understood that our relationship would be precarious. But his presence at our Fourth of July party that day was significant. With every television camera in the country at the celebration, broadcasting the prime minister's remarks, I thought, now he also has skin in the game in this relationship. But as I listened to Viktor Orbán speak behind the red, white, and blue bunting, I again found myself wondering what he would use his tremendous power to achieve.

When we came down from the stage, I took the opportunity to ask him about the bank tax, which was still being heavily criticized by the international business community. Did it have to be so heavy against one sector? Was there a way to spread the impact?

"No," he firmly declared. "They are the only ones with the ability to pay. But we will only have it for a short time, just until the crisis is over." As he spoke, it became clear to me that the size and duration of the special bank tax would be his, and his alone, to decide.

In the days that followed, television and newspapers were filled with pictures of the newly elected prime minister; his ministers Csaba Hende, Sándor Pintér, and János Martonyi; and president-elect Pál Schmitt drinking Starbucks coffee and celebrating with the Americans.

Less than two weeks later, U.S. Supreme Court Justice Anthony Kennedy arrived in Budapest. By then, word had spread among Hungarian government officials that Orbán had sanctioned open doors to the American ambassador and her staff. This was very important for us to do our job properly. And with Orbán's announcement that Hungary needed a new constitution, Justice Kennedy's visit gave us the opportunity to ask officials face-to-face about what would be in it and who would be responsible for drafting it.

Like me, Justice Kennedy had been born and raised in Sacramento, and he served as a federal judge there in the 1970s and '80s. I was good friends with his three kids, and he once joked that he watched me grow up and "always knew that Eleni would be an ambassador one day." Over the years, he had become close friends with my father. In the early days of my process to become an ambassador, my father lamented that he was losing his closest business associate. Justice Kennedy told him, "Angelo, it is important for your family—no, important for our country *and* for your family—that Eleni serve in this way. I know she will do a good job for our country, and beyond that, it is an acknowledgment of all you too have achieved, and of what is possible in America."

Over his many years serving on the U.S. Supreme Court, Justice Kennedy regularly traveled internationally at the request of the State Department. He had been as far as China to talk about the U.S. Constitution and an essential element of any democracy: the rule of law. His visit to Budapest could not have come at a better time.

The first laws adopted by the Orbán-controlled Parliament had been remarkable not only for the weightiness of their content but for the swiftness with which they were adopted—and the lack of the political debate or stakeholder participation that, in a mature democracy, would ordinarily accompany the passage of watershed legislation.

By the summer of 2010, just weeks into the term of the new government, it was clear that Orbán would not stop at constitutional amendments or even cardinal laws (laws that require a two-thirds vote of Parliament to change). He intended to move forward with the passage of an entirely new constitution for the country.

The Hungarian Constitution that was in place in 2010 had been adopted back in 1949, when the country was under Soviet control. In 1989, rather than adopting a new constitution, the newly independent country instead opted to amend the 1949 constitution heavily. However, even at that time the amended constitution was considered a placeholder until a new constitution could be written—one that included such things as a meaningful preamble. Another argument that Viktor Orbán used for the justification of a new constitution was that the 1989 vote to amend the 1949 constitution was not taken by parliamentarians who were freely elected but by the members of Parliament who were originally installed by the Soviets and remained in their seats.

To be clear, the decision to adopt a new constitution was squarely that of the Hungarian people—our friends and NATO allies. For the United States to weigh in was a very delicate matter.

Although there was little to indicate that Orbán would put a new constitution on the ballot as a referendum, or vote of the people, he had set up several advisory groups. It was our hope that the move signaled the powerful prime minister's intention to proceed with some level of inclusivity and stakeholder participation. With so many doors open to us, Justice Kennedy and I visited members of these advisory groups to talk about their vision for the new constitution. Most constitutional experts we spoke to believed that the country's existing constitution functioned very well in terms of protecting the post-1989 democratic rights of the people and ensuring the independence of Hungary's young democratic institutions. Substantive changes, we were told, would likely be minimal.

On July 15, Justice Kennedy and I visited the prime minister. Both sides of the table were packed with advisers. It was a lively discussion, with Orbán speaking confidently about his vision for Hungary and its people. Justice Kennedy regaled the group with tales of his friend Ronald Reagan, a hero to the Hungarian people. When the subject turned to Hungary's new constitution, he described the U.S. point of view very eloquently. "Mr. Prime Minister, there is a certain patina to things that only time can create," he explained. "It is critical that a constitution be an enduring document, one that can stand the test of time." Everyone listened intently. "While Americans come from all different ethnicities and religions, our constitution belongs to us all." I leaned forward, eager to see how Viktor Orbán would take Justice Kennedy's well-articulated point about inclusivity when it came to ensuring the longevity of a country's constitution. Just then, the justice reached into his jacket and removed a small copy of the U.S. Constitution. He quickly signed a dedication on one of the first pages, then reached across the table to hand it to Viktor Orbán.

The prime minister received it with a humble gesture and looked inside to read the inscription. As he looked up at us, he was visibly moved and tapped the small volume against the left side of his chest. "Yes," he sighed. "We the people, we the people."

Justice Kennedy's reception in Budapest had been encouraging. But there was growing concern among our senior staff and officials back in Washington about the lightning speed and lack of consultation with which the Orbán government continued to advance new domestic economic and political initiatives. Several of the laws that had come down were very significant, such as the constitutional amendment that cut the number of members of Parliament by half, a change that would take effect during the 2014 elections. But domestic issues like that one had been openly debated in the country for many years and were recognized as being within the purview of the powerful new Parliament to decide. At this point, our biggest concerns focused less on the content of the laws than on the aggressive way they were being moved through Parliament.

In the midst of the whirlwind, on August 6, 2010, Hungarian lawmakers elected a new president. Pál Schmitt was the country's fourth post-communist president and the second (of three) with whom I would work during my tour.

By the time I left Hungary, in 2013, the country had seen only five post-1989 presidents come and go. I worked with three of them. Pál Schmitt was the fourth post-communist president and my second. It was a special privilege to have been invited to his swearing-in. I was part of a small group, mostly Hungarians, who were invited to share a glass of champagne after the ceremony. Schmitt had won Olympic gold medals in fencing in 1968 and 1972, and he still cut a fine and elegant figure as we celebrated in the Parliament building's grand dining hall.

I brought Máté Hegedűs from the embassy, and he served as my interpreter. Máté was one of our most senior analysts and a real star. Tall and handsome, he seamlessly blended into the group of Fidesz elite. Like many of the other Hungarian men in the room, he had the air of an elegant, dashing baron, minus the ascot.

As Máté whisper-translated discreetly over my shoulder, the new president spoke on assorted matters concerning his country. Then, at the end of his remarks, Schmitt burst out with an astonishing statement. "The young people of Hungary," the Olympic champion declared, "must hear the message that Hungarians are not losers!" Holding their champagne glasses high, the Hungarians in the room nodded and toasted in agreement.

Witnessing this, I was amazed. During our first few months in Budapest, my family and I had been overwhelmed by the beauty and sophistication of the once-imperial city. Venturing deep into the countryside, we discovered libraries, museums, and universities, some hundreds of years old, that would have been sources of envy for any American metropolis. I had been reading Hungarian literature in translation— Sándor Márai, Antal Szerb, Magda Szabó, Miklós Vámos, and others. I'd never read Hungarian authors before I came to Budapest, and now I couldn't get enough. Hungarians are highly educated people with a tradition of culture (composers Franz Liszt and Béla Bartók) and innovation (physicist Edward Teller and inventor Ernő Rubik) that rivals any country in the world. Who were these losers Schmitt was talking about?

Then I remembered something. A few months before, a friend of mine from Sacramento and her husband had come to Budapest for a visit. I asked the embassy's protocol office to help me find them a walking tour. Protocol recommended a native Englishman who had been giving tours in Hungary since the early nineties. With so many gaps in, disagreements about, and unspoken elements of Hungarian history, I was curious: how would a professional guide, favored by the U.S. Embassy, describe the country's past? So I went along with my friends on the tour.

As we stood in front of a flag from the 1956 uprising—a relic that had witnessed the brave and bloody popular revolt against the communist dictatorship—our guide said, "Hungary has lost every war it ever fought in. They are the great losers of history."

"Whoa!" I thought. "What a harsh thing to say!" But I thought back
to what I already knew about Hungarian history: Mongols, Hapsburgs,
Turks, then Hapsburgs again, followed by World War I, World War II,
and the Cold War. The tour guide's remark was not without historical
basis. Nevertheless, I thought, how troubling that a foreign tour guide
would casually boil down the history of a country in such severe terms.

Every country in the world has its own national narrative. Most
countries have narratives that make their people feel proud, and that
everyone inside and—hopefully—outside the country generally agrees
is true. But the narrative that had emerged about Hungary, as expressed
by our walking tour guide that day, was overly negative even if it was
based in fact.

As we continued our walk, I thought about the Jobbik party and
the way that young people were flocking to it. I was still not able to
understand the appeal of the hate-spewing extremists among Hungarian university students. Maybe what appealed to them the most was
that Jobbik offered something else: a national narrative in which "real"
Hungarians were superior people, not losers.

With President Schmitt's comments at his swearing-in reception, I
could see that even the "center right" political leaders recognized the
expediency of getting into the game. But how? How would supporters of the center right attempt to revise the old narrative and give the
people a better story?

The first time that what we had begun to call the "new national
narrative" slammed up against Western sensitivities came during an
official trip to Washington by government spokesman Zoltán Kovács.
Kovács was a historian who had earned his master's at Central European University. While in D.C., he met with Erika Schlager, the top
expert on international law at the U.S. Helsinki Commission, an independent body that dealt with human rights issues around the world on
behalf of the U.S. government. Kovács astonished Schlager by saying
that "while the greatest tragedy for Hungarian Jews was the Holocaust,
the greatest tragedy for the rest of the Hungarians was the signing of
the Treaty of Trianon."

After a highly agitated Schlager told me about this, I met with

Kovács at a little Budapest café. He tried to explain that he had only been trying to help people understand the critical significance of the Trianon trauma. I made it clear that comparing the Treaty of Trianon to the Holocaust and implying that Trianon was worse was not a comparison the United States could accept. I also told him, as a friend, that if he was looking for understanding in the world for the Hungarian people, he would not get far by saying that the signing of a treaty that most people outside of Hungary had never heard about was worse for his country than sending nearly half a million Hungarian men, women, and children to the gas chambers and murdering thousands of others on the banks of the Danube.

Kovács was determined to help me see his point of view. He told me that comparing Trianon to the Holocaust helped people understand how traumatizing the treaty had been for Hungary. He then leaned across the café table, looked at me pleadingly, and said his passion for insisting that people understand the trauma of Trianon wasn't because he was anti-Semitic. "Eleni, you know my wife is Jewish."

Why? I thought. Why was it so desperately important to this government official that the world know about the Treaty of Trianon? It then occurred to me that the Trianon story was the fundamental part of the new narrative: Hungarians weren't the *losers* of history, they were the *victims* of it. The message was that the Great Powers were wrong to redraw Hungary's borders to exclude its ancient villages, and that when foreign powers had too much influence, they would make decisions that were bad for Hungary. The first act of the new Orbán-controlled Parliament earlier that summer had been to amend the constitution to establish a National Day of Unity celebrated on the day of the signing of the Treaty of Trianon. Clearly, that wasn't the end of the issue for Viktor Orbán and his political family; it was just the beginning.

Nothing symbolized the new narrative more than the image of Greater Hungary, the map of Hungary's share of the Austro-Hungarian Empire at the start of World War I. For years, it was a prominent symbol of the neofascists. I remember one photograph from an extreme-right political rally. It was of a very large, intimidating man with a shaved head who sported a tattoo of Greater Hungary from one side to the other of his muscular back. But across the country, the map was evolving from a symbol of the far right to something far more popular. Suddenly, it was no longer limited to the occasional bumper sticker. You could see it everywhere, including on the T-shirts and knickknacks that filled souvenir shops. When Nancy Pelosi came to Budapest, she asked me to find a pair of touristy socks she could give her friend George H.W. Bush. The former president loved fun socks, she told me, and she bought them for him whenever she could. It would be particularly special for her to bring him a pair from Hungary, because his cousin Herbert Walker had been one of my predecessors as ambassador. The idea of Greater Hungary socks set my teeth on edge, but we bought them for Nancy—there was nothing else we could find in their place.

It wasn't just the symbols of Trianon that were emerging around Budapest—popular rhetoric on the topic was heating up. Newcomers and visitors to the capital would often remark that a Hungarian tour guide, taxi driver, waiter, bartender, or other casual acquaintance had told them all about the tragedy that had deprived Hungary of two-thirds of its territory. "Isn't it terrible?" visitors would ask me. "Those poor Hungarians!"

In the fall of 2010, I went to see President Schmitt, accompanied by a dozen representatives of the American Chamber of Commerce to the European Union. The EU changed presidents every six months, and Hungary would take the presidency for the first time on January 1, 2011. These Am Cham representatives traveled to every EU country slated to assume the presidency, to get an idea of how the country would handle the position and what its priorities would be.

We all sat down for tea in Schmitt's office in Sándor Palace, taking our places at a long table. It was the same ceremonial room where I had presented my credentials to Schmitt's predecessor, but it was now set up for a business meeting—albeit one with silk wall coverings and portraits from the Austro-Hungarian Empire.

Though nearing age seventy, President Schmitt still walked and moved like the Olympic gold-medal fencer he once was—no doubt the effect of years of training in precise footwork. But he was not very nimble when it came to the discussion with the AmCham members about the unorthodox economic policies the government had recently adopted, starting with the bank tax.

He told us that the bankers he'd spoken to were not at all upset about the bank tax. "They have that guilty feeling of having taken too much profit," he said. Clearly, the shocked expressions on the faces of the American business advocates did not register, because Schmitt continued in the same vein. "They understood that they needed to give some of it back." I interjected that U.S. banks located in Hungary and affected by the taxes had, in fact, voiced serious concerns, which I'd personally relayed to the prime minister. But Schmitt brushed my comments aside.

Foreign direct investment, or FDI, is the amount of money that foreign companies have invested in a country. Every country has some level of FDI, and almost every country seeks to attract more—even the United States. Hungary's president had just told representatives of some of the biggest multinational companies in the world that "excess profits" should be taken back after the fact. There was no more sure way he could have found to throw cold water on the possibility that these companies would seek additional investment in his country.

But that wasn't the only enlightening statement of the meeting. There was growing concern in the business community that the government was cherry-picking industries that were dominated by foreign companies and levying the highest of the new special taxes on them. When we raised the question, Schmitt responded, "Did you know that of the one hundred wealthiest people in Hungary, ninety-eight are former communists?"

Viktor Orbán's phrase "Bolshevik billionaires" leapt to my mind. I was starting to connect the dots. For twenty years, Hungarians had believed that doing away with communism and joining the West would result in a better economy and more opportunity for their children. With the economic downturn of 2008, many were starting to think they'd been duped. The country's elite was doing well, but everyone else was suffering. In the fall of 2009, as I was preparing for my confirmation hearing, the *Los Angeles Times* reported on a Pew Research Center poll that found that 72 percent of Hungarians surveyed believed they were economically better off under communism.

Hungary's center-right leaders had long been channeling the disappointments of the country's democratic transition into ire against the Socialist Party. But what was also emerging was the accusation that their political rivals had enriched themselves by enabling foreign companies to exploit the country. This argument left out the fact that much of the corruption that plagued Hungary's democratic transition after 1990 had benefited political insiders regardless of party affiliation.

Politically, this allowed the Orbán government to place all blame for the economic crisis at the feet of its already enfeebled political opposition. It also conveniently allowed the government to fill the budget gap by clawing back "excessive profits" from companies it could pick and choose. Finally, it supported the broader lesson of the emerging national narrative, that the only thing wrong with Hungary was the undue influence of foreign powers—including multinational corporations. The Orbán government was fine-tuning its new narrative, and it was steadily gaining traction inside the country.

# 9

# Travels with Csaba

As Prime Minister Viktor Orbán set about assembling his cabinet, he chose Csaba Hende to serve as his minister of defense. Hende was a politician and lawyer from the Hungarian countryside, a smart, affable man who had worked in previous governments, including stints at the Ministry of Defense. But from the moment Orbán appointed him, Hende was rumored to be out of his depth in the military realm—a placeholder, some said, whose primary job was to clean house, replacing top brass with people known to be loyal to Orbán. Hende was also tasked with slashing budgets and stemming the flow of public money into the pockets of high- and mid-level bureaucrats.

Soon after Hende's appointment, my defense attaché, Colonel Robert Duggleby (who had arranged the boar-hunting excursion), and I paid him a courtesy call. Hende's office was appropriate for the defense minister, filled with heavy leather furniture and antique weapons, with maps covering every inch of the walls. Hungary is known for its fine porcelain, and every government ministry was assigned a different pattern from one of the two most famous makers: Herend and Zsolnay. The Defense Ministry used an elegant blue and gold Zsolnay pattern for its coffee service, which was swiftly placed in front of us.

I sat with my talking points on a piece of paper in front of me. We really didn't have any areas of disagreement with Hungary on defense issues. My talking points were essentially the same as those I'd used when I paid a courtesy call on Hende's Socialist Party predecessor just a few months before. I began by recognizing that Hungary was a reliable partner to the United States and an important NATO ally. I thanked Hende for his country's contributions. Then I turned to President Obama's top foreign policy priority.

"Mr. Minister, Hungary's contributions in Afghanistan have been important to the mission of the International Security Assistance Force and are very much appreciated by the United States. I also want to tell you how pleased we are to have been able to support the development of Hungary's Special Forces capabilities." Just a few years before, the country had no Special Forces at all. Now its first unit served shoulder-to-shoulder with the United States in Afghanistan, and another was on the way.

Finally, we discussed the military aid packages that were making their way through the U.S. Congress, a welcome supplement to the assistance that the United States already provided Hungary through our Office of Defense Cooperation. When Hungary joined NATO in 1999, it committed to moving toward the NATO target of each country spending at least 2 percent of its GDP on defense. But it had never made it anywhere near this goal, and as the country's economic situation deteriorated, military spending dropped below 1 percent of GDP. The extra defense aid that we were seeking back in Washington would come at a critical time.

As I spoke, Hende listened attentively, taking notes as his interpreter whispered my words into his ear. Once I'd finished, I picked up my tiny cup filled with strong black coffee and prepared to listen to Hende's points. I expected them to be essentially the same as those of his predecessor. And they were—almost.

Hende told me that immediately after his swearing-in as defense minister he had taken a trip to northern Afghanistan, visiting Camp Pannonia, near the town of Pol-e Khumri, where Hungary's provincial reconstruction team had worked since 2006. Although the international coalition's primary objective was military, Afghanistan's lasting security depended upon a stable society. So in addition to the kinetic activity—the hot part of the war—there were substantial efforts to help the Afghan people develop such fundamental things as sustainable farming practices, schools, and local government structures that could operate responsively, with minimal corruption. A provincial reconstruction team is what its name suggests—a team of military and civilian officers that advances reconstruction outside of major cities. The Hungarians were involved in both the military and civic objectives of our mission in Afghanistan, performing effective and important work.

Although there were more than four hundred Hungarians in Afghanistan at that time, Camp Pannonia was especially significant. It was the only place in the country where Hungary held the command. The base commander and his team of more than two hundred men and women were responsible for the operations there. In military terms, when a country holds a command, it flies its flag. Though Hungarian troops served in other missions around the country, Camp Pannonia was the only place with a Hungarian flag.

As Minister Hende told me about his visit, he became very serious. "Pol-e Khumri has become a very dangerous place over the last year," he said. "My soldiers cannot leave the base to do their work anymore, and I am very, very concerned about their safety." He shook his head from side to side. "Something must be done."

With my cup still suspended in the air, I turned to Colonel Duggleby and indicated it would be fine for him to speak up.

"Sir, with all due respect," he said, "this is a war zone, and yes, it's dangerous. But I have seen your troops in training. They are highly capable, and I know they are up to the job."

Hende pursed his lips and looked nervously at his staff. If he denied this, he would be speaking against his own troops. He wasn't about to say that they weren't trained for it, because then he would be speaking directly against his own leadership. "Yes, yes," he agreed. "They are very capable. They are very brave."

Backing away from the suggestion that he lacked confidence in his own people, he told us that at a minimum there was an immediate need for more, better equipment.

Neither Colonel Duggleby nor I debated the matter with Hende. We let him continue with his points. But we realized that the minister's words about the dangers of Afghanistan indicated that a significant change in Hungarian policy might be taking place.

It was the most dangerous time of the entire Afghan conflict to date. More coalition troops had been killed in the first six months of 2010 than in any other entire year. Several countries with substantial deployments in Afghanistan were feeling the pressure of public opinion back home and beginning to make noises about leaving. Was Hungary looking for a way to pull out too?

More than fifty nations had joined the International Security Assistance Force, the largest number of countries to make up any military coalition in the history of the world. The coalition's objective was to "disrupt, dismantle, and defeat" al-Qaeda in Afghanistan, ensuring that the terrorist group no longer would be able to use the country as a safe haven and training ground. Although Hungary's troops made up only a small fraction of the coalition's 160,000 total in the summer of 2010, they were important for reasons beyond just their military and reconstruction efforts. The United States had worked hard to help former Soviet satellite states transition from the defunct Warsaw Pact to NATO, and we believed that military partnership—in particular, deploying troops side by side—formed a critical bond.

President Obama had campaigned on a promise to work to end the wars in Iraq and Afghanistan. He had made strides in wrapping up our action in Iraq, but in Afghanistan, he decided we would increase, or surge, our troop numbers there before engaging in an orderly drawdown. At the time, it was a challenge for the United States to persuade our friends and allies to stick it out. Around the world, our embassies were tasked with engaging closely with host countries that had troops in Afghanistan and ensuring that they stayed with us.

Because Afghanistan was so important to President Obama, the single most critical part of my job as his ambassador was to make sure that Hungary kept its forces in Afghanistan. After my meeting with Minister Hende, I worried that my host country was going to try to back out of its commitment.

A few days after this meeting, Colonel Duggleby came into my office with some surprising news. Minister Hende had invited me to join him on a three-day trip to visit Hungarian troops in Sarajevo and Kosovo. I raised an eyebrow and thought about it.

A trip to Sarajevo and Kosovo with the Hungarian defense minister would give me an opportunity to advance another U.S. foreign policy objective. Though NATO had enlarged significantly in recent years, from sixteen countries in 1989 to twenty-eight countries by 2010, we believed the alliance should continue to expand, particularly into the Balkan region. Some countries in Europe, however, felt that NATO had grown too quickly and was experiencing expansion fatigue. Because Article 5 of the NATO treaty states that "an attack against one is an attack against all," some argued that the last thing the alliance needed was to include the conflict-prone Balkans. The Hungarians, however, took a view similar to ours.

Colonel Duggleby was delighted by the prospect of a trip with Minister Hende, for several reasons. To his mind, the trip would be just the thing to build our relationship. Rob had made a point of forming deep personal connections with his counterparts wherever he was stationed. He established trust this way and, as he was a very straightforward person, it had gotten him far. He thought the same strategy would work for me, so he'd been eager to arrange the boar hunt with Hungary's previous top military brass. Recently, he had dragged me into another scheme. He got me to agree to join the Hungarian Defense Forces' swim team in crossing Lake Balaton, the largest lake in Central Europe, later that summer.

When I originally asked Rob how far I would have to swim, he said, "Well, ma'am, I'm not sure, but I think it's about a mile across." Thinking back to my days of doing triathlons—more than a decade before—I thought that if I trained enough, I could make it. Imagine my surprise when, after Rob had already announced that I would lead a U.S. team in crossing Balaton, he told me that I'd be swimming about three miles.

My shoulders still ached from practicing for the upcoming swim when Rob made his case for joining Minister Hende on the trip to the Balkans. "It could be very helpful down the road, especially if he's considering an about-face in Afghanistan." He planned to join me.

Hungary had troops in Bosnia and Herzegovina as part of the European Union's lead peacekeeping force. By this time, the United States no longer conducted military operations there. We did, however, still have an active military presence in Kosovo, and that allowed me to accept Minister Hende's invitation—otherwise there would have been no clear reason for me to accompany him. So in September 2010, Colonel Duggleby and I met the minister and his delegation at the Budapest airport, boarded one of the ministry's aircraft—an old Soviet transport plane—and headed to Sarajevo.

As a young business school student at the University of California, Berkeley, in the early nineties, I'd followed the disintegration of Yugoslavia with great interest. The Balkans, often referred to as the "powder keg of Europe," were well known for generations-old ethnic divides. When tensions erupted into full-scale war, I reacted with the same disbelief and outrage that much of the world felt, horrified by the news reports of massacres, ethnic cleansing, and brutality. But I was unprepared for the rawness and destruction that lingered there nearly twenty years later.

When our group arrived in Sarajevo, we were driven directly to a small reception at the home of the Hungarian ambassador to Bosnia and Herzegovina, László Tóth. We stood on the porch of his residence, in the hills above the small city, and surveyed the landscape.

"Back in the winter of 1984," I told him, "I watched the Sarajevo Olympics every day when I came home from school." I'd been a junior in high school and loved the ice-skating and ski competitions. To my Sacramento eyes, Sarajevo had resembled a fairy-tale city, nothing like the stark place I was looking at in 2010.

I asked, "Where were the ski slopes for the downhill races?"

Tóth gestured to the mountains across the city. "They were over there. But of course, almost everything was destroyed—the chair lifts, the lodges, everything. In fact, the Serbs launched their attack on the city from those mountains." They brought guns and rockets over the hills, and laid siege to the city from the high ground. "The people of Sarajevo never saw them coming and had no preparation at all."

"How did they protect themselves?" I asked.

"With forks and knives." The matter-of-fact yet shocking reply left me speechless.

That night, we stayed at the capital's hulking Holiday Inn. It had been built for the Olympics and housed foreign news correspondents during the war. Markos's dear friend and the best man at our wedding in Istanbul, Terry Phillips, had been one of those war correspondents. The shelling was so bad that he and the other reporters slept on the floor near the door, not daring to use the beds for fear of falling glass. Now it was just an old, frayed hotel, empty except for us. Sarajevo resembled no European capital I'd ever seen.

The next morning, we went to the EU base for a briefing by the Austrian commander, who afterward made a point of reminding me that the United States should not forget Bosnia. He told me that with Afghanistan such a high priority, Sarajevo was falling off the radar screen. EU countries were pulling out with the argument that their partner across the Atlantic was pushing them to provide more resources elsewhere. One of the commander's deputies also pulled me aside for a private word. He noted that with Austria, Hungary, and Turkey the largest countries represented in Bosnia and Herzegovina, the pre–World War I dynamics of the Austro-Hungarian Empire and the Ottoman Empire had returned. "We need the United States to pay attention here, at a minimum to avoid raising old ghosts," he said.

Later that day, I had coffee with our ambassador to Bosnia and Herzegovina, Charles English. He echoed the Austrian commander's concerns about the diminishing U.S. focus on his host country. He told me that he had recently seen State Department legend Richard Holbrooke, who then was the U.S. special envoy for Afghanistan and Pakistan. When Ambassador English expressed his concerns that the United States had lost interest in the country, Holbrooke grabbed him by the shoulders and said, "You're the ambassador. Don't let that happen!"

Even before Charles told me this story, I'd been thinking about Richard Holbrooke—it was impossible not to think of him in Sarajevo, given that he'd negotiated the Dayton Accords, which in 1995 had ended the vicious Bosnian conflict. He was a hero to many, including me. I'd met him several times over the years through my political activities and involvement in the Greek American community. Right before I left for Budapest, Richard had spotted me walking through the halls at the State Department. "You can't go to Hungary before talking to me," he bellowed. "Come to my office tomorrow at 10 a.m. sharp!"

Holbrooke, a longtime diplomat, was an expert in the region, to be sure. But he had a special connection to Hungary through his wife, the Hungarian American journalist and author Kati Marton. They had been married years before in the ambassador's residence in Budapest—presently my family's house—and Holbrooke had a great interest in the country.

On the morning Holbrooke ordered me to meet with him, I was in a conference and couldn't easily leave without courting the wrath of State's European Bureau. I sent my desk officer to see if Holbrooke could see me at noon, when we had a break for lunch. She came back and slipped me a note: "Holbrooke can't do noon. He said, 'Don't be shy, just walk out.'" Given his godlike stature at the State Department, that note was a golden hall pass. I left the conference and walked to his office, gripping the note in my hand.

Tall, dashing, and intimidatingly brilliant, Richard Holbrooke was a force of nature, but more than anything else, he was a leader. Packed into his Foggy Bottom office were at least a dozen of the State Department's best and most experienced officers. With their notebooks out, consulting maps scattered all around them, they sparred and debated with Holbrooke about the best way forward in Afghanistan.

The group was hard at work when I walked into Holbrooke's office. It only took him a moment to switch his focus to Hungary.

"Look, Eleni, you're going to a place with a tough history. But they are good people, and they have been loyal partners to us since the collapse of communism. Our operation in the Balkans couldn't have taken place without their help." Hungary had allowed peacekeeping forces to use its air base in Taszár, in the southern part of the country, providing a crucial staging post for air and ground forces. Holbrooke slapped me on the back encouragingly. "Good luck, have fun, and Kati and I will be there to visit soon."

Dick Holbrooke never came to visit me in Hungary. He died suddenly just a few months later, on the job, of a massive hemorrhage. Later, after I heard the news, I found the note from my desk officer, crumpled in my drawer. I framed it with a photo of Dick and me, and I hung it in my office in Budapest.

The Hungarian Ministry of Defense's delegation was very busy with official visits during our visit to Sarajevo. But in between meetings, there was also some time to explore the city. First, we went to "Sniper Alley," the street that had given the Serbs in the hills their best shot at civilians who needed to travel across town to gather food and water. As we walked down Sniper Alley, a man my age rode by on his bicycle—a pleasant enough sight until I noticed that he was missing about a third of his skull. We stopped at the corner where in 1914 a Serbian nationalist had shot and killed Archduke Ferdinand and his wife as they rode in the backseat of a convertible. In 1898, the Prussian statesman Otto von Bismarck said on his deathbed, "One day the great European War will come out of some damned foolish thing in the Balkans."* True to Bismarck's prediction, the assassination of Archduke Ferdinand sparked the beginning of World War I.

As we traveled through the city, we passed buildings still bearing the wounds of the 1990s war, but the damage was as raw as if it had happened the day before. In Budapest, you could see shrapnel and bullet holes in many buildings, remnants of World War II and the 1956 uprising, but they were old, crumbling, small, and random. In Sarajevo, the damage wasn't just fresh, it was modern and industrial. The bullet holes were huge and evenly sprayed across buildings. I imagined trying to survive then, trying to protect my family under that kind of firepower, with forks and knives as my only defense.

The following year, Angelina Jolie traveled to the Balkans with the intention of shooting her film *In the Land of Blood and Honey*. Of course, her project and her presence attracted an enormous amount of attention. But the subject matter was so controversial that she ended

*Winston Churchill, *The World Crisis* (New York: Charles Scribner's Sons, 1923), 195.

up moving both the filming and production to Budapest, which has a well-established film industry. She invited me to watch her direct one morning. As I observed the filmmaking process, I thought, here we are, American women whose country hasn't seen the devastation of a ground war on our own soil since the Civil War. Can we truly understand what others have suffered? Or is it our relative innocence, our optimistic belief in the possibility of a better future, that makes Americans exactly the right people to engage?

As the Hungarian delegation made our way out of the center of Sarajevo and back to the airport, we passed a cemetery with shiny new marble gravestones evenly arranged as far as the eye could see. They glimmered in the sun as we drove along the perimeter of what was otherwise a very old graveyard. U.S. intervention in the Balkan conflict had come late, to be sure. But the current peace, delicate though it was, stemmed from American willingness to follow President Clinton into war and because of Richard Holbrooke's masterful ability to bring two sides together after a brutal, unforgiving conflict.

Our next stop: Pristina, Kosovo.

At that time, Kosovo was the youngest country in the world, having declared independence in 2008. It separated from Serbia with the support of many countries, including the United States, because of fears that the Serbs in the province and in neighboring Serbia would attempt the ethnic cleansing that characterized the war in Bosnia-Herzegovina. Two years later, the potential for violence remained high, especially along the long border with Serbia, and Kosovo was heavily patrolled by the peacekeeping operation organized by NATO, called KFOR (Kosovo Force).

The atmosphere in Pristina was quite different from Sarajevo's. It was wilder and poorer, even though Pristina was the country's capital and biggest city. We drove past the enormous statue of President Clinton presiding over the city center and headed to the home of the Hungarian ambassador to Kosovo. He lived in the same gated compound as the Americans and other Westerners participating in the KFOR operation. The compound was no paradise, but it was secure. I was sorry we weren't staying there when I saw our hotel in the center of town. It was very old, shabby, and dark, and the sounds from the narrow streets outside easily penetrated my room. But security had been provided. I was introduced to Zoltán, a tall young Hungarian soldier who was tasked with spending the night standing outside my door, armed with an AK-47.

The next day, my group boarded an old transport helicopter and headed to northwestern Kosovo. Along the way, I had a request. I'd heard that some of the most beautiful Orthodox monasteries in the world were in Kosovo, designated World Heritage Sites by UNESCO. We would be passing the monastery where the Serbian Orthodox patriarch lived. We were on a tight schedule and unable to land, but the entire delegation was eager to see the monastery, so the pilot dipped down to provide a better look. I've never experienced anything quite like hovering in a military helicopter above a thousand-year-old monastery. It was a privileged view, but it was very disheartening to see this little island of faith in the midst of so much strife.

Whenever the Hungarian delegation landed in a new location, the same protocols prevailed. We were greeted by the base commander and taken to a viewing stand where we stood at attention, listened to the Hungarian national anthem, and watched the parade of Hungarian troops stationed at that base march by. At first, it was a bit awkward. Csaba was very deferential to me as the American ambassador. As we moved from place to place, the minister wasn't sure which of us should walk first. This was compounded by the fact that I was a woman, and Csaba's instincts were to always let a woman precede him. Finally, I told him, "Mr. Minister, I am part of *your* delegation. I think you should go ahead and take the lead."

As he observed his troops, Hende kept one eye on me to make sure I was standing in the proper place. I concentrated on keeping the proper posture: standing at attention meant arms at my side, straight back, head tilted upward with an expression on my face that was serious but didn't make me look like I was sad. Everyone else in the diplomatic corps seemed to have been born with the ability to do this. It took me a couple of tries to get it right.

By the time we landed in Peć, in western Kosovo, our last stop before returning to Budapest, we had the protocols all worked out and there was no more awkwardness. The base in Peć was under Italian command, with the Hungarians serving beside them. The commander had a notably different style from either the Austrian commander in Sarajevo or the German commander in Pristina, providing us with such a bountiful lunch that I wondered how he had managed to find everything—Peć was far off the gourmet grid. The lunch included many courses of delicious but rich food, heavy with meat and gravy. The commander offered us frozen daiquiri–like cocktails, and after we were about halfway through the meal, a female Italian officer appeared, out of uniform, to sing cabaret songs. I have to admit, it was fun, even if I had to use my newfound habit of putting my fork down when I was full and explaining for the rest of the meal that I was too small to eat so much.

When lunch was over, we moved to a more formal room for our meeting with the commander. In an attempt to be gracious, Csaba declared, "Commander, you must be so happy to be surrounded by so many beautiful female soldiers!" The commander looked at me, looked at the minister, and basically pretended he hadn't heard the comment. To be fair, there really were a lot of very attractive women in the Italian forces—I had noticed it too. But I was as astonished as the commander to hear Csaba's words. When Csaba failed to elicit a response, he repeated his assertion. Finally, he must have understood that there was a problem, and he backed away from the subject. Even though the comments had shocked me, I couldn't help but feel sympathetic. To his credit, Csaba never said anything like that again when we were together.

We were both learning.

As the old transport plane was beginning its descent into Budapest, Csaba started to talk about Afghanistan. Again he told me that Pol-e Khumri was too dangerous for his troops. This time he was more forceful than he had been in his office, looking directly into my eyes.

"If someone is killed," he said, "the blood will be on my hands." I drew in my breath, feeling the gravity of his dilemma.

When we were back at the embassy, I asked Colonel Duggleby how we should respond. He was, as always, resolute: "Ma'am, of course it's dangerous. It's a war zone. But the coalition needs the Hungarians there, and if we can't convince them, there will be others in our government and those of other NATO countries who will intervene to try to do so. Believe me, this won't end with you and me."

In August, just weeks after our trip, Minister Hende's premonition came true. A team of Hungarians was rotating out of Afghanistan, with a new team about to rotate in. As they were leaving the base, packed up and ready to return home, their vehicle was attacked with rocket-propelled grenades. Two soldiers were killed, including a twenty-three-year-old woman who was there as an administrative assistant and had young children back home.

I joined a press conference with members of the Hungarian Ministry of Defense and expressed my great sorrow for the families of the soldiers who died. It was very difficult but very important for me to face publicly the costs of war. It was part of the job.

A few months later, Csaba planned another trip, this time to Afghanistan, and he invited me once again to accompany him.

# 10

# Afghanistan: In the War Zone

In December 2010, I packed my bags and headed to the Budapest airfield to meet Minister Hende and his delegation. We would visit four bases in Afghanistan, including Camp Pannonia in Pol-e Khumri. It was a big coup for Csaba that I was going along. I suspected that he hoped to scare me a little bit and to put me in a position where I had to admit that he was right about Camp Pannonia—that it was too dangerous for his troops to stay there.

Although I was excited to go to Afghanistan, I was sorry that Colonel Duggleby was not able to make the trip. It was just before Christmas, and he couldn't change his plans. One of the other officers at the embassy came along, and although this colonel was also very capable, we never managed to forge the kind of connection that I had with Rob. On this trip, I would often feel that I was on my own.

Our first stop was a German air force base where we traded in the Defense Ministry's old Soviet-era plane for a new, more comfortable German military transport plane. We would be flying to Afghanistan with other representatives of the international coalition. After an overnight stop at a base in Uzbekistan, we boarded a German transport plane fully equipped with the necessary defenses to fly over active war zones and headed to Regional Command North (RC North). This base was the command center for all the International Security Assistance Force operations in the northern part of Afghanistan. It was a German command, and two of the largest locations for Hungarian troops fell under its jurisdiction. We would come back to this base later in the trip, but that day we just switched planes and headed to Kabul.

The Kabul airport had become an important military base for the coalition forces. It had once been a commercial airport, but you'd never know that from all the soldiers walking around, clustered more or less by their country of origin—France, Romania, Australia, to name just a few. The Kabul base was very crowded. Of our delegation, only Minister Hende and I had our own rooms. As I unfurled my sleeping bag, I felt a little guilty that I had a room with four beds. I felt less guilty when I realized I would have to walk down the hall to the showers.

The responsibility of providing management services at the Kabul airport base rotated to a different country every three months, and at that time Hungarian forces were in charge. I was surprised to see photos of Greece on the Hungarians' office walls. They told me that Greek forces had just preceded them, and everyone had liked the pictures so much that they never replaced them with photos of their own country. I could understand. The blue water in the images provided a serene contrast to the barren, sandy landscape of Kabul.

We had briefings throughout the day. One of the deputy commanders, a Frenchman, was eager to tell me something. "It's incredible the way the command structures are integrated by country. My deputy is an American! NATO allies and partners are working together as one team. Your country has done a good thing in this respect—everyone feels it." I heard this sentiment several times that week. The German commander of RC North noted that his troops had not seen battle since World War II and that for him to have an American deputy commander was nothing short of historic.

Again and again, foreign military leaders told me that the U.S. troops are the gold standard for performance, capability, and behavior. They regularly asked me how the United States found so many talented and dedicated people willing to volunteer to serve in its military.

Toward the end of our first day in Kabul, we had a meeting with the commander of the International Security Assistance Force, General David Petraeus. I was looking forward to meeting this military legend, an expert on nation-building who had served as part of the NATO stabilization force in Bosnia before leading troops in Iraq and overseeing major reconstruction efforts there.

General Petraeus gave the Hungarian delegation a detailed overview of the mission to date, a sober assessment of what was left to be accomplished, and feedback on how the Hungarian forces were fulfilling their part of the mission. He explained that since he had taken over, the mission had a new direction, which he summarized as the "clear, hold, build" strategy of counterinsurgency: "Don't move into an area if you can't clear it. Don't clear an area if you can't hold it. And don't hold an area if you can't build up and later transfer it."

General Petraeus reminded us that the coalition force's primary mission was to "disrupt, dismantle, and defeat" al-Qaeda in Afghanistan. It wouldn't be enough to drive out the terrorists, then leave. The goal was to ensure that they couldn't easily return. One major focus was to take, hold, and transfer the areas around Highway 1, the 1,400-mile ring road that was being built to connect the country's major cities. This highway, Petraeus explained, would be the main artery of the new Afghanistan and one of the keys to the country's future stability. As a land developer who had helped design and build roads, I was able to quickly grasp the significance of roadway infrastructure for growth and development.

When General Petraeus finished, he asked Minister Hende if he had any questions or comments. Indeed, he did.

"I am worried about my soldiers at Camp Pannonia. Pol-e Khumri is much more dangerous than when we came, and my men are not trained for such conditions. They must stay on base all the time. It is too unsafe for them to leave and perform their duties." He looked General Petraeus in the eye. "I believe that Pol-e Khumri is a very bad place for a provincial reconstruction team."

General Petraeus appeared stunned. "I respectfully have to disagree, sir," he told Hende. "Pol-e Khumri is the perfect place for a reconstruction team, and your soldiers are performing important work there, work that is critical to our mission." He noted that the base was very near Highway 1.

Csaba refused to take the point. But he did say this: at a minimum, the Hungarian soldiers needed more equipment, especially more secure transport vehicles.

The general responded by telling him to work out what additional equipment was needed. "Once you have the list, give it to the ambassador for her sign-off," he said, motioning toward me. "Then send it up the chain of command, and, sir, I promise you it will be seriously considered."

General Petraeus had mastered a quality that I had come to recognize among military men and many State Department officers as well: soft on the outside, hard on the inside. He was friendly and charming, and he strove to put us at ease. As a military leader, it was appropriate that he would address a civilian leader—in this case, Minister Hende—as "sir," but he said it at the end of almost every sentence. Here was one of the most powerful military commanders in the world calling the still unseasoned Hungarian country-lawyer-turned-defense-minister "sir," over and over again. But when Hende launched his attack, Petraeus's softness fell away, and the hardened general appeared. As the interpreter translated Csaba's words, Petraeus gazed at the minister like a panther deciding whether to lunge.

The exchange between Hende and Petraeus left a bit of frost in the air as we rose to leave. The general pulled me aside. "You know, Ambassador, not many of you make it over here like this. Good for you. But tell me, ma'am, how did you manage to get yourself on this trip?" He sounded both admiring and confused.

I explained that I'd traveled with Minister Hende once before and that when he invited me to Afghanistan, I'd jumped at the chance to come. Only later did I learn from an American officer in Kabul that what Petraeus really meant was, "What are you doing here, and how come I didn't know about it?" Though many high-level U.S. government officials took trips to Afghanistan, their trips were almost exclusively arranged by the U.S. government. Petraeus was probably thinking of the complications my visit could create. If so, he was right.

I was scheduled for a dinner that evening with Karl Eikenberry, who was then the U.S. ambassador to Afghanistan. But the embassy was a short drive away from the airport, on a different base, and I had no way to get there. Given my rank, ordinary transportation was out of the question. I would need an escort and a "hardened" vehicle that had been equipped to protect its riders against explosives. There had been a lot of discussion about how to get me to the residence, but no one in the Hungarian delegation had the contacts or connections to work it out. As General Petraeus was preparing to leave, a member of his entourage whispered something in his ear. He looked back at me.

"I hear you need a ride to the embassy, ma'am." He smiled and gestured for me to follow him. The panther had retreated; the friendly general was back. Now it was my turn to hear him call me "ma'am" at every opportunity. We walked out to his Black Hawk helicopter and climbed aboard. A second Black Hawk with the rest of his team lifted off simultaneously, and we headed in tandem toward the embassy, which was on the same base as his command center. Through his headset microphone, General Petraeus asked if I had a little time. He wanted to fly me around Kabul to show me how things were improving.

I was eager to see. As we circled the flat, dust-coated city at sunset, the general noted that Kabul was now safer than Los Angeles and that commerce and traffic had returned to normal. I saw busy, well-built highways intersecting the city. But beyond them, most of the roads were still dirt, lined with poor-looking concrete buildings.

When we arrived at the base, I thanked General Petraeus for his time and wished him the best of luck. As I was escorted into the U.S. Embassy, I noticed that the flag was flying at half-staff. Richard Holbrooke had just died. Sadly, his death came before he could fulfill his mission of bringing peace to Afghanistan, as he had done in Bosnia. I ached not only for Richard's friends and family but for our country, which had lost a brilliant and dedicated diplomat.

Karl Eikenberry was career military, and as a result his 2009 nomination by President Obama to serve as ambassador to Afghanistan had been declared "highly unusual" by the *New York Times*. But like many military men, he was also sophisticated and diplomatic. He'd been in Afghanistan for almost two years. That, along with his military service in the country, made him an old hand there. Whenever one U.S. ambassador visited another country on official and sometimes even unofficial visits, it was customary for the embassy there to offer a country team briefing. Ambassador Eikenberry, a warm and charming man, had not only offered a briefing but invited me to hear it over dinner at his residence, deep inside the security gates.

After the usual pleasantries, we sat down at the table and his team of senior officers provided a comprehensive analysis of their mission, focusing on nation-building efforts. They explained that in 2010 Afghanistan had become the single largest recipient of foreign aid from the United States in the history of our country. Over a billion dollars would be spent by the U.S. Agency for International Development, USAID, for development aid alone, and more was budgeted for 2011. Eikenberry and his officers discussed our priorities for Afghanistan: the rule of law, good governance, anticorruption and transparency, the development of civil society, tolerance, and the role of women. Listening to them, I realized that whether you were talking about a developing country like Afghanistan, a post-Soviet state, or even our own nation, the building blocks of democracy were fundamentally the same. I was also struck by the group's sober recognition of how difficult the mission was. As with General Petraeus, there was cautious optimism that we could prevail, but also a clear realization of the challenges at hand and what it would take to meet them.

The embassy arranged for me to get back to the base after dinner, and the next morning I regrouped with the Hungarians. We had a briefing from their Special Forces unit, which had traveled from a secret location to greet Minister Hende. They were a very impressive group of men, fearless and extremely capable. They were very proud to come out of the training program that the United States had helped the Hungarians build, and they weren't shy about letting me know.

Our next move was to take a transport plane back up to RC North and from there fly on to the remote base of Pol-e Khumri, then to the even more isolated location of Killagai. But we were delayed, and as we sat in the offices at Kabul airport, I told Minister Hende about my meeting with Ambassador Eikenberry. Hende and I hadn't seen each other since the meeting with General Petraeus, and I hoped the general's words had made him consider the importance of Hungary's provincial reconstruction team to the overall mission. Tensions between us had been simmering for a while—I thought I might defuse them by telling him how Ambassador Eikenberry saw things.

After I'd shared the basic elements of what I'd learned the night before, through an interpreter, the minister responded, very smugly, "You know, Madam Ambassador, we Hungarians have a saying for what your country is trying to do here: it's like taking a fish stew and trying to turn it into an aquarium."

It was the final straw. It was an outrageous, disrespectful thing to say about the United States and all of our troops and officers who were serving in this dangerous place. I looked him in the eye, and I raised my voice.

"The cost to my country, in lives and treasure, is enormous. Success or failure will impact the future of my country, our security and yours, and determine the future for our nations' children, yours and mine included. You can be as critical as you want, but you cannot discount our effort out of hand that way, as if nothing is at stake!"

The minister's young interpreter looked mortified, but Csaba himself had staked his ground and refused to back down. Not wanting to give further vent to my anger, I stood up and left the room.

An awkward silence prevailed as we made our way up to RC North. I couldn't help but notice the glances, nods, and gestures I was getting from the minister's top advisers. It suddenly occurred to me that it might be gratitude. Had I finally gotten through to the defense minister in a way that his own professionals had not been able to do? Had they also been trying to tell him that the coalition needed Hungary to stay and finish its mission?

Before leaving RC North for Pol-e Khumri, we all put on helmets and bulletproof vests. As I was handed mine, I grimaced. They were huge, made for a person twice my size, and extremely heavy. I struggled into them and, barely able to see from under the cavernous helmet, lumbered along with the rest of our otherwise all-male delegation to the German transport helicopter.

The helicopter had two rows of benches, one on either side of the hull. Our duffel bags, suitcases, and backpacks were tied down in the middle. Everyone on the helicopter, except me, wore desert camouflage. I'd packed black clothes for the trip, reasoning that black would allow me to disappear, but in reality it made me stand out in a sea of bright sand. I also noticed that of the two dozen or so people on board, everyone was carrying a gun except for myself, Minister Hende, and one or two other members of our delegation.

When we were getting ready to take off, I saw that the back of the helicopter was open and apparently would stay open for the duration of the flight. It was December, a very cold month in northern Afghanistan. I knew I was in for a long ride. Someone pulled out locally made, fluorescent-colored blankets decorated with large images of lion heads. "Authentic afghans!" I thought, and I enthusiastically took one, but it did little to protect me from the icy wind blowing through the helicopter.

The back of the aircraft was open to accommodate a machine gun and the soldier who sat on top of the gun, tethered by a long strap on his back to the ceiling of the helicopter. As we flew, he swiveled the gun from side to side, scanning the horizon. Another soldier sat just a few feet away from him. He also was strapped to the ceiling, and he also scanned the ground below. If the first soldier was shot, the strap would keep him from falling out of the helicopter. Then the second soldier would jump on the massive, high-powered weapon in his place.

When I'm asked if I was frightened in Afghanistan, I always say I wasn't. The intensity I felt there—from the surrounding military forces, from the deadly equipment, from the dusty air itself—was disorienting, but overall I felt inspired and energized.

As we traveled across the mountainous and strikingly beautiful, if frozen and barren, landscape, it occurred to me for the first time that in all my travels—and there had been many since I was a young girl—I had never been in a war zone before. Afghanistan was familiar to me from photos, news coverage, and films, but I don't think you can know what a war zone is like until you have been in one. My heart beat faster. I could feel the adrenaline tick up in my system. If nothing else, this trip was giving me a small taste of what the men and women of our military and foreign services experience.

Hungarian-led Camp Pannonia was a fraction of the size of RC

North. As the helicopter slowly settled onto the ground, I saw that at the edge of the base the ground sloped up to a hillside. Perched on that hillside, so close you could practically touch it, was a village. "That's what Csaba has been talking about all this time," I thought. An armed insurgent up in one of those houses would have a clean and easy shot right down into the heart of the base. I had to admit that you could get pretty jittery staying there for long.

Before dinner, Minister Hende convened the Hungarian troops. He'd had a special medal made for his soldiers serving in Afghanistan. It was the first new medal that had been created in Hungary since the fall of communism. He asked that I stand next to him as he gave them out, one by one.

When the ceremony was over, Csaba asked me to say a few words to the Hungarian troops. It was my honor, I told them, on behalf of the United States, to thank them for their service and sacrifice. It was a dangerous mission, and they were very brave and well-trained soldiers. I wanted them to know that my country was grateful for their service.

Later that afternoon, I was brought down to meet the members of the U.S. Army 541st Forward Surgical Team (Airborne), who were stationed at the base. Major Jason M. Seery, a surgeon, led a team of army medical specialists, nurses, medics, and operating room technicians. They were a very impressive team. Honestly, they looked like they had walked off the set of *General Hospital*—good-looking, fresh-scrubbed, and very young. But these young men and women were the real deal. Not only were they skilled medics, they made up one of only four forward surgical teams in the U.S. Army that had the ability to parachute in to provide aid. Their makeshift facility at Camp Pannonia was little more than a tent.

The team explained to me how they were able to sterilize an area, under very difficult circumstances, for major surgeries. In addition to providing critical care, the unit was also training other members of the coalition forces in the U.S. Army's Combat Lifesaver Course, and they had high praise for their Hungarian colleagues. The Hungarians, they said, were eager for as much training as they could get, and when the sirens went off announcing incoming wounded, the Hungarian volunteers didn't need to be called—they came running.

Just a few months before, an attack nearby had killed two Hungarian soldiers who were traveling to RC North on their way back home. The first one had died instantly, but the second had been rushed into the med unit, where Major Seery and his team struggled to save him. The group grew very solemn as they talked about their efforts to save the Hungarian soldier. He had been their friend, talking with them the night before over mugs of nonalcoholic beer about how much he would miss them, but also about how much he was looking forward to going home. The soldier was airlifted to Budapest but did not survive. The medical team also told me of triumphs. They'd saved two little Afghan girls, sisters, hit by shrapnel after an insurgent launched an improvised explosive device into a local celebration.

I asked the group why they had volunteered to serve in the army and come to Afghanistan. They were talented, disciplined—they could all be in cushy hospital jobs in Florida. What were they doing here? The young surgeon, Dr. Seery, thought about it for a while. Finally, he said, "No matter what else I do in my life after this, I know it will be easy."

That night, I slept without ever completely falling asleep, still flying on adrenaline. As I lay there, I thought of Markos, who had come to Afghanistan in 1991 for the *Los Angeles Times Magazine*. He had grown a beard, put on the traditional cap of the mujahideen, and traveled with a group of anti-communist rebels through the mountains. When Markos was there, the Russians were withdrawing from the unpopular war, which was known in Moscow as "the Great Mincer."

Early the next morning, I woke from my dream-like state to the sound of bombs being dropped by coalition forces only a few miles away from our small, remote base.

As we all assembled for breakfast in the cafeteria, it was unclear if the nearby fighting would keep us grounded for the day. It would be unfortunate, we all agreed, if the minister was unable to visit his troops in Killagai. But as we talked through our morning agenda, it was clear that something had changed. The tension between Csaba and me had diffused, and everyone felt it. I think he finally understood that it would be hard for him to walk away from his country's commitments, and I think he saw that I finally understood that his troops were exposed at Camp Pannonia and needed more equipment to protect themselves.

The corner that we turned was significant, not just for our countries' cooperation in Afghanistan but for everything we would accomplish together for the next three years. Despite—or perhaps because of—our confrontation, mutual respect and understanding had been forged between us. Not more than a few weeks later, a large shipment of new transport vehicles was delivered to Camp Pannonia. Within a short period of time, the reconstruction team received all of the equipment they needed, and they did not lose another member to an attack from that point forward.

While waiting for the transport helicopter, I had a chance to sit down with members of the U.S. Army's 10th Mountain Division who were also stationed at Camp Pannonia. They were a steely, serious group, and I could tell immediately that it was neither the time nor the place to chat about where they were from or what they missed from home. Instead, I asked them if they needed anything. They were in full war mode and made it clear that they were on a mission and they were fine. I thanked them for their service and told them how proud I was to see firsthand that the U.S. military was recognized by our allies as the finest in the world—and that it was our soldiers who made it so.

After the soldiers left the meeting room, a very different group came in: Afghan women who had been singled out by the secretary of state for their acts of courage and resourcefulness. One of them had started the first free radio station in Afghanistan. They described the enormous challenges for women in their country and explained what was in store for them, personally and professionally, if al-Qaeda and the Taliban prevailed. The women across the table from me were prepared to give their lives to achieve freedom within their own country.

That afternoon, we flew to Killagai, a base in northeast Afghanistan that was even smaller and more remote than Camp Pannonia. There, Hungarians served with members of the Ohio National Guard—a different rotation of the unit I had seen off during my first days in

Budapest. This group had a much different mission from the provincial reconstruction team in Pol-e Khumri. They were there to fight. They also were responsible for securing Highway 1 and for training the local Afghan forces to weed out insurgents in the area so that local forces could eventually take the place of the international coalition. Csaba was correct about one thing—there was more fighting in the area than when the Hungarians had arrived. Coalition forces were clearing areas around the highway of insurgents to protect the road for the long haul.

Killagai had far fewer creature comforts than the bigger bases. Knowing this in advance, I'd been traveling the whole time with a big backpack full of dozens of bags of Starbucks Christmas blend coffee and vanilla syrup. I figured the American troops stationed at this remote outpost would appreciate a taste of home and the Hungarians would enjoy a sweet break from the usual military fare.

By the time we left Killagai to return to RC North, I was a bit relieved that we were going back to a bigger, safer base.

At RC North, we visited with more Hungarian troops and had a long briefing by the German commander. Our last obligation of the trip to Afghanistan was a sad one. We attended a church service for the Hungarian soldiers who had recently been killed and hung wreaths at the memorial constructed to honor them and others who had died in service to their countries in that quarter of Afghanistan. We then boarded another transport plane and headed north to Uzbekistan, planning to spend the night and leave the next morning. Soon after we arrived, however, we heard that German chancellor Angela Merkel had made her Christmas visit to RC North that same day. She was on her way back to the base in Uzbekistan. We could see her massive Airbus waiting for her on the tarmac. The Hungarians asked, and her staff agreed, to take us back to Berlin with them that night.

This put me in a tricky situation. Merkel was going to Berlin, which was fine for the Hungarians, because their military transport plane could meet them there that night. But I was booked on a commercial flight the next day to fly from Munich home to California. Markos and the boys were traveling separately, and we would meet at home in California for the holidays. How was I going to get from Berlin to Munich fast enough to make my flight? One of the worst winter storms in history was raging over Europe, canceling flights and stalling trains across the Continent. Should I watch the Hungarians go and stay behind to take the transport plane to Munich that we were originally booked on?

As I contemplated what to do, one of my fellow travelers remarked that when you're in Uzbekistan and someone offers you a ride to Europe on a plane about to take off, you should, as a general rule of thumb, get on the plane. The idea of staying in Uzbekistan by myself at that remote base, with the Hungarian delegation gone, seemed like a bad one. I figured there must be a way to get from Berlin to Munich by morning; I would figure it out when I got to Berlin.

By the time I made up my mind, Merkel had arrived in Uzbekistan from Afghanistan on a military transport plane, similar to the one we had flown in. She disembarked from the transport plane and was met with a brief welcoming ceremony. After a few handshakes, she walked across the tarmac and boarded her waiting Airbus. I joined the Hungarian delegation as we scrambled to follow her. When we passed the chancellor's rooms inside her impressive plane, she stepped out to greet Minister Hende; there had always been a special relationship between the Germans and the Hungarians. As Merkel and Csaba exchanged greetings, I asked if I could take their picture together. The chancellor looked surprised, but the minister was delighted. After I'd snapped the photo, Csaba said, "Now one with you!" and we changed spots. The photo he took would later make me gasp: my nose was red and chafed from the cold, and my hair was matted under a little black Nike cap. But whereas I looked weathered and worn after my trip to Afghanistan, Angela Merkel was as fresh as springtime, if a bit annoyed by the sudden photo op.

We didn't land in Berlin until almost midnight. As I walked down the stairs of the plane, the chancellor's motorcade was tearing away. While the Hungarians loaded up their transport back to Budapest, Csaba pulled me aside to meet the Hungarian ambassador to Germany, József Czukor, who had come out into the cold to greet him. By the time I'd found my bags, almost everyone had disappeared, and I suddenly realized that soon I would be alone on the icy tarmac of the military base. The only buildings I could see were far away and pitch-black. My heart started to race as the Hungarians boarded their plane, waving good-bye to me. Scanning the scene, I spotted one car, and Ambassador Czukor climbing into it. I ran over to him.

"Could you possibly take me somewhere where I can find a cab?"

"Of course! Just tell me where you want to go."

But I had nowhere to go. I asked him to take me to Berlin's main train station to try to find a train to Munich. But the station was almost completely dark, and there was nowhere passengers could wait away from the cold. A ticket seller informed me that there would be no more trains until the next day, though I could try the other station, across town. So Czukor and I drove into the former East Berlin. I looked out at old, impersonal, communist-era apartment buildings, some of which hadn't been touched since the wall came down. The streets were empty, reminding me of the time I had been there with my family, in the late 1970s, a lifetime ago. The East Berlin train station also was closed. A few people huddled in the snow, trying to stay warm until their trains arrived.

My abandonment in the middle of the night, in Berlin, struck Czukor as very funny. As we drove through the empty streets, he relentlessly joked, "My wife will never believe I spent the night with the American ambassador!"

Eventually, I asked him to drop me off at a hotel. He brought me to an elegant one, right next to the U.S. Embassy. The hotel porter relieved me of my luggage and opened the door to another world—a lobby alive with holiday cheer, piano music, and pleasant chatter from the well-dressed guests at the bar. A few minutes later, I lifted my suitcase onto the bed in my stately room and caught sight of myself in the mirror, still wearing the black cap. Just a few hours before, I'd worn a bulletproof vest and walked in a war zone.

When I opened my suitcase, the pale dirt of Afghanistan poured out.

# 11

# God and Country

Exactly one year into my posting as U.S. ambassador to Hungary, I went home to California for the first time, traveling directly from Afghanistan. Driving from the airport to my father's house, where Markos and the boys would meet me the next day, I looked out the window at the familiar scenery. It was almost eerie how much the Sacramento Valley looked like rural Hungary—the flat landscape, the barren winter fields, and the low-hanging fog. The only difference was that whereas Central European winters were unremittingly gray, winter in California had a slight golden tinge.

It felt good to be home. I knew that just a few weeks away from post would give me some perspective and time to digest my first year in Budapest. I still couldn't quite believe that almost overnight I had gone from being a California land developer to chief of mission of a U.S. embassy in a former Soviet satellite country. But by now I could see that the leadership and management style of those of us coming from the private sector brought fresh thinking into the Foreign Service and that somehow the model worked.

As I drove along the familiar roads of my hometown, past neighborhoods that I had helped plan and develop, I remembered that when I first arrived in Budapest, I thought the most useful expertise I brought to the embassy as an outsider was eighteen years in development and construction. At the time, it appeared the biggest challenge I would grapple with during my tour would be the construction of the new annex building. Hungary's transition to democracy was complete, a model of success for other countries in the world. Major, expensive development programs established in Hungary by the State Department and USAID after 1989 to support its transition had long expired. The Peace Corps mission that went in right after the Iron Curtain fell was long gone. Even just a year before, as I made my way through the long litany of State Department briefings, no one could have anticipated that Hungarian democracy would hit a rough patch. But it had been only twenty years since Hungary's new system of government was adopted—less than one generation.

What had truly come into focus for me during that first year was that whether it was Afghanistan, Hungary, or even the United States, a country's democracy is always a work in progress. It was ironic that it hadn't occurred to me sooner, because for most of my life I had been well aware of the delicate nature of democracy. As a lifelong student of Hellenic history, I had worked hard to promote an awareness and understanding of ancient Athenian democracy and its relevance to its modern successor, the United States. Along the way, I had observed that many of my fellow Americans considered democracy and freedom to be their birthright. But I saw it in the context of world history, and I knew that democracy is a rare and precious system.

As a young Greek American, I grew up with stories my father told me about ancient Greece. Some of these stories he'd heard from his father, who had heard them from his own. Others he'd learned as an adult, reading the works of Aristotle, Plato, and the great philosophers and historians of the Golden Age of Greece, the birthplace of democracy.

When I went to college, I majored in English literature. I was passionate about good literature, and I enjoyed writing even more. But along the way I took enough classes in the classics department to warrant Dartmouth's equivalent of a minor in the field. After college, I lived in Greece, auditing lectures by the great professor and rabbi Nikos

Stavroulakis while working as an editor at an English-language daily paper, the *Athens News*. Before I returned to the United States in the summer of 1990, I worked at an archeological site in Episkopi, carefully and slowly excavating 2,400-year-old structures just a few miles from the village where my father was born.

After I returned to California to enter the MBA program at UC Berkeley, my relationship with all things Greek and Greek American expanded even more. When I was a girl, the Greek Orthodox Church had been the center of our family life. As far back as I can remember, all of our friends were Greek. Some were "fresh off the boat"—or at least off a plane from Athens—while others were first- and second-generation Americans, whose parents or grandparents had come from the Old Country. The members of this tightly knit community helped and supported one another, skinned and roasted lambs together, and spent long hours in the church hall socializing after services.

By the time I returned from Greece as a young adult, my father and Sofia had become involved with an organization called Leadership 100. Leadership 100 was—and still is—the most prominent association of Greek American leaders in the country. Though it had been established to support the Greek Orthodox Church, the group brought together some of the United States' most influential and successful citizens—people engaged in U.S. politics, international affairs concerning Greece, and the dissemination of Greek history and culture. Leadership 100 was the epicenter of Greek American influence, sophisticated in its outreach and organization (even if its members still liked to celebrate with whole roast lamb and vigorous ring dancing). But back in 1991, the median age of the Leadership 100 membership must have been about sixty-five, and the group was almost entirely male. A few of the more enlightened members understood that the future strength of the Greek American community would rely on the engagement of the next generation, and many came to the annual conference with their adult children—mainly sons, but a handful of daughters, including me.

My father had long been a respected leader in the Greek American community. He was known for his philanthropy and his prominence within the Democratic Party, but it was his powerful intellect, passion for Hellenism, and ability to mobilize others that made him one of our country's best known and most effective Greek American leaders.

To be honest, my father and Sofia might have first brought me to the annual Leadership 100 conference to find a husband, but when I started to become interested and involved in the community's issues, they were very supportive, encouraging, and proud of me. Throughout the nearly two decades that I worked with my father at our land development firm, we were immersed in a broad range of issues of concern to Greek Americans. Whether it was the illegal occupation of northern Cyprus by Turkey, the question of Greece's sovereign territory, the renaming of the former Yugoslav Republic of Macedonia, or the acceptance of Greece into the U.S. Visa Waiver Program, we were involved. We always advocated for the policies that would be most beneficial for the U.S.-Greek bilateral relationship and for stability in the region around Greece. As Americans first and foremost, we sought the advancement of policies from the perspective of what was in the greatest interest of the United States.

I became passionate about many issues important to the Greek American community, but I was especially drawn to the area of religious freedom. In the early 1990s, Richard Blum, a prominent businessman and the husband of Senator Dianne Feinstein, invited my father to participate in the work of the World Council of Religions for Peace. I jumped at the chance to be involved too. Founded in 1970, the organization is made up of representatives of the world's religions and advocates for the advancement of peace through interfaith collaboration and understanding. In time, Richard asked me to join the board of trustees of the organization, and I served for about a decade.

I first visited the Greek Orthodox Ecumenical Patriarchate in Istanbul, Turkey, in 1989, when I was still a student at Dartmouth, as part of a classics department program. Our student group happened to be visiting sites near Istanbul during the week of Orthodox Easter. When I told my father about it, he arranged for us to visit the Patriarchate during services. The ancient rites were beautiful, but we noticed that everyone entered and left the property from the side gates. We were later told that the massive front gates of the Patriarchate—known as the *phanar*, or "light"—were sealed by the priests in 1821, after the

Turks, furious about the war for independence in Greece, hanged Ecumenical Patriarch Gregory V from them.

It would be many years before I returned to Istanbul. I came back in 2000 with Markos, just three months after we'd met, for our wedding at the Patriarchate. Istanbul—formerly Constantinople—was once the capital of the Christian Empire, but Turkey had become a Muslim country, and over the years the Patriarchate had suffered from legal and political discrimination. At the time Markos and I were getting married, very few people were going to the Patriarchate even to visit, let alone for a big American wedding. We planned everything in just three short weeks, and it was only possible because of our friend Father Alex Karloutsos.

Grounded in his faith and deeply involved with his flock, both at his own parish church and around the world, Father Alex was able to move between church life and the secular lives of its members with ease. He knew that my desire to get married in Istanbul reflected not only my love of our church but also my understanding that the wedding of a prominent American would help raise awareness of the plight of the Patriarchate.

With so little time to prepare, the celebration was a bit chaotic—my policy was "If you want to come, let us know and we'll send you an invitation." Our nearly two hundred guests were mostly friends and family who'd mobilized quickly to get to Istanbul in time. I'd sent an invitation to the president and the first lady, but I doubted the White House would even process the invitation before the wedding was long over.

We expected that a wedding involving a well-known Greek American family at the Patriarchate in Istanbul would be significant to the Turkish media. But imagine our surprise when the Turkish press published what were purported to be quotes from President Clinton, such as this gem: "I told the young couple that there was no better place to have their wedding than in Turkey!" Pictures of our wedding ended up on the front pages of every major newspaper in Turkey. As Turkey aspired to join the European Union, our wedding could be viewed symbolically as a thawing of relations between Greeks and Turks.

———

Markos had also been raised with a strong affinity for the old world of his Greek immigrant parents. Greek was his first language. But as a journalist, he kept a certain level of detachment from the church, just as he did from partisan politics. He made clear early on that I should take the lead in these two areas. As the first years of our marriage unfolded, however, Markos and I began to develop a shared interest in the connection between ancient Greek democracy and what we knew of American democracy from our own education, careers, and life experiences.

After the attacks on September 11, 2001, many Americans asked themselves what they could do to help our country. There was a surge in enrollment at the State Department and in the armed services. As Markos and I contemplated what we could do, we were both struck by something President George W. Bush said soon after the disaster: he explained that the attack had happened at least in part because the perpetrators "hate our freedoms." Markos and I wondered to what degree our fellow Americans knew what this meant. Freedom is so natural for Americans—it is the air we breathe. But we knew that the founding fathers of our democracy had looked to ancient Athens for a model when they devised our system of government. In the intervening centuries between the Golden Age of Athenian democracy and our modern American democracy, most of the world had been governed by kings, tyrants, emperors, aristocrats, and, just as often, chaos. Democracy and freedom are exceedingly rare in world history. Markos and I worried that too few Americans fully understood this.

In 2003, Markos and I were approached by Georgetown University to establish a chair in Hellenic studies. Neither of us had attended Georgetown, but we both recognized the value of giving students at this important Washington, D.C.–based school, many of whom were likely to go on to prominent leadership positions, the opportunity to learn more about ancient Athens. We thought they should know that, as a result of the world's first democracy, revolutionary advances were made in mathematics, astronomy, medicine, architecture, engineering, philosophy, art, and literature. Perhaps the most important advancement of all was the philosophical concept of the value of the individual human being, rich or poor—a concept that led to all the other advances.

Shortly after Markos and I endowed the chair at Georgetown, we began discussions to endow a second chair, at Stanford University. This time we proposed that the chair be held in two departments, classics and political science. Stanford was very receptive to the idea. We had already named the Georgetown chair after ourselves, so this time we named the chair in recognition of Constantine Mitsotakis, a former prime minister of Greece whose assertive policies in the early 1990s had moved the country back toward the West after years of anti-Americanism under Andreas Papandreou. The first person Stanford appointed to hold the chair was Dr. Josiah Ober, one of the country's most prominent classicists, who had previously chaired the classics department at Princeton. Dr. Ober told us that he had been swayed to leave Princeton because he was intrigued by the opportunity to work in both the classics and political science departments. A few years later, he became chair of Stanford's political science department.

When asked to define democracy, Dr. Ober often starts with the meaning of the word itself: "demos" means the people; "cratos" means capacity. Democracy, he will tell you, starts with the question, what is the capacity of the people? What is their capacity to organize themselves and to govern themselves? What is their capacity to work together to create a great culture, a peaceful society, and advanced civilization?

As our trip home to California for the holidays came to an end, I packed up the boys' bags and saw them off to the airport with Markos. The three of them would return to Budapest and the start of the new school semester. As my husband and children flew to Hungary, I headed to Bethesda, Maryland, for the baptism of little Lucas Emanuel Manatos.

Lucas's parents, Mike and Laura Manatos, are part of a prominent Greek American family. As the country's best-known Greek American lobbyists, the Manatos family has served at the center of the vortex of Greek American issues for three generations and has managed to do so while balancing the many points of view and strong personalities that our community is known to produce. The walls of Manatos &

Manatos's Washington, D.C., office are crowded with decades of photographs of family members posed with a countless array of presidents, members of Congress, and political leaders from around the world.

For many years, the Manatos family had been like an extended part of my own family. We worked together on issues and celebrated together at conferences and weddings alike. So when Mike and Laura asked me to be godmother to their new son, I was delighted to accept the honor. According to Greek tradition, the rite would link our families as closely as a wedding links in-laws.

On a cold January day in 2011, some of the country's most active and engaged Greek Americans gathered just outside Washington to celebrate Lucas's baptism. The pews of the Greek Orthodox Church of St. George were brimming with a community of people who all felt like family to me—along with a handful of new Hungarian friends whom Mike and Laura had graciously invited as well.

Archbishop Demetrios of the Greek Orthodox Church of America arrived accompanied by Father Alex Karloutsos. I was pleased to see Archbishop Demetrios. When I was a young woman, I approached him with a litany of tough questions about the church. He answered all my questions patiently, philosophically, and convincingly. The year before I left for Budapest, he awarded me the medal of St. Paul, primarily for my work in interfaith dialogue and religious freedom. It was the highest decoration awarded by our church in America and one that was rarely bestowed—even more rarely was it given to a woman.

The chanting began. Surrounded by shimmering Byzantine iconography, Laura, Mike, our dear friend and the baby's godfather Peter Poulos, and I stood at the front church doors, facing outward.

"Do you renounce the devil?" Father Alex asked, reading from the ancient text.

"Yes, we renounce the devil!" we responded, and we pretended to spit outside the church, away from the congregation and the altar. Such an odd, archaic ritual. Good thing, I thought, that the Hungarians in the crowd did not understand liturgical Greek.

We proceeded to the altar, where little Lucas had his clothes removed and was wrapped in a white sheet. Archbishop Demetrios dipped him into the baptismal font; blessed him with olive oil on his head, feet, and hands; and clipped a bit of his hair as his first offering to God. Then he handed Lucas to me. As I held the wet, slippery, slightly whimpering infant in my arms, the archbishop gave what to me has long been the most meaningful blessing of what is certainly the most important rite of passage in Christianity: "Lord, make Lucas a valiant warrior in the battle between good and evil that rages on this earth."

I knew this blessing well. But for the first time, I didn't hear it just as a member of the Greek Orthodox faith. I heard the blessing as an American. One year into my ambassadorship, I was more convinced than ever that there was indeed a battle between good and evil that raged in the world. I didn't think of this blessing strictly in religious terms—my years of work promoting interfaith understanding had made me respectful and embracing of all the world's religions. To me, it was about the rule of law, democracy, and freedom. Bringing democracy to the world is a slow, painstaking process and not one that can be forced upon nations. But America, despite all of her faults and folly, all of her tragic mistakes, is still the largest force for the advancement of freedom and democracy, the most powerful force for good, that exists in the world.

That's why, though it was such a pleasure to participate in Lucas's baptism and I looked forward to all the wonderful things to come as his godmother, I knew I had to leave the after-party early and get back to my job.

A few days before, Hungary had assumed the presidency of the European Union for the first time. It was a proud moment for Hungarians, and it was also a proud moment for the United States. We had worked closely with our ally in the development of its democracy. Now, as Hungary took a major step forward into the community of democratic European nations, I wanted to share in that rite and offer my congratulations and encouragement. Twenty years after democracy came to Hungary, it was a chance for the world to see the capacity of the Hungarian people.

The Manatos baptismal celebration would continue into the wee hours, but I said my good-byes and headed to the airport and back to Budapest.

With my dad and sisters catching a snake in front of our house on the river in Sacramento. That's me on the far left. *Courtesy of the author*

With my family at Checkpoint Charlie in East Berlin, 1979. I'm third from the right. *Courtesy of the author*

View of the 1989 Freedom March from the U.S. Embassy in Budapest, taken by my husband, Markos Kounalakis. *Courtesy of Markos Kounalakis*

My father and I speak with President Clinton about Greek American affairs. *Courtesy of the author*

Markos and I escort Ecumenical Patriarch Bartholomew into the reception after our wedding at the Greek Orthodox Patriarchate in Istanbul, 2000. *Photo by Thomas Gibbons*

Hosting Senator Obama at our San Francisco apartment. Markos and I were very impressed. *Courtesy of the author*

With my mentor and friend, Congresswoman Nancy Pelosi. *Courtesy of the author*

Secretary Clinton administers the oath of office to me as my father,
Speaker of the House Nancy Pelosi, and U.S. Supreme Court Justice
Anthony Kennedy look on. *Courtesy of the State Department*

Signing the guest book in the Hungarian Presidential Palace just before handing my credentials to President László Sólyom. *Courtesy of Szilárd Koszticsák/MTI*

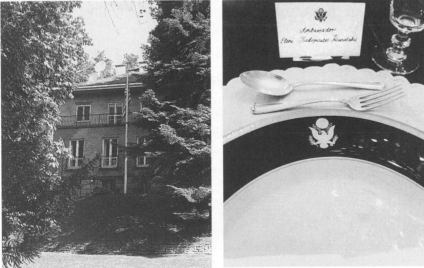

LEFT: Residence of the U.S. ambassador to Hungary, where we lived during our tour. *Courtesy of Barbara Vaughn*. RIGHT: The table was always elegantly set for official functions with the official State Department china. *Courtesy of Barbara Vaughn*

My first boar. My Hungarian hosts were amazed that I brought the boar down with one clean shot. *Courtesy of the author*

Fourth of July 2010. Prime Minister Viktor Orbán had just been elected and attended the reception as our guest of honor, bringing most of his cabinet with him. Images from the event flooded the media for days and signaled mutual hopes for a strong U.S.-Hungarian relationship. *Courtesy of the State Department/Photo by Samaruddin Stewart*

Colonel Robert Duggleby (in uniform) with newly appointed Hungarian minister of defense Csaba Hende (whom I would later join on a trip to Afghanistan) speaking with foreign minister János Martonyi (left). *Courtesy of the State Department/Photo by Samaruddin Stewart*

LEFT: Jeff Lodinsky was the consul general at Embassy Budapest during most of my tour. He was seriously injured in a suicide bomb attack in Afghanistan in 2012. *Courtesy of the State Department/Photo by Attila Németh.* RIGHT: My sons hosted their own parties within our official receptions, usually with water guns or Nerf guns. Here they are with some friends visiting from San Francisco. *Courtesy of the State Department/Photo by Samaruddin Stewart*

Together with minister of public administration and justice (also Hungary's deputy prime minister) Tibor Navracsics speaking at an anticorruption conference. It was one of many events sponsored by the American Chamber of Commerce. *Courtesy of the State Department/Photo by Attila Németh*

U.S. Supreme Court Justice Anthony Kennedy and I speak with Hungarian foreign minister Janos Martonyi after a meeting with Prime Minister Viktor Orbán. *Courtesy of the State Department/Photo by Attila Németh*

During the major floods of 2010, the United States supported the work of the Hungarian Red Cross. Its local president was Georg Von Hapsburg, grandson of the last Austro-Hungarian emperor. The palace where his family once resided can be seen behind us. *Courtesy of the State Department/Photo by Attila Németh*

Visiting Afghanistan with the Hungarian minister of defense in December 2010. The protective vest and helmet were several sizes too big for me. *Courtesy of the author*

After four days in Afghanistan, my skin is chafed and my hair matted under a cap. German chancellor Angela Merkel gave the Hungarian delegation a ride home from Uzbekistan on her plane. *Courtesy of the author*

My second trip to Afghanistan in 2012 as part of a delegation headed by Admiral James Stavridis and a NATO delegation. *Courtesy of the author*

European Union Summit of Justice and Home Affairs. From left: Secretary Janet Napolitano, Hungarian ministers Sándor Pintér and Tibor Navracsics, EU commissioner Viviane Reding, and attorney general Eric Holder. *Courtesy of the State Department/Photo by Attila Németh*

Celebrating the unveiling of the Reagan statue (at right) in honor of the hundredth anniversary of his birth. *Courtesy of the State Department/Photo by Samaruddin Stewart*

Secretary Condoleezza Rice being greeted by Prime Minister Orbán with the customary Hungarian "csókolom a kezét" kiss to the hand. Former U.S. attorney general Ed Meese and I look on. *Courtesy of the State Department/Photo by Samaruddin Stewart*

Political and economic counselor Paul O'Friel (left) speaking with Ronald Reagan's attorney general Ed Meese as we wait for a meeting with Prime Minister Orbán. *Courtesy of the State Department/Photo by Samarrudin Stewart*

Walking through the halls of Parliament with Prime Minister Orbán and Secretary Clinton on our way to the press conference. Everyone's demeanor had become very serious. *Courtesy of the State Department/Photo by Samaruddin Stewart*

The secretary pauses to catch up with deputy chief of mission Tim Betts, our highest-ranking career Foreign Service officer at Embassy Budapest. *Courtesy of the State Department/Photo by Samaruddin Stewart*

Sril Yisrael Jacob (age eleven) and Zelig Jacob (age nine) on the platform at Auschwitz-Birkenau in Poland. The boys were killed in the gas chambers soon after this photo was taken. Notice their patriotic Hungarian clothes. *Courtesy of Yad Vashem*

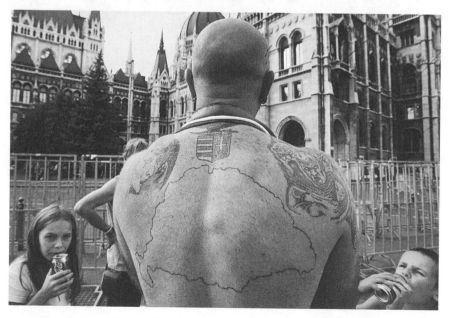

A map of Greater Hungary tattooed on the back of a supporter of Hungary's far-right movement. *Courtesy of Getty Images*

LEFT: The building on the left is the chancery. The smaller "annex" building to the right was the subject of the property swap that I worked very hard to revive and complete. *Courtesy of Barbara Vaughn.* RIGHT: On the roof of the "annex" building during construction with Gergely Horváth of the Hungarian asset management office. Consolidating our embassy offices resulted in major cost savings and the improvement of our security footprint. *Courtesy of the State Department*

From left, Congresswomen Nancy Pelosi, Anna Eshoo, Carolyn Maloney, Jeanette Schmidt, Teri Sewell (not shown), and I meet with Prime Minister Orbán and his senior adviser Péter Szijjártó (in the bottom right corner). *Courtesy of the State Department/Photo by Samaruddin Stewart*

The last group of Ohio National Guardsmen to deploy out of Hungary to Afghanistan during my tour of duty. Seeing soldiers off to war was a new, difficult challenge for me and one that I strived to be worthy of. *Courtesy of the State Department/Photo by Attila Németh*

My official car. I attached the flag to the front of the car only when traveling to high-level meetings. *Courtesy of the State Department*

# 12

# Presidency of the European Union

On January 1, 2011, Hungary celebrated a historic milestone: it assumed the presidency of the European Union. Hungary was one of ten countries that had joined the union in 2004, in the EU's largest single expansion, along with a number of other former Soviet satellites, including the Czech Republic and Poland. With its twenty-seven members, the EU included a broad swath of Europe by 2011. The presidency of the EU rotates among member countries, with each one holding the position for six months. Although the EU's capital is in Brussels, the organization's many committee meetings take place in the country that holds the presidency, and that country gets an extra say in setting the agenda, so it can highlight issues that it considers particularly critical. As Hungary wouldn't have another shot at the presidency for at least thirteen-and-a-half years, this was an important opportunity.

I may have had my reservations about Viktor Orbán, but many highly capable and internationally respected people served in his government. This was particularly true of the men and women at the Foreign Ministry charged with managing the EU presidency. Many of them had worked through the complex process of Hungary's EU accession. They knew the players in Brussels, and they understood the way the union operated. In the fall of 2010, embassy staff and I went repeatedly to the Foreign Ministry to ask and explore two basic questions: what would Hungary's priorities be during its EU presidency, and how would Hungarians advance those priorities?

In many instances, their priorities were very much aligned with U.S. interests. First, they said, they would work to solve the most important issues facing the EU. The top issue at that time, of course, was Europe's economic crisis, particularly the dire situation in Greece and the country's possible exit from the Eurozone. But the Hungarians also planned to propose that every EU member develop a strategy for dealing with Roma integration. Since the end of communism, the former Eastern bloc countries had been struggling with the issue of how to handle their large, impoverished, and often persecuted Roma, or Gypsy, populations. If the Hungarians could get this done, it would be one of the most substantial policy advances for the European Union on this issue ever.

The U.S. State Department was excited that Hungary would be taking the reins of the EU presidency. It was a reminder that the fall of the Iron Curtain had led to a new direction for Central Europe. Coincidentally, 2011 would be an important marker in the U.S.-Hungarian relationship for another reason: it was the centennial of the birth of Ronald Reagan. The Hungarians credited Reagan, along with Pope John Paul II, with helping them to secure their independence from the Soviet Union, and they planned to raise a statue of the late American president to honor the occasion.

At the end of 2010, it looked as though 2011 would be a great year for celebrating Hungary's full-fledged membership among Western nations. We realized that the new prime minister and his supermajority in Parliament added a certain level of unpredictability. Still, we believed Orbán would be careful because of the historic importance of Hungary's first EU presidency, and Hungarians were ready to show the rest of Europe that they were sophisticated, smart, and ready to lead. Towns were spruced up, hotels were booked solid, and seats on flights in and out of Budapest for the next six months were scarce.

On January 1, Hungary took over the presidency of the European

Union, with all the pomp and grandeur of its imperial past. And on January 2, all hell broke loose.

The new Hungarian media law was passed in the final days of 2010, but it came into effect on the first full day of Hungary's EU presidency. Blindsiding both the public and the Foreign Ministry, which took an important lead during the presidency, Viktor Orbán's two-thirds majority in Parliament enacted a law that radically transformed the operation and regulation of Hungary's media. Without public comment, without engagement of the affected media outlets, without any discussion, a Hungarian media law was adopted that handed Viktor Orbán the Sword of Damocles to hold over the head of Hungary's free media. Overnight, a sense of fear of potential reprisal for any criticism of the government spread among Hungary's media outlets. To the shock and dismay of millions of Hungarians and their allies abroad, the media law exploded onto the front pages of newspapers across Europe. The reaction was fierce. According to many political scientists, pundits, and journalists in Hungary and abroad, the new law seemed to prove what they had been saying since Election Day: that Hungarian democracy was dead after barely twenty years.

How much of the outcry was fair and how much was vitriol? To what degree was the new law within the purview of any democratic government to regulate its country's media, and to what degree could it constrain freedom of speech? It was our job to find out. Paul O'Friel and his team began traversing Budapest, talking to officials and journalists alike, looking for answers. The law created a new, very powerful body to oversee regulation: the Media Council, whose five members would all be appointed by Fidesz-controlled Parliament. The law gave the council the power to regulate the content of newspapers, television, and radio. Coverage of national and European news was required to be "balanced" and would be monitored and judged by the council. Any outlet that violated these and other new provisions—as determined by the Media Council in its sole discretion—faced the possibility of debilitating fines. Alleged violators could fight the fines in court, but in many cases they would have to pay them first.

How could Parliament pass a watershed bill that the public knew almost nothing about until it became the law of the land? How could a law be enacted without public debate or even giving the opposition a chance to evaluate the law? In the United States, we have always been wary of too much power concentrated in too few hands. As a result, our system provides checks and balances, and after 238 years of wrangling, power in America is spread across many institutions. But in countries without a long tradition of democracy, countries that have historically been dominated by an aristocratic or political elite, the concentration of power in the hands of the few can feel like the status quo. And for Orbán and Fidesz, their two-thirds supermajority gave them perfectly legal means of passing whatever laws they saw fit. Even though Hungarians protested the media law, the government paid them little mind.

Jeff Levine had completed his Budapest posting the previous summer, and my new deputy chief of mission, Tim Betts, arrived soon after. Tim had spent nine months in Hungarian-language training in Washington and had been well briefed before his arrival. A very experienced officer, he had served in Japan, Turkey, and Australia. Now, six months into his tour, he was already on top of his game. In our efforts to understand the impact of the media law, Tim and I met with news outlets based in Budapest to learn how they would change their practices to avoid running afoul of the new rules. The most common thing I heard was that they planned to be more careful about what they said. That's called self-censorship, and although it's difficult to prove, our embassy media office detected it almost immediately after the new law was passed. People knew there would be consequences for defiance. One popular host of a government-owned radio station, Attila Mong, was suspended directly after holding a minute of silence to protest the media law. Mong never went back to that job.

Some media representatives told us they were cutting back on political news, claiming that those programs had been suffering from lack of interest anyway—consumers preferred entertainment and human interest stories. This trend was apparent everywhere, even in the United States, so it made sense to them to simply dial back political coverage.

The media law had a devastating effect on Hungary's public image at a crucial moment, turning the proud assumption of the EU presidency into a free-for-all of criticism. Orbán went to Strasbourg on January 19 to speak to the European Parliament on general EU matters, but he ended up confronting a hostile gathering. Socialist parliamentarians appeared with duct tape over their mouths to protest the new media restrictions, and "Danny the Red"—Daniel Marc Cohn-Bendit, a German Green Party member—lashed out at Orbán from the floor, comparing him to Venezuelan strongman Hugo Chávez. Orbán calmly rebutted the criticism and promised to abide by the European Commission's forthcoming legal opinion on the new media law—as long as the same standards applied to all EU members. With his cool responses to the circus that the Socialists created, Orbán was able to frame the debate of the Hungarian media law along partisan political lines. When I went to see Péter Szijjártó, the prime minister's senior adviser, a few days after Orbán's EU speech, he gleefully reported that "we are getting calls from conservative politicians from all over Europe, congratulating us for standing up to these liberals. The response from our friends is overwhelming."

Back at the embassy, my staff and I shared our concerns over the new media law with officials in Washington. Foggy Bottom did not disagree, but the U.S. policy of not engaging in Hungary's domestic affairs superseded our concerns at this point. They told me that while it was acceptable for us to register the U.S. government's concerns, I should not forget that "Hungarian laws are up to Hungarians to decide" and that this should be my first talking point when I was asked privately or publicly about the media law.

I mulled this over. We were concerned about their laws, but their laws were up to them to decide—to me, those sounded like contradictory statements. Curious about where red lines were drawn, I investigated the website of the U.S. Embassy in Singapore. Singapore was well known to have very stringent censorship laws. If I had been ambassador there, would I have spoken out about the laws? The answer was clear: absolutely not. Still, wasn't Hungary different? It belonged to the EU and NATO. Both institutions are based on shared values, and their members are among the world's most ardent advocates of democratic principles.

Complicating the issue was the reaction of Hungarian journalists to the new law. At a party at the home of public affairs chief Ed Loo, a group of journalists pulled me aside. "Madam Ambassador, please help us," they pleaded. "We are all very afraid to speak out."

"Tell me. What are you afraid of?" I asked.

"Losing our jobs."

"Listen, you can't be afraid to speak out," I told them. "You are journalists. It's your job to speak the truth. You can't ask the United States to do it for you." I told them that if they lost their jobs, there was nothing I could do. But I knew that one of the first signs of a crumbling democracy was journalists getting arrested. So I added, "If you end up in jail, you can count on me to be there, doing everything possible to get you out."

None of them went to jail, but several did speak out, and more of them lost their jobs. But because they could not prove they had been fired for their beliefs rather than merely downsized, they had no recourse.

In the meantime, we had our hands full with more prosaic, but nonetheless important, elements of the EU presidency. In preparation for this transition, the number of U.S. officers in Budapest temporarily swelled, and the visits from Washington officials intensified. In a six-month period, three members of President Obama's cabinet came to Budapest—the only ones to visit during my time as ambassador. The first two, Secretary of Homeland Security Janet Napolitano and Attorney General Eric Holder, arrived together in April to represent the United States at a summit with the Justice and Home Affairs Council of the European Union.

The fact that they had both come to Budapest for this meeting reflected the importance to the United States of updating an agreement with the EU that allowed us to gather limited but crucial information on passengers flying from European airports to the United States. Immediately after the 9/11 terrorist attacks, the United States and the EU had hastily worked out the Passenger Name Record Agreement. This pact required EU countries to immediately send us the basic information people provided when buying airline tickets that would take them from Europe to the United States. Now the Europeans wanted a new agreement with new constraints. Viviane Reding, vice president of the

European Commission and commissioner for Justice, Fundamental Rights, and Citizenship, would represent the EU at the meeting. She was the most vocal advocate for restrictions to the agreement. A fierce advocate of privacy, she had staked out a very tough position, and it looked as though we might never see eye to eye.

There had already been bad-mouthing and name-calling between Reding and our officials that had made its way into the back pages of newspapers in Europe and the United States. But I was amazed at how fierce the debate was, given that the data we were receiving through the program was pretty basic. It included the standard information people give when purchasing airline tickets: name and address, passport number, and credit card details, as well as departure and arrival information, and whether passengers asked for extra assistance or a special meal. Reding wanted constraints on how long this information could be held, and she wanted us to agree to destroy the records within a particular time frame. Special meals were another sticking point. If someone ordered a vegetarian meal, could that be used for racial profiling against Muslim travelers, many of whom did not eat certain types of meat?

We thought Viviane Reding was being unreasonable. The information being provided was hardly invasive yet had been critical in our efforts to prevent attacks against our country. When we weighed the costs against the benefits, we considered it a fair trade. People expected privacy, but they also expected to be kept safe in an increasingly dangerous environment. If we could have dropped a field, like special meals, we probably would have been willing to negotiate over it. But asking airlines to manipulate the data they collected as part of their protocols, instead of just forwarding it to us directly, would have required more red tape. Hungary's position on the issue was the same as ours. Hungarians knew what it meant to be spied on by the government, and they did not believe that releasing this data came close to that. Because Hungary held the EU presidency, its support was essential to moving the negotiations forward. When Secretary Napolitano visited the offices of Minister of Interior Sándor Pintér, she thanked him profusely for his advocacy in working toward getting the deal done, and she even gave him a bear hug.

Hosting two cabinet members at once created quite an organizational challenge for the embassy staff. Tim Betts and I switched back and forth between Secretary Napolitano's meetings and those we scheduled for Attorney General Holder. While both cabinet members focused on the Passenger Name Record Agreement and U.S.-EU security cooperation, we hoped Eric Holder would engage on other significant issues as well.

While the furor over the new media law had died down somewhat, the process of drafting a new constitution had heated up—largely in secret. Calls from the opposition and civil society organizations for a voter referendum to approve the constitution, which had once appeared plausible, now appeared naive. Orbán had made it clear that he would not propose a referendum, and a voter-driven one would be difficult to get on the ballot under Hungarian law. Stakeholders were demanding to at least have the opportunity to weigh in on the document before it was adopted, but the chances of even that looked slim. We were hearing rumors about what was going to go into the new constitution: laws that would affect churches, universities, courts, businesses, women's issues, voter rights—everything.

In light of the way the media law had come down, we felt we should take the opportunity to have high-ranking U.S. officials meet face-to-face with top Hungarian officials to ask questions and encourage an inclusive process. So we asked Eric Holder, America's top lawyer and the man responsible for managing our judicial system, if we could enlist his help in talking to the Hungarians about our concerns over the new constitution.

We prepared extensive briefing papers for Holder and sent them to his staff before he came to Budapest, but as we sat down to brief him at his hotel, he didn't appear to have read any of the material. Hungarian democracy did not rank on the attorney general's list of things to be most worried about, and anyway, local domestic policy was almost never on his agenda when he visited a country in the EU and NATO for talks. Because I appreciated the vastness of his job, and the unusual nature of our request, I didn't blame him.

But he still agreed to engage with the Hungarians, so we had to get him up to speed—fast. Paul O'Friel delivered a short lecture on

Hungarian history, and I watched Holder absorb the information. For those twenty minutes, his mind was not on the many pressing issues he dealt with as attorney general of the United States; he was fascinated by the Hungarian story—its moments of glory, its periods of great tragedy, and its modern contradictions and complications. When I explained what we wanted him to do to help, he answered that he was in.

Holder and I first went to see Hungary's minister of justice, Tibor Navracsics, who also served as a deputy prime minister. Only forty-four years old, Navracsics was already a star of Hungarian politics, and his advancement by Viktor Orbán was seen as more of a coup for Orbán than an achievement for Navracsics. A trained lawyer, political scientist, academic, and brilliant transatlanticist, he was very well respected internationally. He was also a politician in his own right, with his own following. In aligning himself with Orbán, he provided a powerful and credible voice in defense of the Fidesz government's moves.

As Holder made his way through the talking points we had prepared for him, he raised issue after issue about Hungary's constitutional reform process, specifically questioning the media law and recent moves that appeared to restrict the independence of the country's judiciary. Carefully, he expressed our concerns about what those laws would mean for Hungarian democracy.

Navracsics skillfully deflected Holder's questions and eloquently explained the government's position. Although his English was impeccable, he spoke in Hungarian and relied on an interpreter, periodically offering corrections to ensure that his explanations were crystal clear. He persuasively argued that the Orbán government was engaged in a voter-mandated overhaul of the system that would fix the corrosive and corrupt policies of the past. As Holder listened and nodded to the minister's explanations, I could see the respect of one talented constitutional expert for another. A few pleasantries later, we were standing and saying our good-byes.

Right after this meeting, our delegation was ushered down the long, vaulted corridors of the Parliament building, headed to the prime minister's office. There was no time to debrief, but I sensed that, in spite of the attorney general's agreement to engage as we had requested, Navracsics's skillful answers had caused him to reconsider whether he wanted to be drawn into this discussion. Even though Navracsics had been very polite, he had refused to accept a single point of Holder's, and he'd delivered credible responses to all of them.

When we got to Prime Minister Orbán's cavernous offices—complete with stained-glass windows and thirty-foot ceilings—Janet Napolitano was already there to meet us. We took seats on one side of a hefty table, with a half dozen of our aides at our sides and another half dozen sitting behind us. Opposite us sat Viktor Orbán, Foreign Minister Martonyi, and Navracsics, flanked by their own aides and note takers.

Whenever I briefed visitors about to meet Orbán, I always noted that they would be surprised by how much they liked him. Usually, having heard so many negative reports about him, they didn't believe me, but my prediction always came true. This meeting was no exception. After the usual opening pleasantries, which gave Orbán a chance to charm his guests with clever observations and funny, self-deprecating comments, the conversation turned to the state of the European Union. Orbán made a well-argued case about the mistakes that had led to the euro crisis and the lack of sound decision-making needed to lead Europe out of the mess. Some of the discussion touched on our mutual agreement relative to the Passenger Name Records Agreement. I could see the attorney general nodding slightly as Orbán spoke, pleased that the main purpose of his visit would be successful. I was pleased about that too. Holder thanked the prime minister for Hungary's support for our cooperation on law enforcement, and Orbán recommitted that support. Reassured that our countries' relationship was thriving, Holder turned the discussion over to Secretary Napolitano.

As secretary of Homeland Security, Napolitano was there to discuss security cooperation between the United States and Hungary. Afghanistan and counterterrorism cooperation also were on her agenda. There was a great deal of agreement and head-nodding on both sides as we made our way through the meeting. But I was surprised that before giving the floor to Napolitano, Holder had not raised the issue of Hungarian reforms and the new constitution that we'd discussed with Navracsics. It was right there at the top of his talking points. I figured he thought it would be better to raise the subject at the end of the meeting. So imagine my surprise when Napolitano gave him the floor again and he began to close the session.

"Mr. Prime Minister, thank you for taking the time to meet with us today," he said. "We value the friendship and partnership between the American and Hungarian people, and we wish you and your country the very best of success with its first EU presidency."

Oh my god, I thought. He wasn't going to say anything about the constitution. He must have sensed my agitation, because he turned away from me as he left the table. But I wasn't going to let him go as easily as that.

After the final handshakes and photos, we walked out of Orbán's office, and though I had to trot to keep up with Holder's long strides, I caught him in the hallway. "Mr. Attorney General, why did you decide not to raise the issue of the constitution?"

To talk to me properly, to look me in the eye, he would have had to slow down and lean over a bit. He didn't. "I felt the meeting was going great," he said, continuing to speed down the hall. "He said all the right things, and we agreed on everything." Finally, he looked at me. "The minister of justice really answered all of our questions. I didn't think we needed to raise them at a higher level."

I slowed back down to a walk, lost in thought, as Eric Holder strode on ahead. Suddenly, Secretary Napolitano was at my ear. "Ambassador, wasn't he supposed to raise the question of the new Hungarian constitution, the media law, and all that?"

Yes, I told her, but he didn't do it.

"You should have put it on my talking points," she replied. "I would have raised it." Napolitano had been in town long enough to know that Hungary's reform process was going in a troublesome direction. But she hadn't been in the meeting with Navracsics, so she hadn't heard what Holder believed to be adequate responses to our concerns. The truth was, the AG made a perfectly fair call—if issues are addressed at a lower level, a diplomat will usually let it stand. It was hard to say if Napolitano would have done anything differently after hearing from Navracsics. But in any case, it was too late.

That afternoon, we all headed out for the big event, the U.S.-EU summit on Justice and Home Affairs, in hopes of striking a new

Passenger Name Record Agreement. In preparation for the EU presidency, Hungary had taken a crumbling wing of a two-hundred-year-old palace—Gödöllő, once the favorite home of Empress Elisabeth, wife of Franz Joseph I—and refurbished it almost overnight. The former royal stables had been transformed into elegant and well-constructed meeting rooms. I sat at the table with Napolitano and Holder, and less than two hours later the terms of the new agreement had been struck (though it wouldn't be signed for a few more months). Immediately after the meeting, as everyone stood up smiling and satisfied, Holder and I returned to bilateral issues, thankfully of a less contentious nature.

We sat down with Hungarian prosecutor general Péter Polt in an eighteenth-century gilded parlor that had been renovated a few years earlier. The restoration had been a big job. At the end of World War II, Nazis had occupied the palace, stealing or destroying whatever they could find. Later, during the communist era, the Gödöllő palace was turned into a home for the elderly. Over the decades, nearby villagers had taken a small number of precious items from the palace and hidden them away. When the renovation began, many of these Hungarians, so proud of their local heritage, came forward with missing treasures and restored them to their rightful places.

For many years, the United States and Hungary had worked together closely in the area of law enforcement. We had a significant FBI presence in Hungary starting from right after the fall of the Berlin Wall that included the very first FBI task force outside of the United States, operating side by side with Hungarian law enforcement officials to fight international—primarily Russian—organized crime. We also had a highly successful training center, the International Law Enforcement Academy, where the United States, with the support and cooperation of the Hungarian government, had trained ten thousand mid-level police officers from Hungary, the Balkans, Eastern Europe, Eurasia, and even farther afield.

After Polt and Holder had discussed the mutual benefits of our law enforcement cooperation, the conversation turned to current events. The prosecutor described the rise of Hungary's extreme right with great concern. I could see that Holder was disturbed by the description of the Magyar Gárda, the Hungarian radical nationalist militia, as well as by its politics and methods. Polt told his counterpart, "I want to assure you that we go to great lengths to ensure that they are not able to march in our streets. We have outlawed their uniforms and will not allow them to gather. It would be as unacceptable as if you were to let the Ku Klux Klan march on the steps of Washington." At these words, I saw Holder's face flinch almost imperceptibly.

"I didn't think I would find myself in Hungary defending the rights of the Ku Klux Klan," Holder replied slowly and carefully. "But we do, in fact, allow them to peacefully demonstrate in our country."

As the interpreter translated these words by the first African American U.S. attorney general, Polt's face dropped.

Holder continued, "Freedom of speech, freedom of expression, is a fundamental freedom in any democracy. So long as it doesn't reach into the realm of instigating violence, we defend the rights of people to say things, even if they are odious, horrible things that should be loudly denounced."

After the meeting, Holder sighed and patted me on the shoulder. "It looks like you've got your work cut out for you here. Good luck, Ambassador." He smiled wanly and we left the room for our next appointment. We took a visit to the International Law Enforcement Academy and posed for a photo with all of our beaming personnel there, then the attorney general said his good-byes and headed to the airport. I jumped into my car, racing back to the embassy to meet up with Secretary Napolitano.

I'd met the Homeland Security secretary in 2006, when she was governor of Arizona. Her office had contacted me to ask if I would meet with her on an upcoming visit to San Francisco. I originally turned them down—I figured that she wanted me to make a political contribution, and I already had more causes and candidates than I could handle. But the governor's staff insisted that she just wanted to meet me, no obligation.

We ended up spending an hour in my office talking, and Janet impressed me enormously. Her vision for our country, centrist and practical, as well as socially liberal, was very close to mine. But something else she said really stuck with me. "Women have to help each other, Eleni," she told me. "If we don't, we'll never have a woman president."

Janet's staff had told us that she wanted just a few hours during her visit to take in Budapest and see the sights. They mentioned that she loved opera, so I asked my team to see if there was a performance at the Budapest opera house that night. No, they reported, just the rehearsal of an upcoming ballet, but we were invited to watch it. So Janet and I made our way to the grand Hungarian State Opera House. The most famous building by renowned architect Miklós Ybl, the imposing structure had miraculously survived the Russian bombings of 1944 and '45. Its art and architecture rivaled that of any opera house in Europe, and it featured a resplendent box built for the Austro-Hungarian emperors and now reserved for Hungary's president and prime minister. Because the house was empty that night, Janet and I were allowed to sit in the imperial box to watch the ballet rehearsal.

An opera fan myself, I had been to the Budapest opera house many times by then to see performances. But I'd never had a tour, so I had a lot of questions for our guide. "During the communist times," I asked, "were there particular operas that could be performed and others that were forbidden?"

"No. It was exactly the same then. Puccini, Strauss, Mozart."

I was perplexed. "Really? The same classics were performed during the communist times exactly as they are now? In their original languages?"

"Oh, no," he sheepishly conceded. "They were all sung in either the Russian or Hungarian language."

Inwardly, I gasped. Puccini in Hungarian? Mozart in Russian? How would that have sounded? And how could this guide possibly tell us that performing the classics in Russian and Hungarian was the same as performing them in their original languages? The thought popped into my head that perhaps our guide was from a family connected to the former communists and didn't want to make the old regime sound too bad. More and more, I was coming to this kind of conclusion about the Hungarians I met. In America, we reject the notion that we should be judged by the actions or beliefs of our parents or grandparents. When it comes to political ideology, everybody gets a clean slate. But in Hungary, people more often than not defined themselves by their historical family allegiances. It was hard not to notice.

Though Janet enjoyed the dress rehearsal of the ballet, it was clear that opera was her true love, and she was disappointed that there was only dancing to see that night. I turned to Linda Mézes for help. Linda was one of my two most talented Hungarian political advisers at the embassy. Elegant and professional, she looked to me as her mentor, but I always felt that I was learning more from her.

I asked Linda, "Do you think you could find an opera singer to come to the restaurant?"

"You mean tonight?" Janet and I would be sitting down to dinner in an hour. Linda was puzzled, but the look on my face assured her I was serious, and she hurried off to see what she could do.

Markos and I had invited Janet's staff and members of the embassy staff to join us for dinner. About eighteen of us went to a small restaurant in the old Castle District and ordered a feast of Hungarian favorites—roasted duck confit, foie gras, fruit soup, and on and on. Linda had somehow managed to find the acclaimed Hungarian soprano Borbála Keszei, who at the time was starring in the Vienna State Opera but was commuting back and forth from Budapest for performances. It just so happened that she was at home that night, and Linda had persuaded her to come to the restaurant to sing for Secretary Napolitano.

I don't know what impressed me more, the mesmerizing beauty of the soprano's voice or knowing that Linda, who had initially struck me as a timid young woman, had been able to move mountains, arranging exactly what I'd hoped for, on ridiculously short notice. As this group of tired and dedicated U.S. government officials basked in classical operatic music and Hungarian food, I caught Linda's eye and gave her a grateful, proud smile.

# 13

# Golden Week

Ten days after Eric Holder and Janet Napolitano left Budapest, on April 18, 2011, the Hungarian Parliament passed the country's new constitution, now known officially as "the fundamental law." The Easter Constitution, as it was also called, was announced with great fanfare, but in spite of the assurances we'd been given that the drafting process would be inclusive and that the Hungarian people would have a chance to comment and contribute, Parliament adopted it quickly, with virtually no input from the opposition parties, civil society groups, or the public at large. Even contributions by experts specifically tapped by Viktor Orbán at the start of the process weren't visible to the public, and it wasn't clear they'd had much input at all. Here is how József Szájer, a close friend of Orbán's and a member of the European Parliament, described the process of drafting the Hungarian constitution, a document critical to the freedom of millions of Hungarians.

> Steve Jobs surely will be happy if he learns that Hungary's new consti-
> tution is written on an iPad (in fact on my iPad). . . . On a plane, on a
> train, in a car, during committee, presidency and party group meetings.
> For a representative always en route between Hungary, Belgium and

France there is no more ideal tool. (Thanx Steve Jobs! God bless you!
Get back to Apple, for the benefit of all of us! You are a genius!) . . . As
soon as textual proposal arrives from an advisor, and MP or a citizen, I
can immediately insert it into the text and forward it for further commenting, no matter where I am. I surely could not do this without this
device. . . . We could say that this is a 21st century constitution written
on a 21st century device.

This was hardly the process that Justice Kennedy had advocated
when he told Orbán what would make "an enduring document." Who,
exactly, were the privileged few lucky enough to have Szájer's e-mail
address and the ability to weigh in? Even those who had been announced as advisers to the process were telling us that it had all moved
so fast that their opportunity for input had been very limited.

While the process of adopting the new constitution had been swift
and closed, the content presented another troubling issue. The Easter
Constitution was written with many "placeholders" where major laws
would later be inserted. For instance, it would say, "The detailed rules
for the organization and administration of courts, for the legal status
of judges, as well as the remuneration of judges shall be laid down in
a cardinal act." Cardinal laws were defined as laws that could only be
adopted or later changed with a two-thirds vote of Parliament. Riddled
with placeholders, the Easter Constitution was essentially designed as
a vessel to contain major laws that would have to be written and adopted by January 1, 2012, the day the constitution would go into effect.
The question was, what would the cardinal laws look like, and what
would the process be for adopting them?

As we headed into the spring of 2011—and toward the halfway
point of my time as ambassador—we looked for answers to these important questions. I also realized something: U.S. presidential visits to
any country were rare, and it was not looking very likely that President
Obama would visit Hungary anytime soon. But there was still a chance
that Hillary Clinton would come.

If you're the U.S. ambassador in London, Paris, or any other large
post, you regularly host high-level visitors from Washington, including the president and members of his cabinet. Although that can make

postings at big embassies exciting, being in a midsize embassy like Budapest has its benefits too. If the most-seasoned experts on your host country are at your embassy rather than in Washington, then your country team is more likely to have a central role in policymaking. Of course, we wanted high-level visits as well, because they presented important opportunities to reinforce the bilateral relationship and move the agenda forward.

A U.S. president had not visited Hungary for five years, since George W. Bush came in 2006. That was also the last time a secretary of state had visited: Condoleezza Rice had accompanied Bush. Because of my long friendship with Hillary Clinton, I really wanted her to come to Budapest during my posting. But Hillary didn't fly around the world visiting her friends. She would only come to Hungary if a visit fit in with her agenda of advancing our national priorities. So my staff and I got to work on an agenda that could justify a visit.

First, we argued that Hungary's first turn at the presidency of the EU deserved to be acknowledged. Second, the Hungarian government had commissioned a statue of Ronald Reagan in honor of his hundredth birthday, and they planned to install it in the square in front of the embassy before the end of summer. Finally, Budapest would soon inaugurate the Tom Lantos Institute, a human rights organization established to commemorate the late Hungarian-born U.S. congressman. Lantos was the only Holocaust survivor to serve in the U.S. Congress, and during his nearly three decades of service he was a vocal and effective advocate for human rights. The Hungarian government was funding the institute and had specifically requested that Secretary Clinton speak at the opening. Hillary and Tom Lantos had been close friends, and I knew his legacy was important to her.

If we scheduled major events around these three milestones all at the same time, I reasoned, we might succeed in luring Hillary to Budapest. At the embassy, we began to call the last week of June Golden Week—we called it Transatlantic Week in external communications—and as the month of May ticked away, we waited to hear if Hillary would come. In the meantime, we started to field RSVPs from a cascade of people who found the cluster of upcoming events irresistible.

Two congressional delegations, known as CoDels, were planning visits. One was headed by California Republican Kevin McCarthy, who was mostly enticed to come for the Reagan commemoration. The other group, headed by Florida Republican Cliff Stearns, included members of something called the EU-U.S. Transatlantic Legislators' Dialogue, which would be holding its annual meeting in Budapest. The CoDels would total more than a dozen members of Congress, accompanied by their staff and spouses. Then there was a third delegation, which was coming for the Reagan centennial celebration. The group comprised dozens of dignitaries, including the former president's attorney general, Edwin Meese, and onetime California governor Pete Wilson, and would be led by none other than Condoleezza Rice. They were traveling through Central Europe to attend a series of Reagan commemorations, and they wanted to be present for the statue unveiling in Budapest. Finally, the entire Lantos family would come for the opening of the Lantos Institute. Among all the official events, we had scheduled an eightieth birthday party for Tom's widow, Annette, up at my residence.

Under any other circumstances, it would have been crazy to plan so much for a single week, but I knew it would take all these events together to provide enough justification for Hillary Clinton to come to town. And it worked. Just three weeks before Golden Week began, we received confirmation that, indeed, the secretary would attend the Lantos Institute opening. For a few minutes, my team and I were gleeful. Then we realized what would be involved in handling a secretary of state visit on top of all the other delegations, and we got to work.

Our Hungarian counterparts were thrilled with the news that Hillary Clinton was coming to Budapest, but Golden Week created a lot of work for them too, because they also had to deal with a multitude of logistics on their side. The embassy and the Ministry of Foreign Affairs worked together closely and quickly to make sure everything would be ready.

Aside from logistical challenges, Hillary's visit posed a very big question: Would the U.S. secretary of state comment on Hungary's controversial reform process? If so, what would she say?

I got a call from Tomicah Tillemann, Tom Lantos's grandson and a senior adviser to Hillary at the State Department. Even though the

Lantos family had suffered at the hands of the Hungarian Nazis during the Holocaust, Tomicah, like his grandfather, genuinely loved Hungary and identified himself as Hungarian American. He had been instrumental in securing Hillary's visit and was tasked with helping to write her speech for the opening of the Lantos Institute. Tomicah called to ask my thoughts about how Hillary should address the issue of Hungary's constitutional reform process.

"There is no way that Hillary Clinton, being who she is, could possibly come here and *not* say something," I told him. "It's been discussed and debated in every major newspaper in Europe and beyond. The question is, what does she say and when does she say it?"

Once Washington had my sign-off that it would be appropriate for Hillary to comment, I was fundamentally left out of the process. That was not unusual, and in this case it was more than fine with me, because the cascading events were keeping us all running. When Monday of Golden Week arrived, the delegations began to pour in. The members of Congress had meetings scheduled around the capital, and deputy chief of mission Tim Betts and I traded off on attending them.

The day before the unveiling of the Reagan statue, I was handed a speech for my introduction of Condoleezza Rice. Typically, my staff asked me to outline what I wanted to say, then gave me a draft I would edit. This time we'd been so busy that I'd forgotten all about it—and what they had drafted was impossible for me to deliver.

The speech praised Secretary Rice for her persistence in advancing what members of George W. Bush's administration had called the "freedom agenda." I protested, "I can't say that. It implies that the invasion of Iraq was justified." I wasn't just objecting to the proposed language from a personal perspective. President Obama had campaigned on the assertion that the invasion of Iraq had been a serious mistake and that he would end the war there. How could I imply otherwise? I told my team, "Someone's going to have to rewrite this speech—fast."

For the United States, diplomacy is historically nonpartisan. I hadn't realized until that moment that introducing Condoleezza Rice could present a problem for me. Before handing back the draft, I grabbed a pen and started to edit. What I could acknowledge without question was the former secretary of state's dedication to winning the Cold War.

She was an expert on Russia, the former Soviet Union, and Eastern Europe. "Let's focus on that," I told my staff.

Rice had not yet arrived. But the rest of her delegation was touring Budapest and sitting down with members of the government, who were eager to meet them. This group represented what remained of Ronald Reagan's inner circle, and you couldn't be more loved in Budapest than they were. During the Cold War, Hungarians had slightly more access to information than others on the dark side of the Iron Curtain, and they had seen that many of the Western European capitals were not only resigned to the reality of the Soviet Union but reluctant to poke Moscow in the eye. Reagan, however, had stood up and defied it. By launching a massive arms race, the United States helped push the Soviet economy into collapse—a brilliant strategy on the part of those who devised it, especially Reagan. Hungary, meanwhile, drew hope from the U.S. president's public actions, such as the historic moment in 1987 when he stood in front of Berlin's Brandenburg Gate and shouted, "Mr. Gorbachev, tear down this wall!" The Hungarians knew they were not alone, that Reagan had remembered them, and they loved him for it.

Even for a born-and-bred Democrat like myself, Reagan's shadow was inescapable, going all the way back to the first time I volunteered for a political campaign. In 1984, when Reagan was running for reelection, I painted signs at Walter Mondale's Sacramento headquarters. I was eighteen and very excited that I would soon be voting for the first time—and giddy at the prospect of a woman vice president, Geraldine Ferraro. Wearing a dark suit and tie, I'd played the role of Mondale in a debate at my all-girl Catholic high school. When I heard Ferraro speak in person just a few years later, she was so clear and serious, she gave me a new perspective on how a powerful woman could express herself.

What I didn't know back then—what few people knew—was that many of Ronald Reagan's inspiring words were actually written by a woman, Peggy Noonan. Though Peggy was on the other side of the political spectrum from me, I was awed when she was revealed to have been the genius behind some of Reagan's greatest speeches. So I was genuinely delighted that she was part of the Reagan delegation in Budapest. Markos and I threw a luncheon at the residence for the group, and I selfishly seated my husband on Peggy's right and myself on her left. We had her all to ourselves and peppered her with questions about her time in the White House, as well as what she saw for the future of the Republican Party.

I'd had to scramble to find entertainment for the luncheon. Big U.S. embassies have the budgets to bring in big names, but Budapest had a more modest allocation. So for special events, Markos and I funded the entertainment ourselves. Fortunately for us, we didn't need to bring entertainers all the way from the United States. Hungary is a country with a rich musical legacy, and talented musicians were everywhere. Many were passionately dedicated to the musical traditions of the West, which were denied to them until 1989. For the luncheon, I found a group of Hungarian men who dressed up as a barbershop quartet and belted out tunes from the South. The Reagan delegation loved them.

When I rose to speak to the group, I confessed that I cast the first vote of my life against Ronald Reagan in 1984. But I recalled that on one of my first dates with Markos, we'd talked about Reagan's legacy. "How much credit do you think Reagan deserves for winning the Cold War?" I'd asked him, knowing that his years covering the collapse of the Soviet Union qualified him to answer the question—and that as a journalist he would do it in an unbiased way.

"A lot," Markos had replied. "Ronald Reagan and Pope John Paul II kicked in a door that everyone thought wouldn't budge but was actually rotten through and through."

That night, Hungarian officials held a dinner for the Reagan contingent in Parliament's Hunters' Hall. On the way in, we paused by the Crown of St. Stephen. Possibly dating as far back as the year 1000 and to Hungary's first king, the crown, topped by a tilted cross, is the country's single most important symbol, and its image is everywhere, from the currency to landmark buildings. After World War II, the crown was given to the United States for safekeeping away from the Soviet Union, and it stayed at Fort Knox, in Kentucky, until Jimmy Carter returned it to Hungary in the late 1970s. In 2000, the crown was set in a glass box in the middle of a circular room beneath the great dome of the Parliament building.

Though I was in a nonpartisan mood that night, I had a reminder of my very partisan life in San Francisco. A few days before, I'd called another of the role models of my life, my neighbor, friend, and fellow Democratic Party activist Susie Tompkins Buell. Susie was such a close friend of Hillary's that once we'd publicly confirmed that the secretary of state was coming to Budapest, I called and invited her to visit. But I didn't bargain for Susie's early arrival, right in the middle of the Reagan celebrations. She was seated with Peggy Noonan at dinner in the Parliament building. I tasked Markos with keeping an eye on her to make sure the conversation stayed civil. Susie is very self-composed but very passionate about the issues that matter to her. If someone started delivering a Fox News–style argument on climate change or women's issues, Susie would let them have it. Fortunately, she was able to steer the conversation away from politics and enjoyed the evening. But Reagan's commemorative events were definitely not her scene. The next day, I called my reliable and wonderful friend Eleni Korani to step in and spend some time with Susie. They headed to Vienna to antique hunt and wait it out until Hillary's arrival.

On Wednesday of Golden Week, June 29, Condoleezza Rice arrived for the unveiling of the Reagan statue in Freedom Square. You always can tell how hard people have worked by how effortless a big endeavor appears to be, and I was pleased to see everything running smoothly thanks to our tireless embassy team.

When Deputy Prime Minister Zsolt Semjén had told me, just a few months before, that a statue of Reagan would be selected, cast, and installed in time for the centennial of the late president's birthday, I was very skeptical. But when Hungarians put their minds to something, they can do amazing things. They forged ahead with the plan and asked me to choose between two designs for the statue. I told them that it was their statue and they should pick the design they wanted, but I noted that I preferred the image of a stately Reagan taking a big stride forward with a look of happy determination on his face.

Now dignitaries and onlookers alike gathered in Freedom Square to witness the unveiling. After I'd introduced Secretary Rice and she had finished her remarks, the officials lifted the sheet from the statue and I could see the image I had liked so much, cast in bronze, larger than life.

Viktor Orbán idolized Reagan, and he spoke eloquently about his hero both during the unveiling and afterward, in his office, where he had invited Secretary Rice and the rest of the Reagan delegation. Before the meeting, I had briefed the group about some of our ongoing concerns over the constitutional reform process, and they were very interested in what was going on. These people were the ultimate Cold Warriors. They knew Hungary's culture and history, and they knew that in even the best-case scenario, democracy could not be deeply rooted after barely twenty years. Seated in Orbán's office, they listened carefully as the prime minister laid out his vision to them, describing how the Socialists had destroyed the economy and how he would put Hungary back on track. "They may say we are wrong," he said, "but they can never say that we aren't strong." Orbán reminded the group that he and his colleagues were the freedom fighters of 1989, and continued to fight for freedom. By now, I was very familiar with his talking points.

Toward the end of the meeting, Ed Meese spoke up. "You know, Mr. Prime Minister, Ronald Reagan always left something on the table for his political opposition, just so they would feel they had won something too and be willing to work together for the country."

Orbán's eyes narrowed, and his face took on the stubborn cast I knew all too well. "I couldn't possibly do that," he retorted, lifting his hands off the table.

What had started out as a warm and friendly meeting suddenly went cold. "If I make concessions to the Socialists, I have to make concessions to Jobbik too," Orbán asserted, raising the disturbing specter of Hungary's extremist right-wing party. This wasn't an argument that we ever gave much credence to, but it was one the prime minister and his team regularly used to try to get U.S. officials to back down.

As we made our way out of the room, Orbán pulled Condoleezza Rice into his office, alone. That was not on the agenda—and certainly was a bit of a snub to me. They emerged about ten minutes later, and Condi and I walked together to my car. As we stepped into the back of the Cadillac, I asked her what Orbán had wanted.

"Nothing really," she said. "Just to know if I thought the Republicans would win the next election." As the car rolled away from the Parliament building, she asked me very specific questions about Orbán's policies and the actions of his two-thirds majority.

"So," she asked, "you are saying he's a bully but not a brute?" In her question, I heard her opinion: she was clearly concerned about what Orbán's leadership would mean for Hungary, but the United States had enough brutes to deal with. We didn't have a lot of time for bullies.

That night, the Hungarians hosted a dinner for the Reagan delegation at the Museum of Fine Arts. It was a beautiful event, but it dragged on for a long time. I thought that Condi must be exhausted and would leave after the first course, but she stayed, through multiple toasts and courses, a slow parade of entertainment, and introductions to a long line of people who wanted to meet her. After all of that, she was still happy to sit and talk with me and foreign minister János Martonyi. For the better part of two hours, the three of us discussed everything from Afghanistan to Condi's childhood in Alabama. Given the big difference in our political views, I didn't expect to be so sincerely impressed with her. She struck me as a good person, intellectually gifted, gracious, and willing to engage with people filled with questions about her experiences and the policies she advocated as secretary of state. It made me wonder what her political prospects might have been if she had aligned herself with a different group of politicians.

When the marathon event at the Museum of Fine Arts finally ended, after nearly three hours, I jumped back into the Cadillac and headed to the airport to welcome Hillary Clinton to Hungary.

Tomicah Tillemann had been waiting in the car for me, and as we made our way out of the city, we discussed the final version of the speech Hillary would deliver the next morning. For months, our embassy team had communicated our concerns about Hungary's political reforms to D.C., and these were well represented in her speech. But now that the moment was upon us, I was uneasy as I imagined the upcoming scene: Hillary would arrive early at the Hungarian Parliament; shake hands with the prime minister, whom she had never met before; step up to the podium; and, looking down from the grand platform, give him a lecture on the Hungarian political reform process. And she would do all this before she met with him privately. That seemed wrong to me.

I shared my misgivings with Tomicah. "We keep saying that we are raising our concerns as a friend, but what kind of friend blasts you publicly for the first time from your own podium, without even the courtesy of a private discussion first? The secretary has never even met Viktor Orbán." Why, I asked, couldn't her speech stay focused on Tom Lantos and his commitment to democracy and human rights? That alone was a strong statement that would certainly be heard as a message to the Hungarian lawmakers. After the ceremony, Hillary would have a private meeting with Orbán, and he would have a chance to give her his point of view. "Then they'll do a joint press conference. Tomicah, *that's* when she should publicly talk about our concerns."

Tomicah didn't disagree, but he said that at that point, the die was cast. The speech had been approved up and down the chain of command at the State Department, and it was done.

"Then I may have to resign," I said. The words popped out of my mouth so quickly that they startled even me.

Tomicah gasped. "What? You can't do that."

Back in Washington, at charm school, we were told that although the ambassador was in charge, when it came to the secretary of state, we had to carefully choose when to lie down on the tracks. The implications of this suddenly hit me, and I sensed the faint rumbles of an oncoming train.

"It's not the right way to do this," I explained. "She should give Orbán the courtesy of meeting him before she relays concerns publicly. The Hungarians are waiting for her with open arms—they don't expect to be slapped in the face."

I watched my longtime hero Hillary Clinton emerge from her gleaming U.S. Air Force jet, casually wrapped in a sweater against the cool Budapest evening. When she saw me standing at the foot of the stairs, her face lit up in a bright smile and she opened her arms to hug me. "Hello, Eleni! Hello, Madam Ambassador!"

I smiled too and gave her a big hug. But I knew that I had to say something and that this was the moment to say it.

"Hillary, I'm so happy you are here, but I'm worried about what you are about to do."

She took in a breath and patted me on the back. It felt like I'd just thrown a bucket of cold water on our happy reunion. "Eleni, we have very experienced people who work on these issues all the time." She called over Elizabeth Sherwood Randall, director of European affairs for the U.S. National Security Council. "Liz, Eleni has some concerns about tomorrow. Can you talk to her and see if we can address them?"

It didn't feel good at all to raise issues at the level of the secretary when she had a long list of problems around the world to contend with. But I'd done it. And now, if I was going to make my case, this was the moment to do it. As the secretary's motorcade pulled away, Liz and I hopped into my car, and I started to explain.

"The Hungarians aren't prepared for this speech," I said. "They think Hillary Clinton is coming to Budapest because she loves them— because America loves them. They think it's going to be a celebration of Tom Lantos."

"How can you say that they don't know this is coming?" Liz asked. "What about Eric Holder? Didn't he raise concerns when he met with Orbán?"

"He decided not to do it. He had a good meeting with the deputy prime minister and felt the issues had been addressed there. Look, the Hungarians know that we are concerned. I have told them that we think they are going about their reform process in a way that could damage their system of checks and balances and their democratic institutions. But they don't know they are about to get a public blasting from the U.S. secretary of state from the podium inside their own Parliament."

Liz listened carefully, then started firing away with questions. "So you're saying that Secretary Clinton should raise our concerns about the constitution and the media law and all that with the prime minister privately *and then*, if she still thinks its necessary, address the issue publicly at the press conference?"

"Yes. I firmly believe that she should say something about what's been going on here. But first she gives Orbán a chance to explain. If he can't satisfy her concerns, and I doubt he can, she speaks out. The same message gets delivered, but we've been fair."

By the time I pulled up to the residence, it was nearly one in the morning, and my family was fast asleep. I had left Liz and the others at the hotel, realizing that people at this level of the State Department, including the secretary, didn't sleep much. Just as I walked into our house, Liz called me.

"We're changing the speech, Eleni. Secretary Clinton will address any issues concerning Hungary's reform process—any concerns that she still has once she's met with the prime minister—during the press conference after the meeting, just as you recommended. I wanted to let you know tonight, so you can try to get some sleep. You've got a big day tomorrow."

The tributes to Tom Lantos, delivered amid the imperial splendor of a room that had once served as Parliament's upper house, were worthy of the great man. A Budapest native and a Jew, Lantos was twice sent to labor camps during the Nazi era and twice escaped. He survived the Holocaust thanks to the efforts of diplomat and humanitarian Raoul Wallenberg, who helped not only Lantos but thousands of other very lucky Hungarians. After the war, Lantos emigrated to the United States and married Annette Tillemann, another Hungarian Holocaust survivor, whom Tom had met in Budapest when the war was still raging. His status as the only Holocaust survivor ever elected to Congress made him one of the world's most important voices speaking on behalf of human rights. He represented the San Francisco Bay Area for nearly thirty years. Tom Lantos died in 2008 at age eighty. His tombstone is inscribed with his most famous quote, the mantra of his life and something he knew from personal experience: "The veneer of civilization is paper thin. We are its guardians, and we can never rest."

The Hungarian government had agreed to fund the Lantos Institute, even though it was well known that Orbán and the late congressman had not gotten along particularly well. "We agreed on almost nothing when it came to the political future of Hungary," Orbán noted in his remarks that morning for the institute's inauguration. But within Hungary, across party lines, there was a great deal of respect for Tom

Lantos's contributions to Hungarian independence, and Orbán had supported the founding of the institute. Also, Orbán really loved Annette Lantos, the congressman's widow. As the presentations unfolded, he cuddled Annette with one arm as they swayed back and forth singing a traditional Hungarian tune together.

Hillary spoke beautifully about Tom Lantos and his unrelenting commitment to the principles of democracy. Her words, echoing through the old chamber, were very pointed and, to my mind, appropriate. Her staff must have been up all night making revisions. After the ceremony, she and I, and an entourage of people, headed to the prime minister's office.

As always, our respective staffs flanked both sides of the long table. Viktor Orbán looked tense. He knew the United States was raising concerns about his constitutional reform process with escalating intensity, so he must have braced himself to hear about it that morning. But Hillary immediately put him at ease with comments about our cooperation and questions about some of the challenges our countries faced as NATO allies. When she asked about the constitution, the two of them engaged in a long discussion about what was happening in Hungary. I could see that the secretary was formulating her point of view and that the prime minister knew that to Hillary Clinton, a woman who had seen it all, his arguments for the closed process sounded very, very thin.

As we walked from the prime minister's office to the room where reporters and photographers were waiting for the press conference to begin, Orbán looked worried. Hillary and Orbán made some general opening comments, but one of the first questions went right to the thorny issue of Hungary's reform process: had the prime minister and secretary of state discussed this?

"We talked very openly about preserving the democratic institutions of Hungary," Hillary began, "and making sure that they continue to grow and strengthen, including providing essential checks and balances. As friends of Hungary, we expressed our concerns and particularly call for a real commitment to the independence of the judiciary, a free press, and governmental transparency."

Orbán's face tightened into a frown, but inwardly I sighed in relief. Hillary's response was just right—fair, reinforcing what we'd been saying privately for months, that our concerns about the reforms were real and that they were the concerns of a friend.

Hillary and I drove away from the Parliament building together, with her sitting in my customary place and me on the other side of the car. For the first time since I'd been in Budapest, not one but two American flags waved on the front of the vehicle. I turned to her. "Hillary, I am so sorry that you had to have drama in Budapest. You have so many other places in the world to worry about, it should have been easy here."

She smiled. "I'm very glad you spoke up last night, Eleni. You were absolutely right about how to handle this." I exhaled, and suddenly realized how nervous I'd been.

The secretary went on to ask my views about Russia and China, and how I saw these countries through the prism of working with the Hungarians. I told her about the recent visit of Chinese president Hu Jintao to Budapest and how he had reportedly promised Prime Minister Orbán a large investment sum. "They'll do it too," she responded.

Soon after, the secretary's plane took off. And within the hour, the international news outlets were buzzing with the headline "Hillary Clinton Expresses Concerns over Hungarian Democracy." I knew I had done my job.

There was no doubt that the secretary of state's public expression of concerns during her visit to Hungary had left a chill in the air, but Hungarian officials with whom the embassy was working so cooperatively knew that we'd been fair. I knew instinctively that doors would remain open to us, and we would be able to continue our wide-ranging work with Hungary. We would also, I believed, still be able to engage the Hungarians—as friends and allies—in raising questions and concerns about the fast-paced reform process that was redefining every institution of democracy in the country. To "raise concerns . . . as a friend" was turning out to be a very delicate thing to do. I felt like the tightrope walker my boys loved to watch at the Budapest circus. For the moment, anyway, I was still up on the wire.

As if Golden Week hadn't already been busy enough, Friday was the embassy's massive Fourth of July party. It was my second one, and again the celebration was packed with officials and friends. Hungarian president Pál Schmitt, elegant and charming, had agreed to be our guest of honor.

Later that night, after all the guests had departed, the staff gathered with just our families, in our casual clothes, for our own embassy party. People were happy, if exhausted. Not only had we survived Golden Week, but it had been a big success. Two congressional delegations, the Reagan delegation, and the secretary of state's delegation all had left Budapest satisfied. A few months later, I would distribute a record number of State Department awards for everyone's incredibly hard work. But for now, I was just grateful.

As the band struck up a tune, one of my senior officers, the head of our USAID office, David Leong, who was an old hand in the diplomatic corps, pulled me aside to congratulate me. He had gone out of his way to ensure that he and his staff were available to help with Golden Week, even though it was really not their job. USAID no longer had programs in Hungary. The Budapest offices primarily supported work being done in the Balkans and farther afield. I thanked him for the compliment but insisted that it had been a herculean effort by everyone.

"It's true, people worked very hard to pull it all off," David said. "But all week I never heard anyone complain. That's rare, ma'am, and that's the true reflection of your leadership."

His words brought a sudden sting of tears to my eyes. Quickly, I blinked them away, then spotted Markos nearby, and we joined in the dancing.

# 14

# Seven Hundred New Laws

Once Hillary departed Budapest, the spotlight largely left with her, and we at the embassy were left to deal with the fallout of her highly publicized visit. The next six months would be by far the most dramatic of Viktor Orbán's two-thirds revolution. And our engagement would make headlines again.

In September 2011, the Hungarian Parliament came back into session after its summer recess. Because the new constitution would take effect in January, legislators would use the next four months to rush through new versions of nearly every law of importance governing the country. Ultimately, along with the new constitution, more than seven hundred new laws would be written, amended, and adopted before Orbán's revolution was over, and before I concluded my tour of duty. The most important of them, the cardinal laws, would need a two-thirds vote of Parliament to ever be changed again.

Parliament worked at a frenzied pace. But just like the drafting of the constitution and the media law, most of this work was done behind closed doors, far from the critical eyes of the powerless opposition parties or members of civil society. As all this was going on, the embassy had its hands full with other important elements of our bilateral relationship. In the late summer of 2011, Hungary had agreed to serve as the protecting power of the United States in Libya. Our embassy in Tripoli had been evacuated, and there were few nations that still had a diplomatic presence in the country. In these rare occurrences, the United States asks one of the remaining countries—preferably a close friend or ally—to assume some of our responsibilities, look after any U.S. citizens left in the country, and if necessary act on our behalf. Serving as our protective power in Libya had been a big ask on our part, and that fall the Ministry of Foreign Affairs was hard at work managing a time-consuming and—for its remaining diplomats on the ground—dangerous responsibility.

As we worked with the Ministry of Foreign Affairs on issues dealing with Libya, we continued to closely follow the Hungarian reform process. Because my staff and I had earned the professional trust of many in the Fidesz leadership, we were among the few—maybe even the only—outsiders allowed behind the closed doors of the rapid-fire lawmaking process.

In keeping with our mission to understand events in our host country, Paul O'Friel led a team that worked relentlessly to understand the new laws as they were coming down and evaluate what their impacts would be. It was very difficult, complicated work, but we were fortunate to have staff members capable of doing it, including Steve Weston, Jay Truesdale, Amy Conroy, and Bill McCausland. Our Hungarian team, including Linda Mézes and Máté Hegedűs, were highly capable and had great expert contacts in Budapest who worked with them to explain the significance of the more complicated elements of the proposed new laws.

Just as we kept the lines of communication open with Hungarian lawmakers and government officials, it was our job to stay in touch with the civil society organizations (NGOs, nonprofit organizations, trade groups, community groups, and the like) whose members would be seriously affected by the new laws. These groups ranged from the Hungarian Civil Liberties Union to judges' associations to religious groups. Most of them were operating on scraps of information about what was coming down. The more we talked to members of civil society, the more clear it became that we usually knew more about Hungary's changing laws than they did. This was true not just for the civil society experts, but also for government officials and many legislators. While there were experts who were focused on one or two specific laws, the embassy was fast developing a broad and deep understanding of the bigger picture of overall legislative changes unfolding in the country. It was a highly unusual situation. We advocated that Fidesz lawmakers talk to their constituents themselves before the laws were passed, but most responded that, given the looming January deadline, there was no time.

Because civil society representatives had almost no way to deliver their concerns to their own government, the embassy began to be pulled more deeply into the process. We continued to articulate the U.S. position that "Hungarian laws are up to Hungarians to decide." But we found ourselves in the unique situation of serving as something of a go-between. I have to stress that this was really not our role to play. But we understood that by facilitating communications, we might be able to help.

To keep track of the cascade of new legislation, I asked Jeff Hay, an experienced Foreign Service officer and a star of our political team, to create a matrix of the most significant of the hundreds of laws under consideration, and the proposed changes. With expert help from our Hungarian colleagues, and under the nimble yet focused leadership of Paul O'Friel and Tim Betts, he nailed them all down for us. Jeff became central in keeping track of the reforms and identifying their most troubling elements.

There were many controversial aspects to the new laws that Hungarian citizens could have taken issue with and would probably have liked to haggle over. But the United States was solely focused on the proposed laws that we believed could undermine Hungary's system of checks and balances or weaken the independence of its democratic institutions. We worked carefully to limit ourselves to commenting on these very specific areas. We were engaging in Hungary's internal domestic policies, wading into very sensitive territory, and many were already attacking us for putting our nose where it didn't belong.

In the end, we identified the media law and the proposed laws governing elections and the judiciary as the most troubling. We also had serious misgivings about the new law governing religious groups. The Hungarian government had some good arguments for reforming the "church" law, but it politicized the process of determining which religious organizations would be officially recognized and thus entitled to greater tax benefits and state support. Notably, one large Methodist Church, whose leader had been demonstrating against the government, was already likely to lose its status.

In early November 2011, I attended a lunch at the residence of the German ambassador to Hungary, Dorothee Janetzke-Wenzel, in honor of former president László Sólyom. Germany was probably the second most influential country in Hungary after the United States. Germany had the highest foreign direct investment in Hungary, and the two nations had close historical ties. But Germany and other European Union countries had been silent about the new Hungarian constitution. It rankled us, quite frankly. We believed that Germany and the other EU countries should be engaging, and we tried to push this point to Washington, asking that U.S. officials reach out and talk to their counterparts in the embassies there. But D.C.'s efforts had been fruitless. A few years before, after the extreme right had won a controlling place in the Austrian Parliament, the EU had instituted sanctions against Austria, creating enormous discord and tension among the representatives of member states. So our European allies were not keen on getting involved in Hungarian domestic affairs. This was exacerbated by the fact that the EU was in the midst of a much bigger crisis, grappling with the possibility that Portugal, Italy, Ireland, Greece, and Spain would default on their bonds and drop out of the Eurozone, tearing the EU apart.

The conversation at the German ambassador's luncheon centered not on Europe's economic woes or Hungary's constitutional struggles, but rather on energy security, another hot topic, as energy-rich Azerbaijan would soon decide how its gas would be transported into Europe. After lunch was over, I pulled Sólyom aside and asked him about the new Hungarian constitution. What concerned him the most about the new cardinal laws?

"The language of the preamble is not to my taste. It's not how I would have written it," the former president noted dryly. "But the preamble doesn't mean very much to the rule of law. What concerns me most is what they will do with the judiciary. Everything flows back to the courts—media freedom, religious freedom, free and fair elections. We have had a strong court system over the past twenty years. If the courts remain independent and unbiased, they will be able to ensure that *all* of the new laws conform to general constitutional principles. If the courts can remain independent, our democracy will remain fundamentally sound."

Sólyom had been the first president of the highly respected Hungarian Constitutional Court, created just after the collapse of communism, so I took his response very seriously. It reinforced what Jeff Hay, Linda, and Máté had already identified as one of the most important of the cardinal laws. When I got back to my office, I pulled Tim Betts and Paul O'Friel in. "We need to increase our focus on laws dealing with the judiciary," I told them. By this time, Tim, Paul, and I had formed a very tight-knit team. The three of us would discuss and debate every nuance of how the United States should engage during what was fast becoming a very sensitive situation. I was the one who was most visible—in meetings with high-level government officials, both in Budapest and at home, as well as in the media. But the three of us spent hours together every week planning our next steps. Sometimes I was the one who pointed the way. But just as often, it was Tim and Paul who had done the hard work of managing the research, processing the data, and then devising a strategy for me to deliver.

We already knew that the proposed judiciary reforms would make many sweeping changes. Most significantly, they would create a new administrative body, with management power over the courts, called the National Office for the Judiciary. Its president would have authority over budgetary and financial management of the courts, staffing, appointments, and distribution of caseloads, as well as *the ability to unilaterally decide to transfer cases to courts outside where the alleged crimes had occurred*. This last one was a real no-no in most judicial systems and something that gave me great concern.

A second body, the National Judicial Council, would be made up of judges elected by their peers and would serve as a consultative body to the Judiciary Office, but with no real power to affect decisions. Not only would the Judiciary Office have an unprecedented amount of clout, it would be led by a single individual, appointed by Parliament for up to two consecutive nine-year terms.

After Sólyom's comments, we started working overtime to find out how interest groups were reacting to the proposed reforms. First, I sat down with the head of the Budapest Bar Association, who told me that he was very upset to have been left out of the process and given no opportunity to comment. Two days later, however, I met with leaders of the Association of Hungarian Judges and heard something quite different. They told me that they had been enlisted early on to help with the reform process. They had held meetings with members of the judges' association in towns around the countryside, and in large part they provided the framework for the reforms, with lots of input from their members. This was the most evidence I had seen of outside, expert, nonpartisan professionals' involvement in the reform process, and it encouraged me.

What the judges went on to say, however, was that although most of their recommendations for the new system had been taken, one was not: their proposal had included giving the Judicial Council veto power over many of the Judiciary Office's decisions. In other words, it would be the judges, elected by their peers, who would have had control over the politically appointed administrator, not the other way around. By not taking their most important recommendation, the judges told me, legislators had undermined all of their efforts to reform the system for the better. Instead of being proud of their work, they were very discouraged by the final draft of the bill.

I made an appointment to see deputy prime minister Tibor Navracsics, who also served as minister of public administration and justice, to talk about the judiciary reforms. When I told him about the judges' association representatives' concerns, he was incensed. "But they were the ones who were most involved in writing the reforms! If they didn't like something, they should have told me!" After his frustration subsided, he sighed, "Let me see what I can do." Navracsics was in the center of the storm of the reform process, and I could see the pressure was taking a toll on him.

By this point it was November 2011, only one month before the constitution would take effect. Cardinal laws were flying through Parliament every few days, with nothing stopping them or even slowing them down. In the midst of the chaos, I made my way through the corridors of power to discuss with lawmakers and government officials how the new laws could affect checks and balances and Hungary's independent democratic institutions. I urged them to address our concerns, particularly those related to judicial reform.

Tim, Paul, and I went from office to office, meeting with the Fidesz caucus leader in Parliament, János Lázár; Speaker of the National Assembly László Kövér; and Foreign Minister Martonyi. Wherever we went, we were assured that the Hungarian government recognized the United States' expertise in democratic principles, would take our concerns into consideration, and would address them if officials agreed they were valid. I felt cautiously optimistic.

Secretary Clinton might have left Hungary, but the State Department was still keenly interested in monitoring what was happening there. A few weeks after Hillary's visit, Phil Gordon, the assistant secretary of state for European and Eurasian affairs, called me. Phil was a foreign policy guru, so well known for his expertise that his reputation preceded him. One of Orbán's senior advisers had studied with him in London and told me that when Phil was a graduate student, the students' nickname for him was "God."

He let me know right away why he was calling.

"We didn't consult you enough leading up to the secretary's visit, Eleni. That won't happen again," he said.

Phil's words surprised me, but they confirmed that the State Department would rely heavily on our embassy in Budapest to understand the situation on the ground. In early December 2011, I was called back to Washington and found officers at the State Department and the White House, as well as members of Congress, outraged over the situation in Hungary, from the media and church laws to the reform of the courts to new laws concerning the country's universities and the central bank.

I answered their questions as best I could, trying to separate fact from fiction. I also tried to explain why we were focused on the cardinal laws related to the judiciary. "We say again and again that we are

Hungary's friend," I said. "Friends give friends the benefit of the doubt. We've relayed our concerns over judicial reform, and they have told me that they are listening. If they make changes in response to the comments that we have brought them from their own citizens, they will show that they are working in good faith too."

But as I was making the rounds at the State Department to explain why we should continue to work with members of the Hungarian government behind the scenes, news came from the embassy that the two-thirds majority had passed the cardinal laws related to the judiciary without addressing a single one of the concerns we brought to them.

It's over, I thought, shoulders slumping. My efforts to help the Hungarian government prove its commitment to democratic principles, to encourage lawmakers to listen to all their constituents, had failed. I was disappointed and angry that I'd been misled. But even more, I was worried about what would happen next and how much stress it would place on other important elements of our bilateral relationship. In fact, just as all of this was happening, the Hungarians were helping to rescue American citizens who had been trapped in Libya as Kaddafi's regime crumbled.

As I made my way back to Budapest, I thought about how I vowed at my Senate confirmation hearing to work tirelessly to strengthen the bilateral relationship between the United States and Hungary. And I thought that there might be time for one more effort on our part. Tim and Paul helped me pen an article for a Hungarian news magazine, which we titled "A Second Look." In it, I asked that Hungarian lawmakers reconsider some of the most controversial of the cardinal laws, including those related to the judiciary, religious organizations, and the media. I asked them to ask themselves, "Do the new laws ensure that checks and balances are protected?" Because the article would be in the public domain, it was carefully worded to be very general and to stay away from making explicit the specifics that I had been discussing with lawmakers for months behind closed doors.

To round out the final diplomatic push, Secretary Clinton sent a letter to Prime Minister Orbán asking that he reevaluate some of the troubling laws before the constitution took effect. In this case, since it was intended to be private communication, the secretary's letter included a detailed list of our specific concerns with the new laws. I was very proud to see the hard work of the embassy staff distilled into her letter. But I had been repeatedly discussing these issues with representatives of the government and members of Parliament face-to-face for months. Even though this letter came from the secretary herself, the new constitution would go into effect on January 1, 2012, which was just a few weeks away. There wasn't enough time left, and I had little hope that the secretary's letter would spur any last-minute changes.

I underestimated, however, what might happen if the secretary's letter became public. Many people had been given copies—we handed it to the Hungarian ambassador in Washington, the foreign minister in Budapest, and several others. Somewhere along the way, someone with access to the letter gave it to the press. However it happened, it caused a sensation. Headlines roared of the specific concerns that Hillary Clinton and the United States were expressing over Hungarian democracy.

Despite Orbán's efforts to downplay public outrage over the new constitution, the tipping point finally arrived. Hillary's leaked letter to Orbán spurred Europe to take notice, at last, of what was happening in Hungary. One by one, European leaders began to engage, followed by officials in the EU's headquarters in Brussels.

On January 3, two days after the new constitution became law, the Hungarian government held a massive celebration at the opera house. I was invited to attend, along with other members of the diplomatic corps. One State Department official suggested that I take a quick trip to Vienna so I could be conveniently out of the country. I disagreed—if I wasn't going to attend the celebration, I wasn't going to be coy about it. So I stayed home in my slippers and watched the coverage on television. This was without a doubt the lowest point of my ambassadorship. Reports that the American ambassador was snubbing the celebration of Hungary's new constitution circulated in the press. More important, what should have been a great day for Hungary had degenerated into a partisan battle. Thousands of protesters gathered outside the opera house demanding to be heard. The state-owned television stations covered the protests but downplayed them in a way that justified concerns that they were softening the news in favor of the government. Their reporters stood facing the crowds so that the cameras would pick up the empty streets behind them instead of the mobbed ones in front.

The long-simmering controversy over the new laws exploded into a full-blown crisis. Hungary's currency, the forint, took a nosedive. In a series of interviews with Hungarian media, I explained that the United States had engaged actively with Hungarian officials regarding their reform process, sharing our expertise on how the new laws would affect their democracy. We had raised concerns and been assured that they would be considered, but none of them had been. "U.S. Ambassador Disappointed," shouted the headlines.

With the value of the forint plummeting and the international community's concerns soaring, the government had no choice but to respond. At a luncheon at the home of the ambassador from Slovenia in the early winter of 2012, Foreign Minister Martonyi declared to a group of ambassadors that "the two-thirds revolution—though I have never favored that expression—is over, and now it is time for consolidation to begin." He went on to say that Hungary's leaders recognized that they had moved very quickly, but they'd had to move fast. Now that everything was done, they would go back and "make corrections."

Officials agreed to begin a process to work with the European Union to ensure that their reforms did not violate EU law. It was time for the diplomatic architecture of Europe, bodies created to help answer questions and resolve disputes, to be put to use. The Hungarian government agreed to consult with several important European and EU organizations—the Venice Commission, the Council of Europe, and the European Commission. It volunteered to hand over English translations of the constitution and several of the most controversial of the cardinal laws. If experts from these organizations found elements of the law that were inconsistent with EU standards, Hungarian government officials agreed to work with Parliament to modify them.

This was a significant turning point. We at Embassy Budapest knew that our role, unconventional and nuanced as it was, had been instrumental in getting the Hungarians to this point.

As the consolidation process began, spurring new glimmers of hope among the international community that the Hungarians would come around, something else happened. Hungary's active engagement with the EU changed the United States' role substantially. For many months, we had been nearly alone in pushing for Hungary to address concerns. The European Union had remained almost completely silent, even though it was far more appropriate for Hungary to work with EU and European institutions, given its membership in the group. As one European journalist tartly noted, "It takes Hillary Clinton writing a letter before we are willing to take notice of a problem within our own Union."

As far as we were concerned, EU engagement was better late than never. Admittedly, this was hardly a time of great optimism. Everyone had been bruised by the events of the past months. But a new process had begun that we hoped would result in a better constitution for the people of Hungary, our friend and ally.

To a land developer like myself, and to most people, the word "architecture" conjures up a very tangible image of buildings and construction. However, in foreign policy terms, it means something far less tangible but critically important for our security and economic prosperity. Though entities like the Venice Commission and the Council of Europe sound mysterious and vague, they are part of diplomatic architecture that allows countries to talk to one another and solve problems together and allows laws to be enforced on the international level.

The United States relies on diplomatic architecture to engage with the world, through countless treaties and membership in organizations including the United Nations, the International Court of Justice, the World Bank, and the World Health Organization. The treaties that formed the European Union created an important element of diplomatic architecture.

On my first day in Hungary, when I urged President Sólyom to work through the Organization for Security and Cooperation in Europe to resolve tensions with Slovakia, I had urged him to employ elements of the European diplomatic architecture. Two years later, it was only appropriate that the United States encourage the Hungarians to work within the context of the European institutions to review their new laws and their new constitution. We were very gratified to see the Hungarians enter into these discussions willingly. That isn't to say that we agreed with every outcome or that all of our concerns about the new laws were addressed. But we recognized the jurisdiction of the EU and threw our support behind the process. We vigorously followed what was happening, but now it was from the backseat.

Through the spring of 2012, negotiations seesawed between the EU and the Hungarians. That summer, the Hungarians adopted a major amendment to the constitution addressing many of the concerns that we had raised and that the Venice Commission and Council of Europe had expanded upon. At the embassy, we were very proud that our intervention had resulted in many tangible improvements. But we could also see that in spite of the modifications, Viktor Orbán was growing more and more powerful.

Throughout the next year, even after the first amendment, flare-ups would continue to break out and subside. At one point, it was the religion law. Then it was a proposed law, later abandoned, that would have instituted a new system of voter registration in which the old rolls would be thrown out and every eligible voter in the country would have had to sign up again from scratch. Debates over the independence of the central bank and the constitutional court were ongoing. Concerns about laws reforming the university system became central for a few weeks and ultimately were resolved or at least improved. Some of the resolution was satisfactory to critics. Much was seen as an improvement, but the overriding theme was always the same: the new laws were resulting in the concentration of power in the hands of fewer people and ultimately weakening checks and balances in Hungary's democracy.

Our engagement had been persistent and ultimately helped preserve some important elements of the fundamental democratic institutions for which the Hungarian people had fought so hard. But as consolidation progressed and the rate of lawmaking wound down, our role steadily diminished. Soon it was clear: the United States had done its part.

My staff insisted that I should feel proud of what we had accomplished. "They're making changes and working with the European organizations that are designed exactly for this purpose," they told me. "You should declare victory, ma'am."

   The European process would eventually run its course, and the laws would no doubt be better and technically in compliance with EU law. Once this happened, it would be up to the Hungarian people, and their institutions, to again be the sole stewards of their democracy. It was progress, of a sort. But I couldn't help but continue to worry about the direction it all was taking.

   One afternoon, my friend Karin Olofsotter, the Swedish ambassador to Hungary, and I stood watching our boys and their friends run around an outdoor laser tag park. As the boys and girls dodged through trees, shooting at one another, Karin and I reflected on the situation. She put it this way: "It seems to me that while the laws are getting better, the situation is getting worse."

# 15

# Family Life II . . . the Royal Treatment

Though I continued to be very busy at the embassy, my family was happily settled in Budapest. The house was in much better shape thanks to herculean efforts of the management team, which did everything from digging up and replacing old shower pans to rewiring the house all the way to the street. Several new staff members made all the difference too. Márton Benkő, our new house manager, was always smiling, always eager to go the extra mile for an official event, and always willing to build snow forts with the boys. He and our housekeeper, Albert, and our new chef, Tamás, livened up the residence so that even when we didn't have visiting family, we felt like we were home. With their help, we added American touches to our parties: margaritas in the summer, chocolate-chip cookies year-round. Márton rented bounce houses for the community parties in the summer and launched a gingerbread cookie decorating event during the Christmas holidays. My big fat Greek (American) embassy was in full swing.

The boys' weekends were still taken up by Chinese school, and they rarely missed a day. Their fluency was growing dramatically, but the seven-day-a-week classes restricted our family travel. So whenever Neo and Eon had school holidays, we took full advantage. We visited places that would be harder to get to once we'd returned to San Francisco, such as Egypt and Dubai, and places that were better seen in the months when tourism was slow, including Moscow and Istanbul. We also went to Israel, where my aunt Maria, a great inspiration to me, had been living for more than twenty years as an Orthodox nun. Instead of returning to the States on breaks, we met with friends who were traveling in Europe. One year, we spent the holidays in Paris with our dear friends the Pappas family from New York. Another time, we went to London with our friends the novelists Ayelet Waldman and Michael Chabon and their entertaining brood.

Of course, we traveled to Greece more than anywhere else. I flew in and out of Athens fifteen times during my posting. Sometimes we went for quick visits, such as when I proudly received an honorary doctorate of law from the American College of Greece. But most of the time, we went to our home there, on the small island of Spetses, just a couple of hours by boat from Athens. Markos and I had bought the vacation house in 2005 in the hopes of bringing the boys there every summer. During our years in Hungary, Spetses became our home away from home. On this little island, there were no street signs because there were no street names. No cars were allowed, either. But there were many wonderful people, and we spent afternoons lounging on the beach or diving off old fishing boats with friends from all over Greece and all over the world.

Though we loved spending time at our sunny retreat, those were very difficult years for the country we loved so much. In 2010, the possibility that Greece would leave the Eurozone was very high. And though the crisis was somewhat under control by the time we left Europe in 2013, it deeply changed Greece. People were angry, but they were also uncharacteristically sad, worrying about what the future would hold for their children.

Greece's entry into the European Union and the Eurozone had sparked years of prosperity, but those boom years turned out to have been based on a mirage—the growth was fueled by massive amounts of borrowing. The country's economic base, built on manufacturing and the production of goods and services, had scarcely grown over the previous two decades. Much of Greece's debt had been taken on by the government and siphoned off through elaborate corruption schemes. By 2010, there was no more easy money flowing into the system, but there was a half-trillion-dollar bill to pay, the equivalent of more than $28,000 for every man, woman, and child in the country. To grapple with the disaster, officials launched a brutal austerity program that outraged citizens and set off violent protests.

Our frequent visits to Greece gave us a front-row seat at the crisis. We spent a lot of time there talking to our friends old and new, everyone from high-ranking government officials to the guy who ran our favorite pizzeria. They told us how they and their fellow citizens were suffering. Schools didn't have supplies for the students. Hospitals were running out of medicine because they couldn't pay their massive overdue bills. We heard the fear in our friends' voices of what would happen if Greece defaulted: the complete collapse of the country's economy and the dissolution of orderly society into chaos.

After Hillary Clinton visited Greece in 2012, Foreign Minister Stavros Lambrinidis—the former ambassador whose visit to San Francisco had brought Markos and me together—called me in Budapest.

"Hello, Ambassador Kukla!" *Kukla* is the Greek word for "doll."

Normally, I wouldn't have been keen on a term like that, but Stavros had played an important role in my life, so I responded in kind. "Hello, Foreign Minister Cupid!"

Stavros delivered a very gratified report on Hillary's visit. "Eleni *mou*, she was wonderful. She told us how strongly the United States is with us and how she and President Obama are doing whatever they can to urge the Europeans to work with us to resolve the crisis. You know, Eleni, I lived so many years in the United States, there was a time when I almost felt like I was American. Now I am 100 percent European. It is so important that we keep our union together, and I am so proud that America, your country, is standing by us when we need you."

It was true. The United States was pushing Germany, France, and the rest of the European Union to resolve the crisis and not allow the problems in the Greek economy—which amounted to a small sliver of the EU's gross domestic product—to break the union apart.

During this troubled time, I was fortunate to forge a friendship with our ambassador to Greece, Daniel Smith. Dan invited Markos, me, and the kids to stay at the U.S. ambassador's residence in Athens. He and his wife, Diane, had just moved in a few weeks before; there were boxes everywhere, and the walls where I had seen my first original Andy Warhol pieces so long ago were bare.

As we sat down to tea, Dan told us that he was bothered by the stereotyping of Greeks as lazy—an all-too-common opinion during the crisis. "They work very hard," he noted. "There are clear statistics that show the average Greek works more hours than the average German. There's some terrible stereotyping going on," he said, shaking his head.

A few months later, after they had settled in, Dan and Diane offered to host a dinner in Markos's and my honor at their home. We were humbled and delighted by the gesture and we knew exactly whom we wanted to invite.

Among our very best friends in Greece are the Constantakopoulos family. The clan's patriarch and matriarch were the best friends of my father and stepmother. Years before, my dad had helped one of their three sons, Achilles, come to San Francisco to intern at the Fairmont Hotel. I was living in San Francisco at the time, and the two of us became fast friends. Achilles would be our boys' godfather, and to Markos's delight he later married Costantza, who like him was a Cretan. Now in their early forties, Achilles and his brothers were successful businessmen in Greece, and their wives were enormously talented people in their own right, all of them dedicated to helping find solutions for Greece as it confronted a difficult future.

Along with the three brothers and their spouses, Stavros Lambrinidis came to Dan Smith's dinner for us. So did our close friends Dora Bakoyannis and her brother Kyriakos Mitsotakis, who were the daughter and son of the former prime minister after whom Markos and I had named our Stanford chair. Dora was the only woman to serve as mayor of Athens in its 2,500-year history. She had also served as Greece's foreign minister. Dora and Kyriakos, who both sat in the Greek Parliament, were in the opposition party, while Stavros's party led the government.

The guests gathered around the table had differing political viewpoints and strong opinions. At one point, the conversation got so heated that everyone switched to speaking Greek. Dan could pick up most of it, but Diane's Greek was more limited. I jumped in and urged everyone to please return to speaking English. We were, after all, at the U.S. ambassador's house.

In spite of the rigorous debate, or maybe because of it, the dinner left me feeling optimistic. Everyone at the table wanted what was best for Greece, and though they didn't all agree on what should be done, they were very civil and respectful of one another's opinions. I noticed that the kinds of wrenching political divides I saw in Hungary were not as obvious in Greece. Political affiliation, while important, didn't define you as much there. Even within the Constantakopoulos clan, family members supported different parties and had diverse points of view.

When the conversation had settled down and we were enjoying our coffee, I offered the group my Greek American take on the situation facing my ethnic homeland. "Greece and the United States are fortunate in that the strength of our relationship is based on our historic ties," I noted. "These aren't limited to the classical democratic values of ancient Greece that were carried forward with the foundation of America. Greece and the United States fought together in World War I and World War II, and together we helped repel the forces of communism." Around the table, people nodded in agreement. "Greece has been on the right side of history again and again," I pointed out. "I believe that it will come through this crisis, through the strength of its people and the support of its friends."

Glasses were raised, more toasts were made, and we celebrated the tight bonds of friendship between the United States and Greece. For Markos and me, that night gave us an overwhelming sense of having come full circle. Our Greek grandparents could not have imagined that their grandchildren would rise up as leaders in America, walking the halls of power with capability and confidence. After I was sworn in, my father told me, "Never forget that Markos is the son of a truck driver and you are the daughter of a farmworker."

We never do, and it has made us cherish our opportunities all the more.

During our time in Hungary, some of our favorite experiences happened while visiting friends in other American embassies. On that day when I was so crushed at losing Singapore, Nancy Pelosi pointed out that most people preferred postings in Europe to anywhere else in the world. I'd assumed that was because of the prestige, but after living in Budapest I understood that part of the attraction was Europe's community of embassies. With so many capitals so close to one another, we could, by traveling just a few hours in any direction, drop in on our neighbors. Ambassador William Eacho in Austria, for instance, regularly invited his fellow ambassadors to stay with him and his wife, Donna, during Vienna's ball season; these visits usually included lessons in how to dance the quadrille. We visited Ambassador Norm Eisen in Prague when he held his annual conference on good governance and transparency. We took the kids up to Sweden to visit Ambassador Matthew Barzun and his family, and the Barzun clan visited us in Spetses. We also traded visits with Theodore Sedgwick, who was just up the Danube, in Bratislava, Slovakia.

We'd bonded with Tod Sedgwick over his love for classical Greek culture, but I was a little worried when the Sedgwicks came to Budapest. One of Tod's cousins had been Edie Sedgwick, Andy Warhol's beautiful young muse, who died at twenty-eight after years of drug abuse and, some said, emotional manipulation by Warhol. By this point, the Warhol lithographs had arrived from the United States, and our walls were filled with the Pop artist's bright images. But if Tod noticed, he didn't say anything. (In another irony, Andy Warhol's parents had emigrated from Slovakia, Tod's host country. So it's likely he was used to seeing Warhols everywhere.)

Living in Europe had a "small world" aspect to it as well. One time, Markos went golfing with one of the dads at the American School, who was so impressed that Markos could speak Greek that right on the links he called a Greek friend of his who lived in Switzerland and put Markos on the phone. A year later, Markos and I were at a dinner in Greece, and Markos realized that the man sitting next to him was the same person he'd spoken to by phone on the golf course.

These overlapping circles of society were especially evident when it came to the royal families of Europe—in particular, the deposed royal families of Europe. I got my first taste of this when U.S. ambassador to Serbia Mary Warlick invited Markos and me to visit her in Belgrade.

I'd met Mary preparing for our confirmation hearing, which was also the hearing for her husband, Jim Warlick, nominated to be our ambassador to Bulgaria. It was the first time a husband and wife "tandem team" would serve as ambassadors at the same time.

Mary's invitation to see her in Belgrade coincided with another invitation we received, from Princess Katherine of Serbia, to attend the twenty-fifth anniversary of her wedding to Crown Prince Alexander.

Katherine and Alexander's story was quite complicated.

During the creation of Yugoslavia, Marshal Josip Broz Tito deposed the royal family of Serbia. Prince Alexander was born in a suite at Claridge's hotel in London. The British Parliament passed a special law declaring the hotel room a sovereign territory of Serbia so that Alexander's claim to the throne would not be weakened. Many years later, after the dissolution of the Soviet empire and Yugoslavia's disintegration into separate states, Alexander was invited by none other than Slobodan Milošević to return to Serbia and regain his title of crown prince. Milošević, who was looking for ways to build Serbian nationalism, gave Alexander and Katherine the former royal palace but stopped short of declaring them king and queen.

Princess Katherine, as it happened, was born and raised in Greece. Our paths had crossed in California when she was raising funds to rebuild Serbia's hospitals after the devastation of the Balkan wars. She called me in Budapest not long after my arrival.

"Congratulations, Eleni darling! I only wish that you had been sent here to Belgrade. This new lady seems very nice, but someone like you could truly understand us." Katherine meant that another Orthodox Christian could understand. Religious differences, every bit as much as ethnic differences, were behind much of the strife in the Balkans. On my trip to Kosovo with Minister Hende, I'd seen the ancient Orthodox monasteries from the windows of a low-flying military helicopter. From the sky, they appeared to form links of a chain cutting across what had become a primarily Muslim nation.

I demurred on the question of whether I might be able to change posts, but I accepted Katherine's invitation to her anniversary celebration. Not only would the party be a special event, but Markos and I would be able to visit Mary.

In some ways, Belgrade reminded me of Sarajevo. Many of the buildings still showed damage from the conflict with NATO more than a
decade earlier. One massive structure in the middle of town looked as if
it had just been bombed: it was the former Ministry of Defense, partly
demolished by U.S. military planes during the war. Over a decade later,
the Serbs had neither torn down nor repaired the building, which provided a constant reminder of the siege of Belgrade by the Americans
and our allies—and remained an open wound for the people of Serbia.

Mary was a wonderful hostess, welcoming Markos and me to her
residence, a beautiful neoclassical house in a wooded neighborhood of
Belgrade. The house was meticulously maintained, giving me, not for
the first time, a pang of "residence envy." As it happened, Mary also
planned to attend the anniversary party for Alexander and Katherine.

The Serbian royal palace must have been exquisite at one time, but
it had fallen into crumbling disrepair. Katherine complained that the
government gave them no budget to adequately maintain it. Despite
the general dilapidation, the rooms where the anniversary celebration was held were magnificent—lush silk draperies, intricately carved
stone walls, and elaborate flower arrangements. Dozens of white-
gloved waiters in white tie and tails glided around the room, offering
silver trays with cocktails and hors d'oeuvres. But the most glamorous
element of the event was the guests, members of royal families from
Europe and beyond. Young ladies and gentlemen with titles and long
lineages drank and laughed in elegant clusters, wearing their finery as
comfortably as San Franciscans wore fleece jackets and running shoes.

To me, all this Old European splendor was a bit surreal. As far as I
could tell, some of these dukes, duchesses, earls, lords, ladies, princes,
and princesses did little more with their lives than move around Europe from party to party like a traveling circus. But Markos and I spotted two familiar faces in the posh crowd: Constantine, the former king
of Greece, and his Danish-born queen, Anne-Marie, stood chatting
with friends at one side of the party. The sight of these two royals made
me smile, though no one looking at me—except my husband—could
have guessed the reason.

Markos and I had met the king and queen in Beijing in 2008, when
Dora Bakoyannis, then Greece's foreign minister, invited us to the

Greek embassy for a dinner the night before the opening ceremony of the Olympic Games. We'd brought Eon and Neo, then six and seven years old, to Beijing to support their Chinese-language studies. We didn't have a babysitter with us, and Dora insisted that we bring the boys to the dinner. When we walked into the room, we saw that there was only a small number of guests and that half of them were members of the former Greek royal family. Of course they were there, I thought, since the former king had been an Olympic sailor. Realizing I had brought small children to what was definitely not a family affair, I was mortified.

Dora, however, was unfazed. She took the boys by the hand. "Come, children, I am going to introduce you to a real king!"

She didn't know that back in California we'd explained the steady flow of politicians through our house by telling our boys, "Once, there were only kings, and they could tell everyone what to do. They made all the rules and could change them at any time. That was terrible for everyone except the king! Now we have presidents and senators, and they represent the people instead of ruling them."

So the boys balked at the prospect of meeting the man who had served as Greece's king until the monarchy ended in 1974. "Kings are bad!" Neo asserted, a little too loudly. Dora assured them, "This one is very nice, and anyway, he's not a king anymore." With wide eyes, Neo and Eon approached the former ruler, who smiled broadly, knelt down, and chatted with them. We couldn't hear the conversation, but we could see the boys warm up to Constantine.

My father, always very dismissive of royalty, loved the story of the boys and King Constantine. But his father, my grandfather Kyriakos, had kept a portrait of the young king on his bedside table until the day he died. He, like many others who had fought the communists during the bloody Greek civil war, remained loyal to the king for the rest of his life.

Constantine himself was a very likable man, personally gracious, with a philosophical view of his past and his own role in history. He had been a young boy during the Greek civil war (1946–49) and became king in 1964. He lost the monarchy less than a decade later amid Greece's ongoing political tensions. Constantine had been the best man when Alexander married the sprightly young Katherine, then known as Klary. Now, as he toasted the couple twenty-five years later, he looked over at me and Mary Warlick and noted, "Tonight we have not one but two American ambassadors present. It's a great honor that they have joined us. As they are both ladies, it makes me wonder, has the United States discovered the wisdom in only sending women envoys these days?"

Katherine had arranged for little crown-shaped, gold-wrapped chocolates to be set beside all of our plates. As he sat back down, Constantine picked up his chocolate, reached over, and handed it to me. Everyone at the table watched to see how I would respond, and for a moment I wondered what I should do. I decided that simplest was best: I politely nodded at the former king, quickly unwrapped the candy, and bit into it.

I could see Markos stifling a laugh.

Of all the royalty I met during my posting, no one impressed me more than Georg von Hapsburg, a descendant of the family that had once ruled Hungary and much of Europe. I met Georg in the summer of 2010, when flooding was devastating villages in northeastern Hungary. USAID had agreed to contribute $50,000 to disaster relief, and Georg was the president of the Hungarian Red Cross. The embassy had arranged for us to ride together to the flooded area. I knew next to nothing about Georg, but the embassy's protocol office had put together a profile for me—a profile that was like a Cliff's Notes version of Central European history.

Born Paul Georg Maria Joseph Dominikus, Georg was known as Georg Hapsburg-Lothringen in Austria; as Habsburg György in Hungary; and by his royal name, Archduke Georg of Austria, in Europe's titled circles. Born in 1964, he was the second son and seventh and youngest child of Otto von Hapsburg, the last crown prince of Austria-Hungary, and Princess Regina of Saxe-Meiningen. Georg's father had been four years old when his uncle Archduke Franz Ferdinand was shot and killed. The murder resulted in Georg's grandfather, Charles I of Austria and IV of Hungary, ascending to the throne, but also sparked the outbreak of World War I. Because the Hapsburg monarchy was dissolved at the end of the war, Otto never became emperor. Although he held no official positions during his life, Otto von Hapsburg was well known for his devotion to the liberation of Central Europe from Soviet control and then his support of the creation and expansion of the European Union.

Markos, working at *Newsweek* in the late 1980s, had met Otto. The Hapsburg scion was still alive when I arrived in Budapest, but passed away in 2011 at age ninety-eight. His son Georg had moved to Hungary after 1989 and lived with his family on an understated but beautiful horse ranch just outside Budapest. I was looking forward to meeting a member of this extraordinary dynasty, which stretched back over five hundred years of European history. But as I read the profile, one thing worried me. I put down the paper and walked over to Jeff Levine's office.

I asked Jeff, "What do I call this guy?" I knew Jeff had a good rapport with Georg. I also knew that, as a fellow Californian, Jeff was accustomed to a far more casual environment than the one that swirled around Central European royalty.

"I'm not sure," he shrugged. "I've always just called him Georg."

Sitting in the backseat of the Cadillac, racing through the Hungarian countryside on our way to Borsod County, Georg and I talked about Hungary and all the changes that he and his family had witnessed since the collapse of communism. Georg had seen a lot over those tumultuous years and relayed his stories with extraordinary details and sharp insights. The whole while, I carefully avoided saying his name.

As we arrived in the town of Miskolc, evidence of the devastating floods was everywhere. Historic houses with mud roofs had collapsed into unrecognizable piles, and roads had been completely wiped out. The work that Georg was doing there was much needed, and I could see that the American contribution would go far in helping support the Hungarians' work. As we made our way to the office of the president of the Borsod County Assembly, Ferenc Ódor, I turned to Georg and asked:

"Do you know Ferenc Ódor?"

"Oh yes, he's a wonderful fellow."

"I suppose I should address him as *President* Ódor. Is that right?"

"But of course!" Georg replied.

"And just so I'm correct, how should I address *you*?"

Georg burst out laughing. "Oh, I've been called everything under the sun! 'Georg' is just fine for me."

Here was one of the last direct descendants of the last Austro-Hungarian emperor suggesting that I refer to a Hungarian county president by his title but brushing off the notion that he should be called by anything other than his first name. How could I not like him?

Even after all the upheavals of history, the Hapsburgs' love for Hungary remained strong and deep. I saw it in Georg's demeanor as we toured the flood-wrecked neighborhoods. When Georg's father, Archduke Otto, the last crown prince of Austria-Hungary, died, his body was interred in Austria, but his heart was buried at the Pannonhalma Archabbey monastery in western Hungary.

I would meet one more royal during my time in Budapest. Britain's Prince Charles came to town for a conference on climate change, an issue he had long been passionate about. I participated in several of the meetings and found the prince very knowledgeable and dedicated to the subject. His accent, however, caused me some problems. It sounded much more exaggerated than that of other English people I'd met throughout the years—none of them royalty, of course. To my Sacramento Valley–girl ears, the prince sounded like someone trying to impersonate a member of the English royal family. Throughout the meetings, I had to bite my lip and concentrate on the points he was making, and not his accent, to keep myself from transforming into a giggling schoolgirl.

Later that day, there was a small reception for Prince Charles. My stepmother, Sofia, was visiting at the time, and Markos offered to stay home so she could come with me to meet the prince. Of course, Sofia was delighted. As we moved through the receiving line to greet Prince Charles, I hoped I'd be able to keep my composure when confronted with his accent.

Up close, the prince was a soft-spoken gentleman, and he was intrigued when I told him that Sofia was my stepmother.

Rather than moving on to the next guest, he paused.

"Really? You brought your stepmother? How lovely," he said, before turning to Sofia with a big smile and wagging his finger for emphasis. "You must be a very good stepmother!"

Face-to-face, as it were, with the royal accent, I didn't laugh—in fact, I was completely charmed, touched that a member of one of the most consequential families of history had reached out to compliment a member of mine. And Sofia went home thrilled to tell everybody what had happened.

# 16

# The Three-Legged Stool of Democracy

For twenty years, the United States held Hungary up as a model of democratic transition—one of the world's great success stories of how a country could transform itself from an autocratic government with a centralized economy to a democracy with a free-market economy.

Yet as the Orbán government's two-thirds revolution marched along, and the reform process raged through Parliament, one of the world's great models of democratic transition was rapidly tarnishing. How could this happen so quickly? Certainly, the economic crisis of 2008 had been a fundamental catalyst. It led to the near-total collapse of one of the two largest parties in the country, leaving only one political party that mainstream Hungarians felt was legitimate. It's also true that the economic crisis drove the rise of the radical Jobbik party, which fed on discontent and the desire for scapegoating.

But surely democracies are designed to be strong enough to resist the challenges that arise during economic downturns—even what my father called the "economic tsunami" of 2008. How could all the hard work in building Hungary's democracy over the previous twenty years—work that Hungary had put in, with the help of the United States and other European countries—come apart so quickly?

As I looked for answers, I was reminded of my own family's experience with American democracy as active members of civil society.

Back when I was in high school, I was given an assignment to write about someone I considered a hero. Pondering the question, that night at dinner I asked my father, "Dad, do you have any heroes?" My father was an inspirational figure to me, but I couldn't imagine who had been inspirational in his life.

"Yes, of course," he said. "Cesar Chavez."

When he was about the same age I was then and living in Lodi, California, with his uncle, my father went to high school during the week, just like the other kids. But after school and on weekends, he worked as a farm laborer. Like the mostly Mexican immigrants with whom he toiled in the fields, he would ride the bus out to the farms and be paid in cash at the end of the week.

As we sat together that night at our family dinner table, my father recalled his time as a young man in America. "We were in the fields one day, and I started to hear people talking about Cesar Chavez. They were excited, saying that Chavez was demanding that the farmers give us better working conditions. Back then, there was nowhere for us to even go to the bathroom or wash our hands."

My father continued, "I shook my head at this nonsense. I thought they were dreaming. How could one person get the farmers to do these things? But then it happened. Changes came. At first, I couldn't believe it, but it was the moment I understood something about America that I couldn't have understood before, coming from Greece. In this country, if you have a good idea and you get a lot of other people to go with you, you can change anything. The government has to listen to you."

Back in Lodi, Angelo started to develop business skills that allowed him to make significant profits for a high schooler. Once, he was able to buy large, delicious, but misshapen watermelons at a deep discount from a farmer. The melons couldn't fit in the boxes used to ship them to the stores, but that didn't stop Angelo and a few friends from selling them beside a highway, at double the price he'd paid. He was a very industrious but also very friendly kid. When a new family moved into town, he left a basket of fruit on their porch to welcome them. This was how he met the Fitzer family, a warm and wonderful brood with lots of kids.

One day, when he was about nineteen and a senior in high school, Angelo stopped by "Mom and Pop" Fitzer's house to say good-bye. He was moving out of his uncle's house, he said, and into downtown Lodi.

"Where will you live, Angelo?" Mom Fitzer asked.

"The Tokay Hotel!" he answered proudly. The Tokay was located on what they called Skid Row. Angelo was attracted by the cheap rent and not terribly worried about the conditions or the neighbors. His childhood in war-torn Greece had prepared him for much worse.

But Mom Fitzer was horrified. "That's not the place for a young man your age. We have an extra bed in Tim's room. Why don't you stay here at least until you finish high school?" She wouldn't let him refuse.

My dad always told me that living with the Fitzers gave him his "American education." After he had lived with them for a few weeks, it was report card time. Pop told Angelo that he would have a meeting with him to discuss his grades, as he did with all his children. But Angelo had already signed his card himself and turned it back in to the school. At Pop's order, he got it back, and the two of them sat down together to review it.

"Angelo, your English grades are terrible, but you're doing pretty well in history and math. Have you thought about where you want to go to college?"

"College?" No one had ever said that word to Angelo. "Pop, I can't go to college. I have to go to work. I have to make money and send it back to Greece, to my family." By that point, Angelo's entrepreneurial farming endeavors were becoming quite profitable.

Pop had a different vision for Angelo. William Fitzer had served as a colonel in the U.S. Army, stationed in Heidelberg, where he helped implement the Marshall Plan. Like Angelo, he had seen the evils of war, but he was a stalwart believer in the importance of education.

"Angelo, imagine that Lodi is at the bottom of a great valley," he said. "Going to college is like climbing out of the valley, up a tall mountain. As you climb, you will meet philosophers, kings, presidents, generals, and you'll get to talk to them and ask them questions. When you get to the top of the mountain, you'll be able to see far beyond anything you can imagine from the valley. Angelo, you are an entrepreneur. You will always make money. Go to college and get an education first."

Angelo was convinced. He had an uncle in Chicago, so he traveled there and spent a winter at the University of Chicago's temporary facility at the Navy Pier, where World War II veterans were still benefiting from the GI Bill. But Chicago was too cold for him, so he returned to California and enrolled at Sacramento State, in the business program. With my father's newly minted education and natural business skills, and the lessons he'd learned from working in the fields, the world opened up to him just as Pop Fitzer said it would.

My father learned many things during his first years in America. But I have always believed the lessons of Cesar Chavez and the farmworkers' movement made the most profound mark. Along with my dad's education and the Fitzer family's generosity and love, Chavez's example helped him truly understand the nature of his adoptive country and provided him with an essential part of his value system. Because I worked with my father for many years, I came to see that that value system was the foundation of our business engagement. We were businesspeople, yes, but we were citizens first. The way we saw it, being an active citizen wasn't just a privilege that came with being an American; it was an obligation. The documents I submitted to the Senate Foreign Relations Committee included a list of all the civic organizations that I had been affiliated with over the preceding ten years and any positions I held. Thanks to the incredible record keeping of my executive assistant Lynne Banez, I was able to list fifty.

Like many Americans, I considered involvement in civil society a natural part of life. But Hillary Clinton had long recognized that outside the United States, the role of civil society often was not strong enough. In her autobiography, *Living History*, she wrote about visiting Central Europe in 1999, as first lady of the United States. It was ten years after the fall of the Iron Curtain, and Hillary gave a Fourth of July interview on Radio Free Europe: "Building and sustaining a free society is like a three-legged stool: one leg is a democratic government, the second is a free-market economy, and the third is a civil society—the civic associations, religious institutions, voluntary efforts, NGOs, and individual acts of citizenship that together weave the fabric of democratic life. In the newly free countries, civil society is as important as free elections and free markets to internalize democratic values in citizens' hearts, minds, and everyday lives."*

Clearly, Hillary had been using the concept of the three-legged stool of democracy for a long time. But as secretary of state, she made building awareness of the role of civil society a key element of U.S. foreign policy.

Hillary traveled to more countries than any secretary of state in U.S. history. In addition to visiting with key government decision makers and political leaders, she regularly met with members of civil society. Many high-powered individuals would have given their right arms for a few minutes of private conversation with Hillary Clinton, but when she came to town, wherever she was, she treated the leaders of civil society as VIPs. She brought them together and asked them to share their perspectives on important issues facing their countries.

When she came to Budapest for Golden Week, it was no different. We gathered leaders of the largest and most active civil society organizations, such as Transparency International Hungary, a few leaders of smaller efforts, and representatives of the enfeebled opposition parties to meet her.

After the initial buzz of excitement at being in the room with the U.S. secretary of state subsided, the group settled in for a discussion. Taking turns speaking, they explained that they felt systematically shut out of the decision making of their country. Parliament had adopted a new constitution, but most of the people in the room had seen drafts of the document only days before it was voted into law. They had no opportunity to comment on it or contribute to it.

Secretary Clinton listened intently, nodding in understanding. Then she asked the group what they were going to do about it.

*Hillary Rodham Clinton, *Living History* (New York: Simon & Schuster, 2003), 359.

The question surprised them. The unspoken response seemed to be "That's why we're talking to you."

"Look," Hillary said, "I'm not the one you need to convince that there is a problem here. You need to talk to the people of your country and try to convince *them* that there is a problem. If the media law has made it harder to get your message out, you'll have to work harder. You have the Internet. You have tools. Get out there and talk to people about your concerns. Build support for your point of view. It's not just about finding people who agree with you, it's about convincing those who don't agree with you that you are right. That's where change comes from. As leaders of civil society, this is your job."

It was a sobering message and a powerful one. There is a lot of talk about what the United States can and should do around the world to help countries on their paths toward democracy. We do a lot, more than any other country in history. But we cannot supplant the role of civil society. In a country like Hungary, we cannot take on the daily role of serving as a check on the power of government or the ambitions of business. No one's saying this is easy. But ultimately, citizens in their own countries have to do it for themselves.

My father's American parents, Mom and Pop Fitzer, eventually moved from Lodi to San Francisco, to a quaint row house on Army Street. Pop Fitzer passed away in 1984. He died at our home in Sacramento, in a hospital-type bed that had for months been placed in my father's room, next to his own bed. After her husband's passing, Grandma Fitzer, as I called her, became passionately involved in a cause of her own.

It was 1992, and the San Francisco Board of Supervisors had voted to change the name of Army Street to Cesar Chavez Street in honor of the great activist. Grandma Fitzer—ironically, given my father's respect for Chavez—disagreed with the renaming. She contended that Army Street had not been named randomly; it honored U.S. veterans who had died in the First World War. Pop Fitzer had served proudly in the army, and she felt that it was wrong to take the honor away from army veterans. She, along with the veterans' groups that had mobilized on the issue, argued that instead of Army Street, San Francisco's Nineteenth Avenue should be renamed Cesar Chavez, as it was bigger, longer, and more trafficked. And no army vets would be disrespected in its renaming.

In fact, Nineteenth Avenue had been considered, but the street's business owners and their associations had come out in full force. There were many more businesses on Nineteenth Avenue than there were on Army Street, and they all would have to change their ads in the Yellow Pages, their stationery, and their receipt forms. Their voices were strong enough that the Board of Supervisors opted to rename Army Street. But the matter didn't end there. The veterans' groups collected enough signatures to put the issue on the ballot as a referendum. For weeks on end, my septuagenarian grandmother would sit in front of the Safeway in the Castro District, gathering signatures and advocating for her position. I was in graduate school in Berkeley at the time, and I visited her a few times out in front of the supermarket, just to make sure she was okay. The Castro's residents were interested in any good debate, and I saw people huddled around my grandmother's table, listening to her pitch.

Dozens of interest groups and points of view were involved in this heated San Francisco debate. In the end, it came down to a vote of the people. Army Street became Cesar Chavez, and Nineteenth Avenue stayed as it was. Grandma Fitzer was disappointed but satisfied that she had done her part and that her voice had been heard.

Episodes like this one make up the story of American life. Government for the people and by the people relies on the constant involvement of the people. When Secretary Clinton spoke about the three-legged stool of democracy, she was making it clear that if people waited for business or government to solve all their problems, they would wait forever. If they expected government to get everything right on its own, they would be sorely disappointed.

Civil society was not unknown in Hungarian history, but it had been badly beaten down during the communist times. In the systems of the Soviet Union and its satellite states, the stool had only one leg: government. There was no business sector, no civil society. The Communist Party apparatus was everything.

With the exception of personal effects such as clothes, and larger assets such as cars for the lucky few, people were generally not allowed to own private property. The state owned the land, the companies, the buildings, the houses, and almost every head of sheep on every farm. As for civil society, in the 1950s about one-third of Hungary's population was under investigation as possible "enemies of the people." Openly criticizing the government landed you in jail, or worse. It took only a few years of public examples—citizens tried and executed after false charges and forced admissions of guilt—before people fell in line.

In later years, a system in Hungary developed that was far more subtle but every bit as effective as the show trials. Very early in my Budapest posting, I attended a luncheon held by the American Chamber of Commerce and was seated beside a Hungarian businessman I'll call Tibor, because I'm not sure he would want me to recount his story. Tibor had become very successful in post-communist Hungary. But that day at lunch, he told me of his experiences growing up under the totalitarian regime, and to help me truly understand he recounted a personal family crisis. In the late 1970s, Tibor's eighteen-year-old sister had traveled to Switzerland to visit relatives there. Tibor's family was privileged enough to have blue passports, which allowed them to travel outside the Soviet bloc (red passports allowed travel only behind the Iron Curtain). Even so, they were not permitted to travel to Switzerland all together. This was standard in Hungary, as a way to prevent defections. So Tibor's family would visit their relatives in Switzerland one at a time. In effect, those family members left behind were hostages, ensuring that the traveling family member would return from abroad.

After Tibor's sister had been in Switzerland for a few weeks, she called home and dropped a bombshell. She had fallen in love and was not coming back. She was going to stay in Switzerland and marry her new love. Her parents were beside themselves. Daily, they beseeched her to return. After about a week, a man visited Tibor's father, a prominent engineer, at work. "I understand you are having some trouble with your daughter," he said. "It would be a pity if she didn't return to Budapest. You probably would no longer have this nice office or such an important job. And your son probably would not have a spot at the university."

After much pleading and many tearful phone calls, Tibor's sister came home. His father lost his job anyway and was reduced to a clerk. Tibor was allowed to go to university, but only after a four-year delay.

"The worst of it," he told me, "is that I never saw my sister happy again."

Another friend, a woman from the Ministry of Foreign Affairs, who was about my age and a university student when the Iron Curtain fell, put it this way over drinks one night: "In my house, my parents would whisper at the dinner table. Every day, they told us kids, as we went to school, that we should never, ever, tell anyone anything about what went on in our house—not who came over, not what we talked about, not what we were doing or saying or thinking. I understood that it was a matter of our survival, so I always kept quiet."

There had been twenty years of freedom. But I could see that Hungarians were not able to easily forget the consequences of government tyranny. Just a few months after I arrived in Budapest, I personally cut the ribbon on the capital's first Starbucks store (I would be invited to cut the ribbons on all of the half-dozen Starbucks that opened during my time there). I'm very fond of Starbucks, but only partly because of the coffee. I love that its stores are natural gathering spots for civil society at home and abroad.

At one point, talking with the woman who trained the Hungarian baristas, I asked what her biggest challenges were.

"When Hungarians go to a Starbucks counter for the first time to give their order, they are sometimes stunned when the barista asks for their name," she told me. "Some customers don't know what to say. They get nervous and don't want to do it. So we tell the baristas not to push, just to say 'Okay, I will write Mr. Orange Shirt or Miss Blue Scarf.' Usually, after a few visits, they get more comfortable and give their names. When that happens, I feel like we are achieving a victory over the past!"

As the Starbucks anecdote shows, communism's legacy continued to reverberate in the hearts and minds of the Hungarian people. It didn't take long for me to realize that civil society in Hungary was still very weak and that citizens had only limited participation in the political process.

In April 2011, the mayor of Budapest declared that the name of the most trafficked square in the city, Moscow Square, would be changed back to Széll Kálmán Square—its name before the end of World War II. A few weeks after the mayor announced his intention to make the change, the city council voted in favor, and it was done, along with the renaming of about twenty lower-profile streets and squares around the city. There was no public debate, no opportunity for citizens to comment. Several council members voted against the measure, but if members of the public at large had a problem with the decision, no one ever heard about it.

Compared with the Army Street saga in San Francisco, this was an astonishingly swift, noninclusive, and no-recourse government action. I'm not suggesting that every place in the world can be like San Francisco, but in Budapest there were neither activist grandmothers nor organized neighborhood groups to protest, and the names of squares and streets could be changed at the direction of an elected official almost overnight—with no public testimony, letter-writing campaigns, or petition signings.

In January 2012, Secretary Clinton launched an eighteen-month State Department initiative she called Strategic Dialogue with Civil Society. She knew that by directing embassy staff, especially ambassadors, to meet regularly with leaders of civil society in their host countries, the United States would be helping to validate and empower those leaders. Because of the circumstances, we had been doing a lot of this in Hungary already. But I wondered: the United States had instituted robust programs in Central Europe after the fall of communism, and those in Hungary had not really taken root. What more could we do now, when Hungary no longer qualified for the kinds of programs, and the budgets associated with them, that were run by USAID for transitional democracies?

As I tried to come up with high-impact, low-cost options, I thought of my friend from back home in San Francisco, Christine Pelosi. Christine had written what some considered the bible for how to organize and grow a grassroots movement, *Campaign Boot Camp*. She had attended Georgetown's Edmund A. Walsh School of Foreign Service before going to law school and had a solid base of knowledge about international affairs. What if we gathered up members of civil society from across Hungary and offered them Christine Pelosi's civil society boot camp?

That's what we did. Christine came to Budapest, and over two days we guided several hundred people through her twelve steps for starting and running a campaign. I was aware that this was a delicate situation—pro-government conspiracy theorists had already started to accuse the embassy and me of plotting against Viktor Orbán. So I was very clear that Christine should focus on campaigns for causes, not campaigns for candidates. People loved the program, which gave them not only a big shot of inspiration but also a practical road map to use as they built up their organizations.

One thing I always heard from Hungarians was that you couldn't start an NGO (nongovernmental organization) without funding from the government.

"Nonsense," I told them. "All you need is someone with a living room and a couple of couches, and someone to make coffee and bring a few snacks." As I shared a lifetime of civil society experience with the Hungarians, my own activist instincts boiled up, but I tried to keep them under control. It wasn't for me to do this work for them, just to help them see the path.

My next step was to establish an award, which I called the Ambassador's Award for Active Citizenship. I figured I had the authority to do this, and my team agreed. The award cost nothing more than the price of the paper on which the certificate was printed, but it meant a great deal to its recipients. I challenged my staff to look around Hungary for people who were the best examples of active citizenship or active civil society, staying away from political groups or controversial subjects.

I gave eighteen Active Citizenship awards over the term of Secretary Clinton's eighteen-month Strategic Dialogue with Civil Society. All along, I stressed that most of what civil society engaged in wasn't controversial at all, just people coming together to make their communities better. In fact, one of the most memorable awards I gave was to a man in the town of Karcag, in eastern Hungary.

István Kurucz was a Hungarian judo master who had started an after-school program for disadvantaged kids. No one had hired him to do it or even asked him to do it. He simply loved judo and thought it would be good for kids in his community, keeping them out of mischief and improving their self-esteem. In the United States, such programs are ubiquitous, but for an individual in Hungary to create and run a free program like this was a rarity.

When we walked into a classroom at the local high school to present the award, we saw that it was standing room only—everyone whose life the judo master had touched had come to show support. The local mayor was there too.

With the flags of Hungary and the United States behind us, I gave the award to István Kurucz. Citing the importance of civil society to all democracies, young and old, I said, "Your community recognizes the importance of your work. But I want you to know that the United States recognizes it as well."

The huge, muscular man melted into tears, and the room exploded in applause.

I also gave an Active Citizenship award to Háttér Society, the largest and most active organization for Hungary's lesbian, gay, bisexual, and transgender community. The organization operated a hotline for young people struggling with their sexual orientation and for people who had been infected with HIV. It delivered food to the sick, found jobs for the destitute, and provided a vital safety net for people who had nowhere else to go. It was heartbreaking how many LGBT people in Central and Eastern Europe were shunned by their families. In addition to the many indignities they suffered at the hands of strangers, they often found themselves abandoned by the people who should have been there for them.

In a December 2011 speech in Geneva, Hillary Clinton addressed the issue in the boldest terms the United States had ever used, saying, "Gay rights are human rights, and human rights are gay rights." It was an echo of her groundbreaking statement in Beijing about women's rights, back in 1995 when she was first lady. For members of LGBT communities around the world, it was just as important. To me, it was a license to engage more directly in an issue that had always been close to my heart. From a very young age, I felt a surge of outrage whenever I heard someone make fun of people who were gay. Who got to decide what was normal?

When I first arrived in Budapest, I was saddened to learn that members of the diplomatic community, along with most Hungarian government officials, didn't march in the gay pride festival. In San Francisco, every government official who wants to be reelected shows up at the parade. Many Hungarian officials stayed away from the festival for political reasons, but for the diplomatic corps it was primarily an issue of security. The Hungarian police told us they had their hands full just ensuring the safety of the participants, many of whom had been attacked in previous years. If they had to look after diplomats as well, it would take away from protecting participants.

I accepted the argument in 2010 and 2011, but I didn't stay away completely. As I've noted, tolerance is an important message in U.S. foreign policy. The first year I was in Budapest, my public affairs counselor, Ed Loo, proposed, and I agreed, that we provide financial support for the events surrounding Budapest Pride Week. It was the first time the embassy had done so, and we allowed our insignia to be used by organizers in all of their advertisements. I was proud of this decision, but I felt that after Hillary's Geneva speech, as well as her direction to engage in the Strategic Dialogue with Civil Society, I should do more.

In June 2012, I marched in the Budapest Pride parade. My security team had worked it out with the police that I would enter the parade after it started, march for about five blocks, and then leave through a barricade. Images of my participation lit up the Internet. It's the closest I came to crossing the line of participating directly in Hungarian civil society. But I knew that after Hillary's Geneva speech, I could justify my actions as advancing U.S. foreign policy. Many people expressed gratitude. More expressed anger and disgust. But my participation, and the parade itself, proved what I had long known to be true: when people stand up for things they believe in, other people pay attention. Things don't always change as much or as fast as activists want them to. But one thing is certain. Without the engagement of civil society, democracy cannot flourish.

In fact, it cannot even be sustained.

# 17

# Anti-Semitism:
# The Bizarre and the Tragic

I had been in Hungary only a few weeks when I was invited to speak at the Budapest Holocaust Memorial Center on International Holocaust Remembrance Day, which is held every year on January 27. My speech had been crafted by a very capable young embassy officer named Aaron Feit, whose portfolio included tolerance issues. It was very well written, I thought. I was proud to be quoting President Obama, who had recently spoken of the Holocaust with the powerful words "Never forget. Never again."

Waiting for my turn to speak, I listened to testimonials by people who had lived through the Holocaust. One by one, they mounted the podium and shared stories of suffering, loss, and grief. I had seen many movies and read books about the Holocaust, and I'd visited the Holocaust Memorial Museum in Washington, D.C., but these testimonials made clear the yawning gap between my own education on the subject and the victims' actual experiences. Just before my speech, Dorothee Janetzke-Wenzel, Germany's ambassador to Hungary, took the podium. She spoke of her regret and the regret of her country for the atrocities it had committed, and as she did, she broke down in tears, unable to complete her remarks.

After that, it was my turn. I took the podium, standing in the same spot where the German ambassador had just broken down crying. Though my speech had seemed strong the day before, it now sounded very different to me. Following Dorothee Janetzke-Wenzel's passionate regrets and the testimonials of people who had personally experienced the horror, my words sounded inadequate, like a eulogy from a distant friend.

I doubt that the audience realized my discomfort, but from that moment on, I learned everything I could about the Holocaust in Hungary. I read and studied. I visited Hungary's synagogues, which had been filled with worshippers in the country's "golden age" at the turn of the twentieth century; then emptied by the Hungarian Arrow Cross and German Nazis; then appropriated by the communists, who turned them into libraries, community centers, and television studios; then turned back into synagogues again, albeit for much smaller congregations.

I came to understand that there was almost no part of Hungarian history or culture that wasn't interwoven with the history and culture of Hungary's Jews. Starting in the late eighteenth century, Jews living within the borders of the Hapsburg Empire emerged as industrialists, bankers, and businessmen. After 1867, the first Jewish families were ennobled, granted titles for their loyalty to the emperor and their contributions to society. In the 1860s, the Austro-Hungarian emperor, Franz Joseph I, gave Jews full equal protection under the law. The ranks of the Hungarian nobility included names such as Goldberger de Buda, von Rosenberg, Baron von Korányi-Tolcsvai (originally Kornfeld), and Baron Samu Hazai (born Sámuel Kohn). These and other Jewish families made enormous contributions to the Austro-Hungarian Empire and to Hungary itself, helping the country to become an economic powerhouse at the end of the nineteenth century. In addition to their economic contributions, Jews were among Hungary's most influential scientists, innovators, mathematicians, artists, musicians, and writers.

At the turn of the last century, Hungary's Jews were thoroughly assimilated into the country's life. Some married gentiles, while others converted to Christianity. Often it was hard to know who was Jewish and who wasn't. After World War I, when Hungary's borders were dramatically rewritten, many Jews moved to stay within those borders because their freedom seemed so assured in Hungary. That changed in the 1920s, when the government ordered Jews to register with the government as part of numerus clausus and other anti-Semitic laws that limited the number of Jews at universities and within the professions. If at least one of your grandparents was Jewish, you were legally a Jew. The government had your name, and it knew where you lived. After more than a century of living in Hungary as respected, patriotic, and prominent citizens, Jews found themselves in a hostile and increasingly threatening country.

Foreign Minister Martonyi once told me about a Hungarian writer named Jenő Rejtő. "Every Hungarian knows his name. Every Hungarian knows that he helps define the very essence of Hungarian humor. What was funny to him is funny to us." But, Martonyi lamented, "many Hungarians don't know that Jenő Rejtő was Jewish. What would they think if they did? Would it help them understand that our culture, who we are as a people, has been influenced so dramatically by our Jewish brothers and sisters?"

When the foreign minister asked me this question, Hungary was seeing a rapid resurgence of anti-Semitism, harnessed and fed by far-right extremists. During my years at Embassy Budapest, rarely a day passed when we did not interact on the issue. Rarely a month passed without some odious act of anti-Semitism: an anonymous man brutally accosts an enfeebled rabbi, who had survived the Holocaust, as he walks to the bus on the streets of Budapest; an old Jewish cemetery in the countryside is desecrated, tombstones painted over with swastikas; someone hangs a necklace of pigs' feet around the neck of the statue of Raoul Wallenberg, heroic rescuer of Jews during World War II.

Before I arrived in Budapest, I had been heavily briefed about anti-Semitism in Hungary and the growing political power of the radical nationalist Jobbik party. When I was asked about this troubling trend at my confirmation hearing, I said, "It is a small but vocal group who is responsible for these words and acts. Most Hungarians do not share their sentiments."

I spent nearly four years reminding myself of these words, which though I still believe to be true felt less and less true with each passing incident. In my mind, it was becoming increasingly urgent for Hungary as a nation to come to terms with its role in the Holocaust and battle the virulent anti-Semitism that was poisoning its present. For those who respect and admire the Hungarian people, as I do, this is a painful and difficult matter to address. But in my opinion, anyone who cares about Hungary must urge its citizens to confront these issues openly and diligently.

My friend the novelist Ayelet Waldman came to visit me in Budapest soon after I arrived. Ayelet is what I would call a heat-seeking missile— as a writer, she is drawn to controversy. The more uncomfortable her readers are likely to be with the subject matter, the more interested she is in exploring and writing about it.

Ayelet and I are very close friends. She supported and encouraged me during my difficult confirmation process and helped me keep going when things looked dim. So I was excited when she said she was coming to Hungary for a few weeks to do research for a novel about the Holocaust. She asked me to find historians who could help her paint a picture of Budapest at the dawn of the twentieth century. Ayelet's book, which she would title *Love and Treasure*, was based on the true story of the Hungarian Gold Train. Filled with valuable property that Hungarian Nazis had confiscated from the Jews, the train was seized by American soldiers in 1945. At first, I was confused as to why Ayelet was researching turn-of-the-century Budapest when her story was centered on the Holocaust. But she knew that the best way to describe the Gold Train's contents—and show the vastness of what had been lost—was to describe the extraordinary community that had owned the stolen objects.

One day after Ayelet arrived in Budapest, we stopped at the New York Café, which had been the center of the city's rich intellectual and cultural life before World War II. The café was a masterpiece of fin de siècle architecture, a white-and-gold wedding cake of a restaurant, every surface of which was lavishly decorated. Ayelet, who had studied its history, ordered us two slices of Esterházy torte, one of the café's specialties.

As we dove into our pastries, Ayelet described the place she was researching. "Turn-of-the-century Budapest was one of the most intellectually and culturally sophisticated places the world has ever known, and Jews were totally accepted. They were rich, powerful, and integrated into society at large." She put down her fork and looked at me seriously. "I think of it this way: Budapest was Manhattan."

As she worked on her novel, Ayelet shared her findings with me. The juxtaposition of stories from Budapest's cultured, inclusive past with the twenty-first-century desecrations and acts of anti-Semitism we heard about regularly at the embassy—and the chasm of the Holocaust between them—disturbs and haunts me even today.

An important part of U.S. foreign policy is advancing the issue of tolerance and minority rights. Living in a country of immigrants, Americans have not only coexisted remarkably peacefully, but we have benefited from our diversity. Telling our own story is one of the most important tools we use as we advocate for tolerance and minority rights in countries around the world. Another important teaching tool is Holocaust education, because there is no sharper or more compelling example of the violation of minority rights in Western history. Despite living in some of the most advanced societies in history, more than six million human beings—men, women, and children; friends and neighbors; philosophers, poets, and scientists—were brutally and systematically slaughtered. Understanding why and how it happened is not just an important way to combat anti-Semitism, it is an incomparable teaching tool used by U.S. ambassadors and embassies around the world in advocating for tolerance of all minority groups.

Since 1989, every U.S. ambassador to Hungary has confronted the challenge of Holocaust education. In the decades following World War II, the German people carried out an intense national debate over what it meant to be a German citizen after the war and the Holocaust. The conversation was unflinching and painful, but Germans doggedly carried it out, determined to come to terms with the horrors of recent history. But despite the enthusiastic and effective participation of its own Arrow Cross, civil servants, and police in the genocide, Hungary did not go through any similar process. This was partly because in the communist era people were not allowed to speak freely about the past. But even after the Iron Curtain was torn down, Hungarians seemed to prefer to stay silent on the issue—to let the horrors of that time fade from their collective memory. With the communist era quickly following the Holocaust, many Hungarians adopted the view that "we all suffered" and preferred to let it go at that. As a result, I could see there was no real national awareness of what had happened. There was no common understanding of how to talk about the tragedy and what it meant to Hungarians.

Certainly, what happened in Hungary isn't a footnote. In 1944, when the war was almost at an end, more than 450,000 Hungarian men, women, and children were rounded up, detained, deported from Hungary, and killed at the Nazi death camps. One out of every three Jews who died at Auschwitz-Birkenau was a Hungarian citizen. Thousands of Jewish men, women, and children were marched from the ghettos to the banks of the Danube, shot, and thrown into the icy river to die. Today only a small memorial of cast-iron shoes marks the site of that massacre, which the accompanying plaque blames on Arrow Cross militiamen—a reference to Hungarian fascists that does not mention Hungary.

As I rode to work one morning in the winter of 2011, I was reading the English translation of the news on my BlackBerry when a short item in the daily *Népszava* jumped out at me.

EVIDENCE SUGGESTS SKELETONS FOUND UNDER BUDAPEST BRIDGE
ARE HOLOCAUST VICTIMS

Traces of bullets have been found on the remains of skeletons found by divers during the reconstruction of the Margaret Bridge, Népszava reports. A source speaking on condition of anonymity said forensic tests show that the remains could be those of 20 or 21 people.

Traces of bullets were found on the skull, shoulder and pelvis of five or six skeletons.

The bodies apparently date from the early or mid 1940s, meaning it is increasingly likely that they were Jews executed during the Holocaust, Népszava speculates.

Police have promised to provide a briefing at a later date.

Reading about this tragic discovery, I expected an outpouring of community horror and regret, or at least curiosity, but the story came and went with little impact. There were no follow-up announcements by the police, no memorial services. When I spoke later with Jewish groups, they said they hadn't been informed about what had happened to the skeletons after the police were done with them and were not given the opportunity to be involved in handling the remains.

The problem in Hungary, I realized, wasn't just the rise of anti-Semitic, neofascist voices and acts. Hungarian society at large was responding to those radical voices with disproportionate silence and apathy. In the case of the skeletons under the bridge, it seemed that most people preferred to keep old memories submerged in the cold waters of the Danube.

As my time in Budapest unspooled, far-right extremism and intolerance continued to grow in Hungary, fueled by economic upheaval and uncertainty. The State Department tasked the embassy with reinforcing our efforts to help Hungarians combat it. The United States had a special envoy for Holocaust issues, Doug Davidson, and a special envoy for monitoring and combating anti-Semitism, Hannah Rosenthal. They spent a great deal of time focused on Hungary. I myself regularly issued statements or attended ceremonies in response to egregious acts.

Most of the anti-Semitic acts happening in Hungary were anonymous. But every once in a while, there were overt, high-profile public acts. In the winter of 2012, a Jobbik member of Parliament named Márton Gyöngyösi demanded in a speech—right on the Parliament floor—that a list be drawn up of all the Jewish parliamentarians and all the Jewish members of the government. He declared that as Jews they were a threat to Hungary's national security. In another case, a vocally anti-Semitic member of Jobbik named Csanád Szegedi was kicked out of the extreme-right party when it was learned he had been paying a blackmailer to hide the fact that he was Jewish—the grandson of an Auschwitz survivor.

When we discussed the rise of anti-Semitism with our interlocutors in the Orbán government, they regularly held up examples of some of the unprecedented steps they were taking to try to deal with the problem. It was true that Viktor Orbán and the Fidesz-controlled Parliament made efforts, such as outlawing Holocaust denial and even speaking at pro-tolerance rallies. "Look at all we are doing—isn't it enough to show you our commitment to the issue?" was the constant assertion. But as far as the United States was concerned, if the problem was still growing—and it was—then whatever these enormously powerful political leaders were doing was obviously either not enough or simply not the right approach. There was also the problem, as I saw it, of the effort by many high-ranking Fidesz officials to advance the establishment of a new national narrative. Historical figures whose profiles supported the narrative of national pride were being rehabilitated, and they were often ultranationalists who in many cases also turned out to be committed anti-Semites.

In early 2012, speaker of the Hungarian Parliament László Kövér started a campaign to rebury the remains of a famous Hungarian poet named József Nyírő in his native Transylvania. Nyírő was considered one of the greatest lovers of the Hungarian homeland and had fought in the period between the world wars to reunite lost Hungarian territories. Honoring him with reburial in his native village, in a territory that had once been Hungary—and adding his wistful poetry about Hungary to the new national educational curriculum—was part of the celebration of Greater Hungary, so important to the new narrative. Inconveniently for Speaker Kövér, this poet had been an enthusiastic supporter of Nazi Germany and a fierce anti-Semite. After a bizarre series of communications between Hungary and Romania—and rumors that jars of fake ashes were being transported across the border to see if a smuggling operation could be successful—the Hungarian leader finally dropped the project.

A seriously troubling part of the new national narrative held that Hungarians were not to blame for the Holocaust. Just as with the Treaty of Trianon, Hungary had been the victim of foreign powers. In this case, Germany, not Hungary, was responsible for the deportation of the Hungarian Jews. The preamble of the newly adopted constitution explicitly stated that Hungary's "self-determination" was lost on March 19, 1944, the day the Germans occupied Budapest and deportations began. I witnessed this attitude spreading over my years in

Budapest, but something happened a few months after I'd returned to the United States that is worth noting.

In 2014, the government announced it would raise a statue to commemorate the occupation of Hungary by the Germans in 1944. The artist Imre Párkányi Raab described the piece as follows: "In my composition, [the Archangel Gabriel] has been laid low. . . . He is depicted as handsome and tranquil. . . . The monument explains that his dream will turn into a nightmare. A culture, its wings broken, is being crushed by a greater power: the Third Reich and the symbol that represents it: the Imperial Eagle. The depiction of the eagle is the exact opposite of the Archangel Gabriel's. The Imperial Eagle is an assemblage of mass produced icons and symbols. It sweeps in flight across the world. Soon it will reach us and engulf Hungary, putting its inhabitants in chains."

In Raab's sculpture, Germany is the big eagle swooping down on innocent Hungary, represented by the Archangel Gabriel. Actually, Hungary and Germany were Axis partners for most of World War II. Germany only invaded Budapest in 1944 after learning about Hungary's secret peace negotiations with the Allies, just as the Russian army was making its way to Budapest. With its warped take on history, Raab's statue drew controversy, but Viktor Orbán defended it, calling the work "morally exact and immaculate." Although the artist said that the angel represented Hungary, Orbán put his own spin on it. He publicly stated that, in fact, the angel represented the innocent victims of Germany, including the Jews.

Government officials were sending strong messages to Hungarian citizens who were increasingly drawn to the drumbeat of the new national narrative: that every Hungarian loss had been the fault of foreign powers. When the West raised questions, government officials always had an answer to explain why things were not as they seemed to us, the foreigners. Again and again, we were told that we simply didn't understand. As early as 2012, the Nobel Prize–winning writer Elie Wiesel, a Holocaust survivor from a part of Romania that once had been part of Hungary, had seen and heard enough. He announced that he would return the Great Cross honor that had been bestowed on him by the Hungarian Parliament a few years before, to protest what he believed to be the Hungarian government's efforts to "whitewash history."

At the embassy, we continued to do what we could to push hard against the rise of extremism in Hungary. We brought in speakers, we funded programs, and we met with Hungarian officials to urge the government to act more aggressively against hate. I gave speeches and attended memorials, marches, and rallies. I traveled to Auschwitz with the Hungarian chapter of the March of the Living organization and spoke on the steps outside the Hungarian House, a museum located in one of the former barracks. As usual, my remarks felt woefully inadequate in the presence of the few remaining survivors, but I marched with them and thousands of others through the factories of death.

I had seen taped interviews with survivors over the years, but I had never personally met one of them before moving to Budapest. Early in my tour, in 2011, a woman named Aranka Siegal came from her home in New York and asked to meet with me. What was marked on my schedule as a fifteen-minute office call ended up stretching to over an hour as Aranka and I sat together on my office sofa and she shared what her family had suffered.

When Aranka was a baby, in a village named Beregszász, her mother had a close friend who lived across the street. Aranka's mother didn't have enough milk to nurse her, so the friend, a Christian, nursed her instead. But by 1944, when Aranka was thirteen years old, the village had been poisoned by anti-Semitic propaganda. Most of the inhabitants, including the woman who had nursed Aranka as an infant, stood by as the young girl, her mother, her two sisters, and her little brother were deported to the camps.

Aranka would later write a memoir about her experiences, ending with the liberation of the camps by the Allies in 1945. Only she and her older sister survived the ordeal. On my office sofa that day, Aranka told me the details of what happened between her family's deportation and her rescue. It was the story of millions of people who didn't survive to tell it.

Aranka and her family were taken from their house in Beregszász and detained at an empty factory, along with the other Jews from their area. Next, they were packed like animals into a cattle car and transported away from Hungary, traveling for days, surrounded by the sick and dying. Then they arrived at Auschwitz and were put through the "selection": those aged fifteen to thirty-five stood to the right, and everyone else lined up on the left. The first group was kept alive for slave labor, and the rest were sent to their deaths. (On the platform, a man had whispered in Aranka's ear that she should lie about her age.) After the selection, Aranka and the others who were chosen for work were stripped of their clothing, put into rough shirts with holes for their arms, and shorn of their hair. Aranka and her sister worked in a kitchen. Every day, a thick stench hung in the air. "I could see the smoke coming from the nearby chimneys," she recalled. "People told me what the smoke was from. But I continued to hope that somehow it hadn't happened to my dear mother and little brother and sister."

After liberation, Aranka made her way through Sweden to the United States and settled in New York. For many years, she hid her experience from her children because she didn't want them to know what had happened to her. As she explained to me sitting on my sofa, "I just wanted to be a normal American mother, do you understand?"

Two years after Aranka's first visit to my office, we invited her to return to Hungary as part of our well-established embassy speaker program. She did television interviews and shared her experience with students around the country. She and I went together to light candles of remembrance at the Holocaust Memorial Center, a renovated synagogue not far from the center of town. As we left, I had my driver, Zoltán, fasten the American flag on the front of the car. I usually only put the flag up when I was going to a ministry or the Parliament building, but I wanted it waving as Aranka and I rode across town. In the car, Aranka told me something that had happened to her the day before.

She had gone back to Beregszász. There she met someone who used to play with her little brother, Sándor, who had been a small child when the family was deported.

"He told me that he and Sándor would play together all the time. They would play in his yard and pretend they were airplanes, mimicking the warplanes they could see overhead. He said he was too young to understand when his friend suddenly disappeared, so he imagined that Sándor had been taken away on one of those airplanes. All those years, whenever a plane flew overhead, this man told me, he thought of little Sándor." Aranka said that for nearly sixty years she thought that only she and her surviving sister had any memory of their brother. Her eyes welled with tears. "And yet all that time, here was another person in the world who *remembered* him."

I was once told that in the Jewish faith there is a belief that people die twice: once when the body dies, then again when all memories of you are forgotten. At Greek Orthodox funerals, we urge, "May his memory be eternal" and "May her memory be eternal." Hundreds of thousands of people died during and after the Hungarian deportations, from March to July 1944, along with all of the members of their families and many of their friends. So essentially, most Hungarian Jews died twice at the same time: they were killed and forgotten simultaneously, because almost everyone who knew them died too.

Even though I was born in 1966 on the other side of the world, I decided that I would try to remember—really remember—victims of the Holocaust. At the Hungarian House in Auschwitz, I saw a photograph of two young Hungarian brothers standing near a train at the death camp. Just arrived and waiting for the selection, the boys are dressed in traditional Hungarian suits and coats, which appear to be a year or two too small for them. When I look at their shocked, scared faces, I see my own boys' faces. I want to grab them and hug them and reassure them, but they were killed in the gas chambers not long after the photo was taken.

Their names were Yisrael and Zelig Jacob. I will never forget them.

Toward the end of my time in Budapest, former Massachusetts governor and 1988 presidential candidate Michael Dukakis called one day to tell me that he and his wife, Kitty, were coming to town to look for information about her long-deceased grandmother, who had been born in Budapest. They had a few names but little else.

We wouldn't typically get involved with something like this. But I thought Kitty's visit would provide an opportunity to help other Americans find their roots, so we decided to help her look for information about her family's past. By using Kitty's family as a case study, we would be able to create a record of the many resources that existed in Hungary for people to find information about their long-separated families. Hungarians kept meticulous records about everything—not just birth certificates but documents dealing with legal transactions and court cases—in archives and libraries spread around the country. In the end, we found the birth certificate of Kitty's grandmother and the address where her parents had been living when she was born. There were also court documents related to a business dispute, which might have been the reason Kitty's family emigrated to America in 1906.

When John Kerry succeeded Hillary Clinton as U.S. secretary of state in the winter of 2013, some Hungarians rejoiced, but others groaned at yet another reminder of their country's complicated past. When then-Senator Kerry was running for president in 2004, the Hungarian ambassador to the United States, András Simonyi, visited him at his office. Simonyi, himself Jewish, had brought the senator a special gift: a copy of the birth certificate of Kerry's grandmother, who had been born in Hungary. On the certificate, next to her name, was a little letter "i" for "Israelite." Kerry had reportedly known almost nothing about this chapter of his family history.

I don't know if Secretary Kerry will go to Budapest, but I hope he does. I hope he will go there to honor his grandmother and the world she once lived in. I hope he will visit the Dohány Street Synagogue. Built in 1859, it is the largest in Europe. I hope he visits in winter, when there are no tourists, so he can warm it with human life on a day when it would otherwise sit empty. I hope John Kerry will go to the Jewish cemetery, where he can put a stone on one of the 200,000 Jewish graves, including that of Alfréd Hajós-Guttmann, who became Hungary's first Olympic medalist in 1896. I hope he will marvel at the thousands of stained-glass windows of the Parliament building, handcrafted by a Jewish master artisan. I hope he will go to Budapest to meet the wonderful Hungarian people, who have an exceptional sense of humor—sometimes light, sometimes dark, sometimes simple, sometimes complicated—inherited, at least in part, from their Jewish brothers and sisters.

# 18

# Security Overseas

People sometimes ask me what the most exciting moment was during my time as ambassador. I tell them it was the morning we found a fifty-kilo bomb in front of the Chancery building.

I was on my way to the office from a meeting when my BlackBerry buzzed. It was Rick Gregory, the embassy's chief regional security officer.

"Ma'am, I need you first off to tell your driver to turn the car around." He was speaking in an urgent, all-business voice I'd never heard him use before. Instantly, my mind filled with dire possibilities. I didn't know where to go, so I told Zoltán to head to Starbucks.

"What is it, Rick? What happened?"

"Ma'am, the workers in front of the embassy this morning uncovered a live ordnance embedded in the sidewalk."

Ordnance? It took a moment for the unfamiliar word to register. "A bomb? Rick, are you saying they found a bomb?"

"Yes, ma'am. It's an old one from World War II. If it explodes, it won't bring down the structure of the Chancery, but it will blow out all the windows and create quite a bit of damage. Are you willing to give me the order to evacuate the building?"

"Yes!" To make sure there could be no doubt, I added, "I hereby give the order to evacuate the building!"

A few hours later, Rick called me at the residence and reported that the Chancery had been emptied and the ordnance defused and removed. I asked if he could tell which country had dropped the bomb. I hoped it wasn't one of ours. To my relief, Rick identified the bomb as Russian-made. It must have fallen during the Soviet Union's siege of Budapest, gotten buried under rubble, and rested undetected as the capital was rebuilt all around it. The embassy's construction project finally brought it back to the surface.

Later that night, we had a farewell party for my friend György Szapáry, who was leaving soon to serve as the new ambassador from Hungary to the United States. As we enjoyed the sweet cake, decorated with U.S. and Hungarian flags, György leaned over and said, "I understand you found an old Russian bomb today. But you didn't need to evacuate your embassy. We find those bombs all the time here in Budapest, and they never explode."

Maybe so, but I was glad we hadn't taken any chances. The events of the day—the long-buried bomb suddenly appearing amid the BlackBerrys and high-tech construction projects of the twenty-first century—reminded me once again that in Hungary history was never far below the surface.

The incident happened in the summer of 2010, very early in my service. I will never forget how Rick and his staff, junior and senior officers alike, reacted, snapping into action while maintaining absolute calm. They handled the emergency as if they had been waiting for it. In fact, they had been trained for just such an event.

Before leaving the United States, I took the State Department course required for all Foreign Service officers: Security Overseas, a classified seminar designed to scare you so thoroughly that you would never forget what you had learned.

They showed us actual footage from security cameras of government buildings being blown up and embassy cars being attacked. They showed videos of what would happen if you were caught in a stampede or if you ran to a window to investigate a commotion and were standing next to glass when a bomb went off. They told us what to do in case of a chemical attack: "If you smell something strange, don't sniff—don't even breathe." If we did happen to inhale deadly gas, they taught us what to do: "You have about thirty seconds to retrieve your mask from the kit under your desk and put it on. If you think you've been contaminated, inject yourself in the leg with the syringe full of serum."

At that, I timidly raised my hand. "How often have officers had to stab themselves in the leg with the syringe?"

"It's never happened before, but there is enough of a risk of a biological attack that you must be prepared."

Our Security Overseas instructors brought in the most common rudimentary pipe bombs and laid them on a table so we could get a good look. They also showed us how easy it was to make them.

Perhaps the most important thing Security Overseas taught was something they called "situational awareness." Wherever we went, we should pay attention to what was going on around us and who was nearby. We should always be prepared to notice anything odd out of the corners of our eyes. I have to admit, I've never been particularly situationally aware as a security precaution, but Foreign Service officers in general are very good at it. According to my husband, foreign correspondents are too—not just to get the story, but to see if they are being targeted.

Security Overseas provided loads of specific information about how to handle myself as an ambassador abroad, but nothing surprised me more than a general message I absorbed before I left Washington. Even though the State Department would be taking precautions to protect Embassy Budapest and its hundreds of personnel, and even though the government of Hungary was officially responsible for my personal security, my safety was ultimately in my own hands.

Before we left for Budapest, Markos and I had a farewell party at our home in San Francisco. It was wonderful to see friends and family as we set off on our Hungarian adventure. At one point, Nancy Pelosi and I managed to pull away from the crowd to chat in a corner. At the time, she was speaker of the House of Representatives. For the party in our ninth-floor apartment, Nancy's security detail had split up. Guards were with her upstairs in the living room, and I suspected that others were poised wherever they needed to be to protect the woman who was second in line for the presidency after Vice President Joe Biden.

Nancy said that while I might at first think it was exciting to have a security team with me everywhere I went, it could be frustrating and took some getting used to.

But I would have no such team, I told her. "State's Diplomatic Security office briefed me on this a few weeks ago. They said they consider Budapest safe enough for me to travel around by myself." I wouldn't have any security except for my driver.

Nancy had visited many embassies around the world during her twenty years in Congress, and she was surprised to hear that I'd be on my own in Budapest. Her surprise gave me a moment's pause—should I be more concerned about safety? I knew that several of my fellow ambassadors in Europe at the time, like Bill Eacho in Austria and Charles Rivkin in France, were surrounded by security details wherever they went. But others were in the same open-air boat I'd be in. Lee Feinstein, our ambassador to Poland, hopped on a Warsaw streetcar to go to work, all by himself.

Part of me was relieved not to have a security detail. I wanted to be able to roam around anonymously, under the capital's radar. Markos and I were avid walkers, fond of weekend rambles that could last for many miles and many hours. Getting lost in Budapest would be a great way to get to know the people and see the sights, and if nobody knew who I was, I'd be treated like any other American in the city. But at the same time, I was confused. Why did some U.S. ambassadors have so much security and others so little? Even in Budapest, it had swung widely from one ambassador to another. If one of my predecessors ate at a restaurant, he would demand that traffic be shut down on the entire block. My immediate predecessor, April Foley, had arrived to a full detail when she came to Budapest, but after she had lived in the capital a few years, the government of Hungary decided that the security measure was no longer necessary, as well as too expensive to continue.

When I arrived in Budapest, one of the bridges over the Danube was closed for renovation. This caused traffic gridlock during the morning commute and made the already long drive from the residence to the Chancery even longer. Worst of all, the bridge closing limited the routes I could take to get to work. At about the same time each day, I found myself stuck in traffic at the entrance to one of the two bridges that remained open. I called Rick into my office to talk about it.

"In Security Overseas," I noted, "they said we should avoid having our car blocked in the front and in the back at the same time. The traffic on these two bridges is terrible. I'm stopped for long periods of time. Not only that, but since I leave home at eight each morning, right after the boys get on the school bus, my travel is very predictable."

One of Rick's duties was to approve the routes my drivers took to and from the Chancery each day. These routes had to be varied to avoid predictable patterns. "With the Margaret Bridge closed," I said, "I have even fewer routes to work. Can you persuade the police to let my car go in the bus lane?" The Cadillac's license plates indicated that the vehicle belonged to a diplomat, but everyone knew it was the American ambassador's car.

Very shortly, Rick returned with an answer for me. "Ma'am, they won't let us do it. They said you can ride in the bus lane, but you will have to be accompanied by police."

In that case, I asked, would they escort me just during the morning commute? My days had a lot of variety, and I left work at different times, so I figured I could do without an evening police escort. On the weekends, I remained on my own, though Rick gave me some basic guidelines: "Don't make reservations at restaurants unless you do it at the last minute, and don't go to the same place the same time every week—like that yoga class I know you go to every Saturday morning."

He advised me to break up my schedule. "There's no better way to stay safe than having random, unpredictable patterns."

Someone once asked me how President Obama could simply show up at Washington burger joints and schmooze with the patrons when he couldn't go to a D.C. fund-raiser without taking major security precautions. I explained that many people knew the president would be at the fund-raiser at a certain time on a certain day, but no one would ever guess that he was going to stop at a random burger place on a random weekday.

I was not President Obama, and Hungary was one of the safest posts in the world. Even so, I was surprised at first that my security team regularly deferred to me on the topic of my safety—I'd assumed they would lay down the law and tell me how they planned to protect me. Instead, they often noted that I should do whatever I felt comfortable with.

After a few months of morning police escorts, I was scheduled to have lunch with Interior Minister Sándor Pintér. When the hour came, deputy chief of mission Tim Betts and I walked the few blocks from the embassy to the restaurant. At the time, Tim had been in Budapest for only a few weeks. I had been there for about six months.

He said, "It's so strange to be walking with the ambassador without any security at all." Tim had come to Hungary from serving as consul general in Okinawa, Japan, in a country where the U.S. ambassador had a sizable detail. He really wasn't comfortable with this casual arrangement.

As we sat down with Minister Pintér, I noted that we had walked unaccompanied from the embassy. "It's a testament to how safe and secure Hungary is, Mr. Minister, that I could walk here from my office without an escort."

He smiled at me. *"Nagykövet Asszony, ön nagyon bátor."* Máté, who had met us at the restaurant, nervously translated the minister's words: "Madam Ambassador, you are very brave."

I may have been able to walk around the city on my own, but Embassy Budapest had layers upon layers of security. As regional security officer, Rick Gregory oversaw these efforts, which were housed in different places. The members of the marine security detachment, commanded locally by a gunnery sergeant, made sure that classified data located at the embassy stayed secure. During the day, they guarded the front door, standing behind bulletproof glass and checking in visitors. At night, they swept through the embassy looking for any classified information that might have been accidentally left out, such as a cable, and checking for breaches in the information security, like an unlocked safe. I grew accustomed to finding the knickknacks in my office slightly out of place each morning.

The embassy building itself was surrounded by a large contingent of Hungarian security guards. Hired and managed by the regional security officer, they stood at every entrance to the embassy property. Guests had to go through them and a series of metal detectors and scanners before they ever set eyes on the marines. Several of these guards were stationed at other embassy properties around Budapest, including my family's residence.

Many people don't realize that the host country's government is responsible for the security of the ambassador. In Washington, where foreign embassies are located, and in New York, home to the United Nations, the United States ensures the safety of foreign diplomats, often in partnership with local law enforcement. After Minister Pintér's comment about my bravery, Tim and I asked Rick Gregory to go back to the Hungarians to reopen the question of my security detail.

Rick reported back that the Israeli ambassador was the only diplomat in Budapest with a detail. However, he said, the Hungarians now wanted to include me as well.

"I think we should accept, ma'am. As a general rule of thumb, it's never a bad idea to accept the highest level of security that the host country offers. More and more people know who you are now, so it's probably a good idea that you've got company."

That sounded fine, but I hoped to preserve some independence. "Rick, see if you can pitch this. During the workweek, they can follow me everywhere, but if I don't have any official events on the weekend or if I'm leaving the house to do something personal, I can go on my own."

That was the deal we struck. Every Friday, Rick sent a message to the detail to let them know when I didn't have any official events and therefore would not need them over the weekend. As a result, I was free to go to yoga classes, take my kids to the park, and spend time with friends, incognito. But I had to be smart about it.

When I did have the security detail in tow, it was something to see. Trained professionals, they moved their cars around mine quickly yet safely. At crowded events, they formed a circle around me that no one could breach. Before long, I began to feel that I couldn't go anywhere without causing a stir. Once, I wanted to buy a bathing suit before going on vacation in Greece, and I figured I could pick up something simple at the mall. After the cars and security pulled up to the front of the building and I walked inside, the security detail became nearly invisible. But when I walked into the store, one of the members of the detail followed me in, pretending to be shopping for ladies' sleepwear, and I knew I couldn't stay. The last thing I wanted to hear were complaints that Hungarian taxpayers had to fund a team of burly guys to shadow the American ambassador when she got it into her head to buy lingerie. I began to limit my weekday activities to work matters and shop only when absolutely necessary.

The September 11, 2012, attacks in Benghazi, Libya, which killed four Americans, including Ambassador Christopher Stevens, sent shock waves through the Foreign Service. No serving ambassador had been killed since 1979. Officers throughout the State Department, including at Embassy Budapest, had known Chris Stevens, been mentored by him, and loved him. Almost overnight, the department ramped up security at its diplomatic posts around the world as a precaution. I was in no position to reject the regional security officer's firm recommendation that I no longer travel unaccompanied. By then, I was used to the members of the detail, and they were truly professional and dedicated. When I left Hungary to return to the United States, the wife of a member of my detail embroidered two pillows for me with American flags and the words "USA Forever."

The career diplomats at Embassy Budapest had taken the same Security Overseas class that I attended, but their ongoing training went a lot deeper. Emergency drills were frequently held at the embassy. Sometimes they were fairly simple drills, such as what to do in case of chemical weapons contamination: staff gathered outside the building to watch a training officer strip down to his skivvies in order to demonstrate how to take a decontamination bath. Some of the training took hours. The more complicated drills took days. These started with an imaginary scenario—say, a plane had crashed on its way from New York to Rome. Embassy Rome would lead the drill, but officers in embassies all around the region would participate in a mock crisis.

Ambassadors were not required to do these drills. When I asked why, someone joked that in an emergency another officer would be tasked with saving me. The fact was that because most U.S. ambassadors were career Foreign Service officers, they had risen through the ranks of the

State Department and were already very well trained. They were also far more likely than political appointees to be sent to high-threat posts. But I never missed a chance to learn more about how the U.S. Foreign Service functioned, and I wanted to be trained too, so I participated in the drills whenever possible.

During one daylong training I attended, focused on a mock terrorist attack on the Budapest subway, the trainer made an interesting point. He said most people do the same thing in an emergency: they freeze. Foreign Service officers are often the only ones to break out of the shock, because they've had experience in drills and role-playing, preparing for the real thing.

The trainer's point confirmed what I had already come to believe: U.S. Foreign Service officers are among the best-trained people you will ever find during a crisis. Not only do they keep cupboards full of bottled water and supplies, they'll never be caught with less than half a tank of gas in their car. And most important, when there's a crisis and everyone else freezes up, these people begin to mobilize.

The issue of security was constantly on my mind as we worked on the property swap agreement. The real estate deal had been one of my most important projects from my first days in Budapest, and we'd made tremendous progress with the Hungarians on moving it forward. From the beginning, I knew that if I could get it done, there would be huge cost savings for the State Department. But I also realized early on that there would be an even more important benefit.

The Marine House was located on the other side of the Danube from the Chancery. Until the late nineteenth century, Budapest had been two cities, Buda and Pest, separated by a wide, fast-moving section of river. If there was an emergency and the bridges were closed, the protocol the marines would follow required them to climb down the steep side of Castle Hill in old Buda and swim across the Danube to the Pest side of town. Under the property swap, the marine security detachment would move closer to the Chancery.

The improvement in the marines' location from a security standpoint provided a big incentive for me to get the agreement back on track. But at one point, although the Hungarian side of the deal was progressing, I realized that I had another problem, in the State Department itself.

For the property swap to be successful, the Hungarian government had to rebuild the building next door to the Chancery to our very demanding, very particular specifications. The Hungarians had been spinning their wheels for years, unable to meet the complex building codes. I traveled to Virginia, to the headquarters of the State Department's Bureau of Overseas Buildings Operations, to brief them on what I thought it would take to get the deal done. I felt fairly sure that I had the Hungarians ready to move forward on their side. But I said I didn't think the Hungarians would be able to figure out on their own how to renovate the building to satisfy us.

"We have to help them through this process," I explained to a room full of senior officers. "We have to tell them how to build it."

The response was not reassuring.

"Madam Ambassador, it sounds like you're telling us that we need to hold their hand every step of the way."

"Yes, that's exactly what I'm saying."

"We absolutely cannot do that. If we do, we will be incurring liability for a building we didn't build."

"But if we don't," I said, "the Hungarians won't be able to perform. They've already tried, wasting millions of dollars on plans that don't even begin to address the structural requirements. If we can't walk them through it every step of the way, we should end the deal right now."

Fortunately, the next day I had an appointment to discuss the swap with the State Department's undersecretary for management, Patrick Kennedy.

Pat and I had met before I left for Budapest, and we'd really hit it off. He told me that he was a junior officer when President Carter decided to return the Crown of St. Stephen to Hungary and part of the team that moved the crown from Fort Knox to the plane that would fly it home. He told me how the security officer at the plane had refused to accept the box unless Pat verified that the crown was inside. "I had no choice but to unbolt the locks and open it up."

When I walked into Pat's office for our meeting, I presented him with a gift I'd found at the Budapest airport: a Lucite cube with a three-dimensional etching of the crown hanging inside. He was de-lighted to get this present-day reminder of his exploits as a junior of-ficer. As I took a seat, I saw that everyone from the preceding day's meeting was in the room. But this time there was no conflict. They nodded in agreement as I explained the dilemma we faced in Budapest.

"There are a lot of good reasons to do this," I told Pat, "but by far the most important is our security footprint. We have the opportunity to move the marine detachment from far away, across the river, to a loca-tion much closer to our Chancery and where most of our U.S. govern-ment employees work every day."

Pat was quick to agree. Right then and there, he directed the over-seas buildings staff to put aside the liability issue just enough to be able to work with the Hungarians, guiding them throughout the process and doing whatever it took to help them design and construct the new building to our complex specifications.

On those orders, the Bureau of Overseas Buildings Operations staff unleashed a team of its most talented people. Thanks to their hard work, the plans were soon completed and approved, and the long-awaited construction on the new building went forward.

One morning not too long before the end of our tour, I went into my boys' room to wake them for school. As I gently shook my older son, a cell phone slipped out from behind his pillow.

"Neo, why do you have a phone here?"

"Kidnapping," he sleepily replied, before rolling back over in his bed.

In Budapest, my boys were an important part of my team. They politely served cookies to adult guests, patiently entertained kids of all ages, and never complained about anything Markos and I asked them to do. I knew they loved our life as representatives of our country, but until that moment, seeing Neo's hidden phone, it hadn't occurred to me that they might have fears they kept to themselves.

As Neo was getting ready for school that morning, I sat him down to reassure him about his safety. "We have a team of embassy guards, plus the Budapest police out in front of the gates, and there are cameras all around the property. No one is going to kidnap you."

"I know where the guards are, Mom, and I know where cameras are. But this is a big property. Someone could break in and enter the house without the guards seeing him."

When we first moved into the residence, I had my own concerns about security. The house was at the bottom of a hill, and the yard not only extended upward, out of eyesight, but it was packed with thick trees and snarled shrubs that hadn't been pruned in years. Cameras were trained on the front of the house because the overgrown foliage obscured the view of the residence from the guard station just a few feet away. I launched a major tree-trimming and shrub-removal effort, which had improved security and allowed more light into the house. Neo knew all of this, but he still wasn't convinced that he was completely safe.

So I said, "I'm going to tell you something, but you have to promise me that you will never repeat it at school or to anyone." I carefully chose my words, wanting to reassure my son without raising more alarms about the dangers in the world. "Before anyone could get to the gate of our house, our security team would already know they'd hatched a plot against us. I can't tell you how, exactly, but I promise you that we don't just rely on the guards and cameras."

Neo understood that there were aspects to my work that I couldn't discuss, so he let the matter drop. After that, though, he seemed convinced that he and his brother were safe.

As an American ambassador with a top secret security clearance, I came to learn something about the highly talented people who work hard to ensure the security of the United States and our allies. Many of these people are truly brilliant and receive little or no acknowledgment for their important work.

One time I had the privilege of being in the room when an intelligence officer received a medal for gallant service. I can't say anything about where, when, or who was there. But I can tell you that there were no cameras, no family, and no friends. When the ceremony was over, the officer looked at the medal and I witnessed a brief moment of pride. The officer then looked up and handed it to a superior officer for safekeeping. The officer might never see that medal again, and unless the information is one day declassified, only those of us who were present will ever know about the service for which it had been awarded. The United States government employs many such dedicated security experts. I feel very fortunate to have been able to meet a few and personally thank them for their service—as an ambassador, as an American citizen, and as a mother.

# 19

# The New Deal, Same as the Old Deal?

During his 2010 election campaign, Viktor Orbán railed against red tape and bureaucracy. He promised to simplify the tax code, fight corruption, and pave the way for Hungarian entrepreneurs to succeed. Since 1989, corruption and unpredictable regulation had stymied the emergence of a true entrepreneurial class in Hungary. No one who knew the profile of this small but talented country could deny that the right reforms had the potential to transform its economy. At the time, Hungarian talent, from waiters to doctors, was fleeing to work elsewhere in Europe or to start companies in the United States. All Orbán had to do was create a business climate that would entice them to stay and pursue their entrepreneurial ambitions at home. Given that he had overseen the creation of more than seven hundred new laws and a new constitution, surely it was within his power to do this.

But as Orbán's economic policies took effect, it became obvious that they weren't helping business—at least, not most businesses. The tax code was more complicated than ever, and regulation had reached new levels of unpredictability. Along the way, the embassy offered to bring in experts from the States to talk to government officials about how to help small and medium-size enterprises—how to give them the information and tools they needed to be able to start and grow their companies. But these offers were never taken. As time passed, hopes that the reform process would simplify and clarify what businesses needed to do to succeed and create a level playing field for robust competition started to dim.

Then there was Közgép, a company controlled by Lajos Simicska, a college roommate of Viktor Orbán's. Közgép's revenues were estimated to be approximately $182 million in 2009. But in 2010 and 2011, the first two years of the two-thirds revolution, the value of publicly financed projects that Közgép reportedly won from the government (financed in part through grants and subsidies from the European Union) was an estimated $1.3 billion. International companies located in Hungary that ordinarily would have bid for the projects told us it was no longer worth the time and money required to submit proposals, because Közgép was sure to win. As a result, Közgép's bid was often the only one, allowing the company to name its price.

When in May 2012 Gergely Karácsony, a green member of Parliament, accused the prime minister of promoting the interests of Hungarian oligarchs, Orbán responded with patriotic indignation: "Hungary needs large Hungarian companies in the financial sector, the insurance sector, the building sector, the energy sector, the car manufacturing sector, the pharmaceutical sector, the food sector, in information technology, the hotel industry, as well as in every significant sector. Yes, we need highly capitalized, successful companies possessing many billions of forints. If not, then the foreigners will take everything in this country, and I am convinced, whether or not you are aware of this, that in reality when you speak against Hungarian capital, you are conducting labanc politics, which I reject."*

"Labanc politics" was a pointed reference to the seventeenth-century Austrian troops loyal to the House of Hapsburg. These royalist soldiers were easily identified by their long hair wigs, also known as "lobonc." In the context Viktor Orbán used the term, he meant the Hungarians

* http://budapestbeacon.com/economics/kozgep-and-subsidiary-win-public-tenders -worth-huf-32-billion/

who served as labanc soldiers, acting as guards for the Austrian rulers, the Hapsburgs. In his modern usage, Orbán was openly accusing anyone defending foreign investors of working against Hungary's interests and essentially of being treasonous. Here again, we saw the new national narrative in full force: foreigners were responsible for the great disasters of Hungarian history, including the economic crisis that the Hungarian people were currently enduring. The only way for Hungary to reach its potential was to minimize foreign influence on the country. But rather than creating a transparent and predictable business environment that would allow Hungarian companies to rise up through open competition, Prime Minister Orbán appeared to be closing competition to all but a few companies, whose success he sanctioned.

Minister of National Development Lászlóné Németh told me that every week she sat down with Orbán, looked over the list of public works projects, and decided which ones to prioritize and which bids to accept. "If a Hungarian company's bid is competitive with one from an Austrian or German company, then yes, they will win," she explained. "Why should German companies be building Hungarian roads? And if Közgép is the only Hungarian company that can do it, why shouldn't they continue to win the bids?"

The problem was, Hungary's EU membership required it to treat all EU-based companies the same as its own. But even if you were sympathetic to the idea of giving Hungarian companies an advantage in the competitive European marketplace, there was a much more troubling development in the country's business circles.

In the past, smaller Hungarian companies typically joined bids to perform part of the work of the larger companies. Now I had heard from at least three credible sources, in confidence, of a new way that business was being done. If they wanted to bid, they had only one possible partner: Közgép. And if they didn't agree to the partnership terms offered by Közgép, they ran the risk of finding themselves out of business.

The clout amassed by companies connected to Orbán and his cadre was growing daily. In the spring of 2012, the respected anticorruption organization Transparency International reported that the Hungarian state had been "captured" by private interest groups: "Due to the weakening of checks and balances and the inability of the control institutions to limit the power of the government, private interests prevail over public interests." Through the tireless work of our commercial counselor, Rob Peaslee; our commercial attaché, Marianne Drain; and our economic affairs officer, Jay Heung, we came face-to-face with the realities of the new Hungarian economy, and we were forced to acknowledge that the conclusion drawn by Transparency International was fundamentally, and very unfortunately, well grounded in fact.

Just about the time that Transparency International released its report, I received word that Nancy Pelosi would stop in Budapest on her way home from a visit to Afghanistan. Every year, the Democratic leader traveled to Iraq or Afghanistan to visit U.S. troops on Mother's Day. She was traveling with five other members of the House of Representatives, all women, including another Northern Californian role model of mine, Anna Eshoo. The trip was long enough that it usually required a stopover somewhere in Europe. I asked Nancy to take the opportunity to visit Budapest as a way to help commemorate the ninetieth anniversary of diplomatic relations between the United States and Hungary.

When Nancy came off the airplane in Budapest on a chilly May evening, I was there, jumping up and down on the tarmac to stay warm. It was Mother's Day, and the symbolism was very, very special to me. We hugged, then quickly got into the car to escape the cold. I will never forget driving her into town, overflowing with stories about all the things that had happened so far during my tour.

Nancy was a master at finding just the right touch to commemorate an event, and she had tracked down the treaties between the United States and Hungary, signed by President Warren G. Harding and then–Secretary of State Charles Evan Hughes on December 20, 1921. She'd had the ninety-year-old treaties reproduced and bound in stately leather books. We went to the Parliament building, and Nancy presented the books to the Hungarian speaker of Parliament László Kövér and to Viktor Orbán.

This was a powerful diplomatic overture but, truth be told, the two Hungarian leaders gave Nancy and her bipartisan delegation a cool reception. For more than twenty years, U.S. representatives had been warmly welcomed in Budapest regardless of their political party. Though Orbán was polite to the delegation, he appeared to receive us not as close friends and NATO allies but as foreigners whose opinions about the Hungarian reform process were not welcome.

Orbán opened the meeting as he always did when I brought high-ranking American officials to visit: he talked about his own life as a freedom fighter. As he did, something clicked into place for me. Freedom, to Viktor Orbán, did not mean personal liberty within the rule of law, as it did to the ancient Greeks and as it does to Americans. To Orbán, Hungarian freedom meant freedom from the influence of anyone who wasn't Hungarian.

Nancy was slated to deliver a speech that afternoon, but first the members of the congressional delegation and I had lunch in a private room on a restaurant boat on the Danube. Between sips of goulash soup, the congresswomen remarked on the energy that sizzled all over Budapest. Construction projects were rising out of the earth; historic monuments were being repaired and restored; and glorious old buildings, some scarred from bygone wars, were being cleansed of decades of soot. It was difficult to explain why, in spite of the headlines about the negative impacts of Orbán's economic policies that the delegation had seen in their briefing papers, the restaurants were crowded, tourists were everywhere, and business generally seemed to be booming. Nancy had last visited Budapest in the late 1980s, before the fall of the Iron Curtain. Now she could see the contrast from nearly twenty-five years before, and she was amazed by it.

After lunch, it was time for Nancy to deliver her speech at a local museum, the House of Terror. Despite its Halloweenish name, the House of Terror was a serious Budapest institution devoted to illustrating and explaining the horrors of life under fascism and communism. Many eschewed the House of Terror on the grounds that it gave the Holocaust short shrift compared with communism. Even though I agreed with the criticism, I often recommended that visitors go there anyway (but also visit Budapest's separate Holocaust museum). The House of Terror, for all its imperfections, was an important monument to the forty years Hungary had suffered under a totalitarian system.

The museum was run by Mária Schmidt, a historian, a well-known

Fidesz loyalist, and a serious admirer of Nancy Pelosi's. Mária realized early on that I had a special relationship with the Democratic leader, and for two and a half years, she had asked me, "When will she come to Hungary? She is the most powerful woman in the history of American politics, and we want to invite her here to speak!"

Now Mária welcomed Speaker Pelosi to the museum, along with historians, journalists, and women leaders whom the embassy had asked to be invited. We'd also asked a group of young Roma women to come hear Nancy speak, and they were there in full force.

I took the podium of the packed room to introduce the U.S. Democratic Party leader. In saying her name, I was so excited that I accidentally said "Peloshi," pronouncing the "s" the way the Hungarians do. I could hear some tittering in the crowd. My years in Budapest were starting to show.

Nancy began by speaking about Cardinal József Mindszenty, a remarkable man who had suffered in the name of tolerance and freedom during Hungary's long decades of oppression. As the country's Roman Catholic leader during World War II, Mindszenty spoke out against the deportation of the Jews, and the Hungarian Nazis imprisoned him, in the same building that later became the House of Terror. The cardinal was released after the war, then he spoke out against the Soviets, and they jailed him too. Mindszenty was freed again in 1956, during the Hungarian uprising, but when Soviet tanks rolled into Budapest to crush the revolution, he had nowhere to hide—except the U.S. Embassy. No one knows exactly what happened that day, but the marine security guard on duty at the Chancery let the cardinal come inside. Once safely past the threshold, Mindszenty would stay in the Chancery for nearly fifteen years. He lived in rooms that would one day be my office, while U.S. Embassy life buzzed all around him.

Much of the furniture in my office had belonged to the brave cardinal, and I felt his presence all around. Not long after I arrived, I found a portrait of Mindszenty that had been unceremoniously stored in a closet. I pulled it out and hung it over my desk. Often I would turn around, look into the cardinal's steely yet saintly eyes, and remind myself that not many years ago he had lived, prayed, and studied exactly where I was sitting.

The portrait also had a strong effect on Nancy Pelosi, who shared the experience with her audience at the House of Terror. As a young Catholic girl in the 1950s, she said, she had prayed every day for Cardinal Mindszenty. But that wasn't the only reason she had been affected. "It was particularly moving to see his picture this morning because yesterday was Mother's Day in America," she noted. Nancy recalled that when she was a little girl, her mother had penned a poem to her grandmother, inspired by these words of the cardinal: "Mother, I think of you, I dream of you. Who can fathom the true meaning of the word 'mother'? Even when it is said by an old man, it sounds like it's coming from the lips of a child."

As Nancy recited these lines from memory, everyone in the packed lecture hall at the House of Terror—Mindszenty's former prison—sat mesmerized, enthralled by both the cardinal's tender words and their profound effect on an American political leader.

After concluding her remarks, Nancy spoke to a group of local journalists, fielding questions about Hungary's recent constitutional reforms as knowledgeably and deftly as if she had been steeped in the controversy for years. At one point, she was asked about the media law. Nancy responded by talking about the importance of a free media to any democracy. Then she said, "If I had to choose just one freedom—just one—it would be freedom of the press, freedom of speech. Everything flows from there. Don't you think so?"

The Hungarian journalists present represented media outlets from across the political spectrum. By raising the sensitive issue this way, and letting her own opinion be inferred, Nancy made a powerful yet diplomatic point. I could see the faces of the reporters change as she spoke. She was getting through to them. Possibly, I thought, they will gain a fresh sense of courage in this stifling climate, which had been fostering self-censorship.

I'd known Nancy Pelosi for a long time, but more than once during her visit to Budapest I was freshly reminded of her boundless intellect. I have long believed that her achievements and capabilities have not been fully realized by the American public. The four years that she was speaker of the House were four of the most productive in our country's history, including the passage of the Affordable Care Act, which brought health care to millions of Americans. Nancy never seemed to mind personal attacks against her, as long as they didn't inhibit her ability to lead the Democrats in Congress and do a good job for the American people. I felt very fortunate that I had been given a window into her leadership.

Just a few weeks after Nancy's visit, I went to see President Bill Clinton at his New York office, uptown in Harlem. I first met then-Governor Clinton in 1991, soon after he announced his intention to run for president. I started out as a volunteer on his campaign and served as one of his delegates when he ran for reelection. Now it was June 2012 and I was in New York for my younger sister Chrysa's wedding. I asked for a visit with the former president even though I didn't really have an agenda. I just wanted to thank him for his support over the years and say again how proud I was to have grown up as a "Clintonite."

The president, on the other hand, was very keen to talk to me—about foreign policy. How did the Hungarians see the reelection of Vladimir Putin just a few months before? Were they concerned about the effect of his reelection on energy security for Europe? He then peppered me with questions about the various pipeline proposals that were competing to bring gas from Azerbaijan to Europe. He also wanted to know how the Eastern Partnership—the EU and U.S. effort to build closer business and diplomatic ties with countries in Eurasia, especially Ukraine—was going. I straightened my spine and did my best to brief him. President Clinton listened intently, checking once to look at his phone when it buzzed. "Hillary is the only one who has this number," he explained, quickly reading the message, then putting the phone back in his jacket pocket.

President Clinton seemed satisfied with my briefing. But he had one more question for me. "Eleni, you know Viktor Orbán. What do you think of him?"

I considered for a moment, calculating my words carefully.

"Mr. President, some people say he's crazy. I don't think that's right. I see him as a very smart, very rational man. But he doesn't seem to me to have the same concept, the same definitions as we do of democracy, freedom, and even free markets. I think he sees himself as the only one who can protect the Hungarian people from what he believes are corrupting outside influences." I paused. "But when it comes to the larger issues we've been talking about, like energy security for Europe and the Eastern Partnership—and Afghanistan—we are still very much on the same page as the Hungarians. They are as much a reliable partner on international issues now as they have ever been."

Not long after I spoke these words to President Clinton, Hungary faced a decision that pitted its economic interests against its diplomatic ones. The choice would, for the first time, shake our faith in the country's reliability as a partner and cast a pall over our relations.

Ramil Safarov, a citizen of Azerbaijan, was serving a life sentence in a Hungarian prison for the ax murder of an Armenian man named Gurgen Margaryan. The two of them had been in Budapest in 2004, participating in a NATO-sponsored program called Partnership for Peace. The program brought soldiers from non-NATO countries together to train them in English and build friendships among them. It was designed particularly to foster trust between European states and those of the former Soviet Union.

Azeris and Armenians were historically antagonistic, and at the time the men's countries were engaged in ongoing territorial disputes over the Nagorno-Karabakh area. One night, Safarov sharpened an ax he had just bought at a superstore and hacked the sleeping Margaryan to death. He later claimed that the Armenian had been taunting him.

Hungarian foreign minister János Martonyi was a talented statesman and a committed transatlanticist. He was so well regarded that not long after his appointment, the European Union's high representative for foreign affairs, Lady Catherine Ashton, asked him to travel to South Korea and attend meetings in her stead. Though he did so with great distinction, that kind of inclusion ended after the first international outbursts over Hungary's reform process. Martonyi never lost his professionalism or composure, but by the fall of 2012 he appeared to be losing influence.

Orbán's spokesman, a very young, charming, and savvy former public relations professional named Péter Szijjártó, had been given international business issues as part of his portfolio. Members of the diplomatic community were whispering that as business matters grew in importance to the prime minister, Szijjártó—unquestionably loyal to Orbán—was sometimes acting as the de facto foreign minister. More and more, Orbán took his young spokesman, and no one else, to meetings with foreign leaders if the agenda included business issues. Hungary's relationship with Azerbaijan had grown in significance thanks to the latter country's gas reserves, and Szijjártó was tasked with managing it. Azeri gas was expected to be delivered to Europe through one of many competing pipelines. Hungary wanted to ensure that it would have access to the gas and, if possible, find itself in a strategic location along the chosen route.

On the morning of August 31, 2012, the embassy received some shocking news. The Hungarian government had agreed to a prisoner transfer that allowed the ax murderer Safarov to go home to Azerbaijan. This happened very quietly. Our embassy was not notified— possibly not even Foreign Minister Martonyi was notified—until after Safarov was already on a plane and out of Hungarian airspace. The Hungarian government explained that prisoner transfers were very common. As long as the prisoner's home country signed documents promising to carry out the sentence in one of its own prisons, Hungary would transfer him.

As anyone at the Foreign Ministry or our State Department could have predicted, a few hours after his release from Hungary, Safarov landed in Azerbaijan and walked off the plane to a hero's welcome. Within a few more hours, the president of Azerbaijan had given him a full pardon. The ax murderer was immediately promoted to the rank of major and given a new apartment and eight years of back pay.

Armenia was furious. The United States and our allies were stunned. The appropriate place for me to register our dissatisfaction with the decision was the Ministry of Foreign Affairs, but as we sat in his office, Martonyi could barely look me in the eye. He feebly attempted to defend the transfer on the basis of the fact that the Azeris had signed the paperwork saying Safarov would stay in jail. But we both knew this document, like the government's argument, was a charade.

The relationship between Armenia and Azerbaijan had only become worse since 2004, when Margaryan was murdered, and the United States, along with Russia and France, was working hard through the

Organization for Security Cooperation in Europe to defuse the tension over the Nagorno-Karabakh region. The Safarov transfer reverberated through the State Department. The deputy assistant secretary for Central Europe at the time, Marie L. Yovanovitch, had previously been the ambassador to Armenia and knew the issue better than anyone. "Don't they realize that their little trick could cause a war?" she fumed to me from Washington. "Who will clean it up—Hungarians? No, Hungarians won't clean up the mess. We will! We will be the ones left to fix it!"

Though my engagement on this matter should have started and ended with my visit to see Martonyi, my deputy Tim Betts and I decided that we should probably go see Péter Szijjártó too. We found the young PR man cavalier and beaming with pride.

"Madam Ambassador, the agreement was signed in good faith," he assured me. "It isn't our fault that the Azeris went against their word. We can't control their decision-making process." He asserted that rumors that the oil-rich Azeris would give Hungary a large loan or another quid pro quo in exchange for Safarov's release were false. "They couldn't possibly do anything like that now," he said cheerfully.

Of course, I knew very well that such actions were the kind that would never be forgotten. When the dust settled, Hungary would have a new friend. I said so and reiterated to Péter what Ambassador Yovanovitch had said to me earlier in the day. Maybe if he understands what could happen, I thought, he will grasp the seriousness of this. But my argument did not appear to sway his point of view.

Leaders around the world face decisions like these all the time. Usually, the friends and allies of the United States consult widely to ensure their decisions won't hurt international efforts to advance security and stability in the world. These efforts are often led in large part by the United States, and our allies understand we take on this role for everyone's benefit. Our friends and allies often go to great lengths to be helpful, even incurring economic costs, to at a minimum avoid actions that will create instability.

That is what the Hungarian Ministry of Foreign Affairs might have explained to Péter Szijjártó had he checked in with them. As soon as Safarov's release became public, Armenia severed diplomatic ties with Hungary. But because Szijjártó was tasked with dealing with

international business and Armenia held no particular interest for him
in that regard, this serious consequence would not affect his portfolio.

We at the embassy had to accept that with this action, relations had
unquestionably changed between Hungary and the United States.
Hungary had been our reliable partner for more than two decades. Our
cooperation with the ministries of defense, interior, and foreign affairs
remained strong in many areas, from Afghanistan to regional law enforcement. But Hungary itself was now being run by a very powerful,
unpredictable, and—from our perspective—less reliable leader. If Viktor Orbán was capable of letting business considerations overrule larger
issues of regional stability, how could we depend on Hungary to support us when the next problem arose?

One night toward the end of my time in Hungary, I gave a dinner party
at the residence for about a half dozen senior members of center-right
Hungarian think tanks that actively supported Orbán's government.
Some of them were paid handsomely by the government to serve as
pollsters and advisers. Others weren't on the payroll but were philosophically supportive of the government's policies and actions.

I decided to have the dinner because on many occasions during the
previous three years, I had put these same policy experts at the table
with their harshest critics. They were always gracious about attending
the gatherings, where they defended the government and explained the
grand vision behind the two-thirds revolution. Our embassy-arranged
meetings served as some of the only instances during the reform process
when pro-government policy experts faced their critics. It wasn't always
easy to keep them coming back, as the discussions could get pretty
heated—and the accusations against them pretty nasty—but they did,
with impressive tenacity. This dinner was a chance for me, and half a
dozen members of our team, to ask hard questions on our own without members of civil society or the opposition present to launch their
own complaints and criticisms. I was determined that these Hungarian
policy leaders should not feel attacked. I hoped to dig a little deeper,
possibly challenge their thinking, and I genuinely wanted to hear what
they had to say.

On the whole, it was a relaxing night. At one point, as we sat elbow to elbow around my long dining table, splendidly set with the State Department china, the conversation turned to government policies that directly conflicted with my guests' own theories of sound economics—policies that were anticompetitive or led to the nationalization of companies. I asked them how they could harmonize these policies with their own beliefs in free markets.

For a few moments, the group fell silent, stuck; then the sharpest among them took the question.

"Madam Ambassador," he began, "you have served during the most interesting time in Hungarian history since communism ended. We believe what you have witnessed is the New Deal for Hungarians. Some of the changes have been very drastic, and ordinarily we might not support them, but drastic measures had to be taken to fix the problems that have existed here since we started building our democracy in the early 1990s. One day, we will all see whether or not the New Deal worked and lifted our country up."

I could see from the faces of the others around the table that they agreed with him. They were confident that Hungary was on the right track, taking control of their national narrative and bolstering their own national economic interests.

As my guests thanked me for the dinner and said their good nights, I appreciated their willingness to share their beliefs with me. But I had to wonder whether things would work out for them as they hoped. All through dinner, they had recognized that many time-tested fundamentals of economic and public policy were being shunted aside by the two-thirds majority and the prime minister. But they were willing to support these policies because they believed the circumstances justified them. They thought they were getting a New Deal. I reflected to myself that it sounded an awful lot like the Old Deal, with government having too much control over the people of Hungary all over again.

# 20

# Afghanistan, Revisited

In the spring of 2012, Embassy Budapest buzzed with its usual activity, but there was a little sadness in the air. The senior officers who had made up the core of my team from the time I arrived in Hungary were scheduled to depart for their next assignments. Fortunately, my deputy and by then very close associate and friend, Tim Betts, would stay until the following summer. But Paul O'Friel, Rob Duggleby, Ed Loo, Jeff Lodinsky, Rick Gregory, and Tom Larned were all going to leave. Senior officers rotate to new posts every three years, so people were always coming and going. But some years, you had what felt like an exodus, and this would be one of them. Saying good-bye wasn't easy, not just because we had worked together as a close-knit team for the previous two and a half years. It was also difficult because Paul, Jeff, Rick, and Tom had all volunteered to go to Afghanistan.

By any calculation, this was a big number of senior people to rotate at the same time from the same post to Afghanistan. But State Department officers are always encouraged to accept postings in hardship locations at various points in their careers. Why did these four decide to do it now? At least part of the reason was that their families would be able to stay in Budapest. Unlike ordinary posts, extreme hardship posts had shorter durations, usually of one year. Allowing families to stay in Budapest for the extra year, in their same houses, was very convenient for people who generally spent their lives moving from place to place. It was partly dependent on my agreement, and I had told everyone that if they wanted to go from Budapest to Afghanistan, I would work to ensure that their families could stay with us.

It seemed to me that an extra year would provide a reprieve from the constant packing, unpacking, and relocating required of career Foreign Service officers. Three of the four men had kids in high school; it would make a big difference if these children could spend one more year at their schools. I was proud of the choices the guys had made, but I was a bit concerned that my assurance that their families would be taken care of had factored into their decisions to volunteer for this dangerous mission. Although I myself had been in Afghanistan in December 2010, the bloodiest year of fighting, I was only there for a few days. These officers would go for a year, tasked with difficult work in the middle of a war zone. I couldn't help worrying.

In April, as they prepared for their departure, Rob Duggleby walked into my office with some exciting news.

"Good morning, ma'am. I've just heard that Admiral James Stavridis will be traveling to Afghanistan in just a few weeks, and he has invited you to join him." Stavridis was the supreme allied commander of NATO.

Colonel Duggleby and I both knew that even though I'd been to the war zone before, I wouldn't miss the chance to go again, nearly two years later. I would be part of a small delegation of diplomats from NATO member states that often accompanied Admiral Stavridis on his trips.

"This time, you probably won't need your sleeping bag, ma'am." Rob explained that this trip would be quite a bit different from the one I took with the Hungarians.

I boarded Admiral Stavridis's plane at an airfield outside Brussels early on a Tuesday morning in the beginning of May. The NATO commander had about a dozen members of his staff with him, including Stephanie Miley, a woman from the State Department who served as

his senior civilian adviser. In addition to Stavridis's staff, his delegation included four diplomats. Besides myself, there were two women
ambassadors, from Sweden and the U.K., who were posted to NATO,
and another American ambassador, Robert Mandell, who was newly
posted to Luxembourg. I noted that the Swedish ambassador, who
had been to Afghanistan many times before, wore beige and army-
green clothing. I did too, having learned from my previous trip that
black clothes only made me stand out amid all the sand-colored desert
uniforms.

I joked to Stephanie that with so many women making up the delegation, maybe this was a "girls' trip" to Afghanistan.

Our conversation soon turned to a more serious discussion, and I
asked her, "What is it like for you, as a woman, to work at such a high
level within the NATO command?" Stephanie answered that she'd
never had any issues working with other Americans, up and down the
chain of command.

"What about the Muslim men you work with in Afghanistan and
elsewhere? You're Admiral Stavridis's top civilian adviser. Do they
have trouble with that?"

"There are a lot of women in our military and State Department who
have worked very successfully in these environments," she replied. "I've
found that many Muslim men in less developed parts of the Middle
East see three kinds of people in the world: men, women, and American women." American women, she explained, were seen as unique
creatures who drove cars, wore pants, and stood tall with their male
counterparts.

Hearing this, I was quietly proud of the brave American and Western women who had helped to create this perception. If only more
Muslim men were willing to see Muslim women the way they saw us.

My trip with Admiral Stavridis had far fewer transfers than my previous visit and far less waiting around. Clearly, there were advantages to
traveling with NATO's supreme allied commander. We flew directly
from Belgium to Afghanistan, landing at the Kabul airbase, where
I was given a cozy little room in a trailer, with my own bathroom,
shower, and television. Colonel Duggleby was right—I didn't need a

sleeping bag this time. The bed was made up with clean sheets and a soft blanket.

We stayed two nights in Kabul, making day trips to two other large coalition bases. These bases were the best protected, and as a result the most commonly visited by delegations like ours. On this trip, I wouldn't wake up in the morning to the sound of bombs dropping nearby or witness a machine gun operator hanging out the back of a helicopter. This expedition was more typical for a visiting diplomat. But it was no less interesting.

The briefings we received made it clear that things had changed quite a bit in the two years since my last trip. The members of the International Security Assistance Force were preparing for a complete transfer of power to Afghan forces in the spring of 2014, just a year away. I asked the commander how General Petraeus's strategy—"Don't take what you can't hold; don't hold what you can't transfer"—had fared. It had worked very well, he said, but now there was an additional principle. Instead of trying to train the country's police and security forces to our standards, the "Afghan good enough" standard was applied: good enough training to ensure sufficient stability that the rule of law could continue to develop, unhindered by insurgents; good enough progress that the country could continue to build its fledgling democratic institutions. Overall, Admiral Stavridis appeared to believe that postwar Afghanistan had a good chance of maintaining its stability and not reverting to serving as a training ground for al-Qaeda.

Up in the north, at the international forces base in Mazar-e-Sharif, we met with members of the local police, who were ready, willing, and able to take control. This was considered one of the most stable parts of the country, and the first phase of the transfer would start here. The commanders were also optimistic that the training of the Afghan security forces and police was going very well. However, when we went to southwest Afghanistan, the regional command in Helmand Province, the situation was much more sobering. As Admiral Stavridis's plane descended, we saw vast fields of poppies abutting the boundary of the base.

I was pleased we were visiting Helmand because Paul O'Friel would be arriving there in a few months to serve as the senior civilian adviser to the regional commander. I took the opportunity to tell the commander that he was about to get a stellar officer, but the commander didn't seem all that excited. The fact was, he was having a tough time in Helmand. The situation was not stable, and he was about to lose thousands of marines in the drawdown. No matter how talented Paul was, it would be challenging and dangerous work for all of them.

Back in Kabul, on our last night, we were invited to dinner at the home of General John Allen, the four-star marine general who commanded the U.S. troops in Afghanistan. Even though the Afghan food he served us was delicious, the conversation quickly took our attention away from the meal. General Allen had invited several guests to discuss the political situation in Afghanistan. One was a woman who served as a member of Parliament. She was smart and impressive, possessing a vast amount of knowledge and experience related to both domestic and international affairs. But when the conversation turned to the issue of corruption, she said something shocking.

"We are a third-world country," she noted, "so you cannot expect that things can be done here without the elements of a third-world system." Instead of telling us what the Afghans were doing to fight corruption, she argued that we should accept it as the status quo.

Hearing this, I had to respond. I explained to her that I understood the realities, but if the best and the brightest Afghan government officials weren't trying to stem corruption, that was a problem for the United States. "If the American people know that their tax dollars are going to build schools for children, produce clean water, and help teach modern farming techniques, they will support these things," I said. "They'll do it not just because they're generous but also because they believe our leaders, who tell them that funding development makes a difference in achieving global stability. But if American taxpayers hear that their dollars are going into the Swiss bank accounts of Afghan politicians, they won't tolerate giving another penny."

The conversation eventually turned to poppy farming. Again, the Afghan parliamentarian spoke up. "I am trying to get a bill passed in our Parliament that would legalize poppy farming for the purpose of producing medicinal opium." The opium produced in Afghanistan constituted a large part of the world's supply.

"But there isn't anywhere near enough demand for medical uses to justify even a fraction of the supply coming out of Afghanistan," I noted. "And the harm that heroin does is staggering." Once again, the legislator and I found ourselves in disagreement.

Even though the Afghan politician and I could not see eye to eye on these important subjects, I empathized with her personal struggle. She told me that when the Taliban took over in the 1990s, killing working women in the streets and revoking women's rights in general, she'd had to fight to survive. Now, under the fledgling democratic system, she was an elected official, empowered within her country. The International Force and the United States were working in Afghanistan in part to help lay a social foundation that included basic freedoms for women. I worried that night at dinner, and I still worry, about what will happen to these women leaders if the Taliban regains power in their country.

As we were preparing to leave Kabul to return to Brussels, Admiral Stavridis called the members of his diplomatic delegation back, one by one, to his neatly appointed office in the rear of his plane for debriefing. Taking a seat across from the NATO commander, I told him that I'd heard him say during one of the meetings that he could not find another country to provide the security force at the airport base after the Belgians left Kabul. Drawdowns had begun, but in strategic locations like Kabul they were needed for at least another year.

"Admiral, the Hungarians have been stationed in Kabul in the past—maybe we could persuade them to take another rotation."

"Do you really think they would?" he asked, incredulous.

"I think that if we need them to help, they will do their best to help," I replied, quickly adding, "The only thing is, they probably won't have the money to fund such an effort."

"Everyone else is set on drawing their numbers down," the NATO commander said. "We can find grants to help cover the costs. You tell Minister Hende that if he does this for us, he will be my best friend."

Back home in Budapest, I delivered the message to Csaba Hende, the defense minister with whom I had first traveled to Afghanistan, and the Hungarians responded with incredible speed and surprising flexibility. They knew they would have to apply for the funding through U.S. and NATO channels, and that it would not be approved or guaranteed until long after they'd made the commitment to help in Kabul. "I think it will come through, but I can't promise you," I told the defense minister.

It was a different Csaba Hende I met with that afternoon—we had both been changed by our jobs. I was silently grateful for Rob Duggleby's efforts to help me build a strong relationship with him and with the Ministry of Defense. I remembered when Rob had me lead a group from the U.S. Embassy to swim across Lake Balaton with the Hungarian Defense Forces. I placed in the top third of all swimmers, dragging myself out of the water three miles later. Before the news cameras could get to me, Rob's wife, Ginny, waded into the lake to hand me a pair of glasses to replace my swim goggles and a hat to hide my matted hair. Thanks to events like that, our team at Embassy Budapest had developed a genuine kinship and sense of trust with our defense counterparts.

Soon after we asked them, the Hungarians told us they were willing to take a leap of faith, and they made the commitment. While every other nation's troop contributions to the International Security Assistance Force declined, Hungary's would increase by more than two hundred soldiers. Just two years before, Csaba Hende had hinted that his country was looking for ways to pull out of Afghanistan. Personal relationships were important—over time Csaba and I had truly become friends, even bicycling fifty miles together around his home province in southwest Hungary—but this latest decision was based on something much bigger. The mission in Afghanistan was dangerous, and victory would be elusive. But Csaba and his team had come to strongly believe in the importance of Hungary's NATO membership in ensuring the safety and security of their country. They knew they could not contribute as much as other, wealthier countries. But they had an opportunity to do something strategic and very helpful, and they took it.

The continuing dangers of Afghanistan were much on my mind as Paul, Rick, Jeff, and Tom prepared to leave Budapest. They would be arriving during the drawdown, possibly the most perilous time for them to be there. I decided that the least I could do was throw them a farewell dinner. I had heard about a local cooking school that did large groups, and I signed us up. Senior staff and spouses gathered for a night of cooking supervised by Hungarian chefs, but we would be cooking Greek cuisine—the school gave me a choice, so naturally that's what I picked. Hours of chopping, stirring, and drinking later, we sat down to a feast of heavily seasoned Greek delights. After dinner, I asked the four guests of honor each to say a few words. They were all heartfelt and funny, but I will never forget what Jeff Lodinsky said that night.

By the luck of the draw, Jeff was going to a base in southeast Afghanistan, the most dangerous part of the country, near the Pakistan border. Insurgents were still strong in the area. While Jeff did his tour in Afghanistan, his Hungarian-born wife, Judit, and their kids would stay in Budapest.

Jeff had been an important voice as the embassy navigated the fast-moving events of Orbán's two-thirds revolution, going beyond the scope of his normal consular duties. He listened to Hungarian radio, he read the papers, he talked to his in-laws—he was really wired in. I was going to miss his contributions, and I was going to miss him, an all-around great person who had enthusiastically participated in the embassy community, even joining our Balaton swim team. As Jeff stood up to speak, I remembered when, just after the January 2010 Haitian earthquake, he immediately volunteered to fly to Port-au-Prince, where he lived at the heavily damaged airport for two weeks, issuing passports to U.S. citizens who had lost everything in the disaster.

As Jeff gave his toast that night, I noted that even though he wore a brave face—all the wives of those going to Afghanistan were sitting there listening to him—he was worried about the upcoming tour and what he would encounter.

"Sometimes," he said, "I ask myself, why did I volunteer for this? It's so wonderful here in Budapest, and I don't want to leave!" He laughed and continued. "Then I remember that the kind of work we do in Afghanistan—well, that's the reason I signed up for the Foreign Service in the first place. This is what I decided that I wanted to do with my life."

This simple, eloquent declaration of purpose left us stunned for a moment, then we applauded, loudly, inspired by Jeff's words and courage.

———

A few months later, when the summer transition was over and the four guys had settled into the four corners of Afghanistan, I was in a meeting in my office. Suddenly, Tim opened the door and asked me to step out. Foreign Service officers are trained to be steely and calm under pressure, and Tim had the reputation that nothing ever threw him off balance. But I could see by his expression that something very bad had happened.

"Jeff Lodinsky was in a suicide bomb attack," Tim said in a low voice. "He's alive, but he was injured pretty badly, and several of the people with him were killed. Judit already knows." Tim delivered the awful news clearly and concisely; I could just barely make out his eyes faintly watering and a slight twitch of his mouth.

I returned to my office to finish my meeting, trying not to show how shaken I was. For the moment, there was nothing we could do but wait for more news. Eventually, we learned that the suicide blast had knocked Jeff to the ground. He had been wearing his kit: a helmet, a bulletproof vest, gloves, and goggles. But his legs were unprotected, and his right leg was in bad shape. The sergeant major walking on his left and the USAID worker walking to his right were both dead. Their bodies had likely shielded Jeff from worse injury.

The next morning, we told senior staff what had happened. "Let's just pray, all of us," I said, "that he was knocked unconscious and woke up in the hospital."

Medics in Afghanistan managed to stabilize Jeff, who was flown the next day to a military hospital in Germany. Tim made arrangements for Judit to get there immediately. (For months, he and our management team handled the red tape that would ensure Jeff's family was taken care of.) Though very worried, I knew there was nothing I could do just then, so I kept my plans to travel that same day to Greece with Markos and the boys. As we walked into our hotel room in Messenia, my BlackBerry started to buzz.

"Ma'am, this is the Operations Center in Washington, D.C. Are you available to take a call from Landstuhl Regional Medical Center in Germany?" The doctor got on the phone and told me that Jeff was there. He had just woken up, and he wanted to talk to me.

"He is on a lot of medication and may not make sense," the doctor warned. "But he insisted that we call you. Try to let him keep talking as much as he can, since it's good for him to recount what happened." He put Jeff on the phone.

"Oh, Ambassador, it was terrible." The medications made Jeff's speech sound extremely slurred. "Ragei is dead, and the sergeant major is dead. It was terrible." Ragei Abdelfattah was the USAID officer and a friend of Jeff's.

"Do you remember what happened, Jeff?"

He struggled to describe the attack. "We were going from the base to a meeting with the district governor. They said it was too close to take a helicopter and we could just walk there. We were walking along a ditch, and suddenly this boy pushed himself through the barrier to where we were walking. I could see he had something under his robes. I looked right into his face, I looked right into his eyes, I saw him pull back his robe and push the button, and then boom! Ambassador, it was terrible," Jeff repeated. Slurred and halting, he sounded so different from the precise, confident man I knew. "When I woke up, I couldn't hear anything. I guess my ears were all screwed up. I saw Ragei—his eyes were open, but I knew he was dead. I could see the sergeant major was dead too. I looked down to see what happened to me—my left leg wasn't too bad, but my right leg didn't look good at all, and my shoe was gone."

He went on, trying to describe the horror he'd witnessed. "I saw the boy, Ambassador. I locked eyes with him. He was just a kid. I don't hate that boy, Ambassador. I don't hate him—he should have been out playing with his friends. I saw his face at the last second, and I could see he knew what he was doing was wrong."

For what seemed like forever, though it was only about fifteen minutes, Jeff kept repeating what had happened to him and his companions. Finally, the doctor told him it was time to rest. Before he got off the phone, Jeff said in the sweetest voice, "Ambassador, I just have to tell you something. I love you! Don't tell Markos, but I love you for how you take care of my family, for how you take care of all of us."

I started to cry. I told him I loved him too and that everything would be okay. Then I called Tim.

"He saw everything," I told Tim. "He was conscious the whole time." A few minutes later, we hung up and realized that Jeff Levine, the embassy's deputy chief of mission when I first arrived in Budapest, probably didn't know anything yet—and he and Jeff Lodinsky were like brothers. I called him in Washington and broke the news. Then I walked outside to meet Markos, at a party our friends were having at the beach bar of their beautiful resort. Everyone was still in beach clothes, movie stars mingling with Greek politicians as all the kids played in the sand. The contrast with what I'd just heard was too much for me. I walked off and found a place where I could sit, quietly watch the sun set, and reflect on what had happened.

We found out later that the attack had been carried out by not one but two suicide bombers, who detonated their devices simultaneously. Jeff spent several months at the Walter Reed National Military Medical Center, in Bethesda, Maryland, to repair his leg and try to save his hearing. I visited him at Walter Reed soon after the incident, and he shared more details of the bombing. As he lay deafened, surrounded by carnage, his training kicked in, and he'd dragged himself into the ditch in case more attacks were coming. As a result, he wasn't immediately found. As he waited in the ditch for someone to help him, he wondered if he would die there because no one could see him.

Out of the whole terrible experience, Jeff was most devastated by the death of his friend Ragei, who had emigrated to the United States from Egypt and volunteered to go to Afghanistan not long after joining USAID. Jeff and Ragei had worked together at the base. "As we were walking along the pathway, Ragei kept looking around and saying how beautiful everything was, and how excited and happy he was to be there, serving his new country, doing his duty for America."

When Jeff learned he would be honored by the State Department for his heroism, he argued that he didn't deserve it—the honor should go to the men who died. I reminded him that things were different now. He was a symbol to every Foreign Service officer. They all knew that their work was perilous and that over a lifetime of service this kind of thing could happen to any of them. That Jeff had not only survived but recovered was important for all the diplomats who went into dangerous places and risked their lives.

I saw how Jeff suffered through his recovery. But I also saw what kept him going through those difficult days: his love for his family and his faith in the important work he'd dedicated his life to. Jeff was determined to be back on his feet in time to take up his post as the deputy consul general at Embassy London. After a long year of surgeries and therapy, he made it to London on time.

# 21

# Farewell

By the summer of 2013, my time in Budapest was almost over.

President Obama had just named my successor. Once that happens, the sitting ambassador starts to feel a little like a lame duck. Three years is the standard amount of time for a U.S. ambassador to serve at a post, and I had already been in Budapest six months longer than I anticipated, so that my boys could finish out the school year and there wouldn't be too much of a gap before my successor arrived. Of the team in place at Embassy Budapest when I arrived in the winter of 2010, I was one of the last U.S. officers still there. The rest had gone on to new postings around the world. Changes were happening at State Department headquarters as well: Hillary Clinton had passed the baton to the new secretary of state, John Kerry.

My last day at work was set for July 25, 2013. Markos and I decided that we would move the boys to Greece a month early, and that he and they would enjoy the summer there as I tied up loose ends and prepared to move out of the residence. When I packed the boys' suitcases, I loaded them with Neo and Eon's favorite Hungarian sausages and made sure to pack their well-worn collection of Nerf guns. As I ran around the house gathering the last few items, Eon sat down at the piano in the larger of the two connecting salons. A musical boy, he had taken quite a few guitar lessons in Budapest. Now, slowly, he pressed down the piano keys and played a made-up tune that sounded like a funeral march. Remembering the old Hungarian adage, with one eye I smiled, thinking that Eon had somehow picked up the essence of the Hungarian national anthem. And with one eye I cried, realizing how hard it was for the boys to say good-bye.

Neo and Eon had loved their time in Budapest. Not only were they proud to represent their country, and proud of me as well, but they'd had a lot of fun, making Hungarian friends, Chinese-speaking friends, and friends from across Budapest's international community. My two California kids had jumped feet-first into Central European winters, discovering the joys of snow forts and ice skating. They would return to their family and friends with lots of stories and rich experiences, and (we later discovered) a better grasp of Mandarin than many of their classmates in San Francisco.

A few weeks before, I had visited former secretary Clinton at her home in Washington, D.C. She asked me about the boys. I said, "All this time, Hillary, they thought they were working for you too."

She clapped her hands, laughing. "Well, tell them I said they did a wonderful job, and thank them for their service!"

When I shared this with the boys, they received the news straight faced, like professionals, and noted that they had, after all, been well trained in their duties.

Moving around the house, getting the boys ready to fly to Greece, where Markos was waiting for them, I realized that I'd grown comfortable in the old residence. The floors still creaked and the radiators clanged, but the house had slowly become our own, brightened by laughter and love. The residence staff was sad to see Neo and Eon go, and the boys were going to miss them a lot too. But when the three of us got into the back of the Cadillac and we pulled away from the residence, I was the one who started to cry.

"Mom, we've never seen you cry before!" Neo said.

That was true—except for the occasional sad movie or TV commercial, they had never seen tears stream down my face. I tried to explain. "Boys, we came here when you were seven and eight years old. Now you're eleven and twelve. In a way, we're leaving your childhood behind in this place."

I wasn't sure if they completely understood, but I knew that one day they would.

I had already started making my farewell calls—bookends to the courtesy calls I had paid upon my arrival. Protocol required that before leaving Hungary I make the rounds of government officials, opposition leaders, business leaders, and civil society members. I discovered that saying good-bye was very different from saying hello. I had spent years immersed in Hungary's changes and controversies, giving me a much deeper understanding of the country. I also had developed a strong affection for the people and their culture. As I said my good-byes, I was sad that my ambassadorship was over, but I knew that I would see many of these people again. I knew that I no longer was just an American, and a Greek American, I was also part of the greater Hungarian diaspora. Hungary is such an opaque and complicated country that once people have an intimate experience with it, they tend to stay connected. Just like my predecessors, who had regularly returned for visits after I'd taken the ambassador's office, I intended to come back one day. Then *I* would be able to sit on the sofa.

The best farewell call of all was with Foreign Minister Martonyi, who hosted a lunch for me at the historic Gundel restaurant, in the heart of Budapest. Members of both our senior staffs attended. The menu included foie gras, roasted duck, and other of my favorite traditional Hungarian dishes.

Before presenting me with an exquisite vase made by the renowned Hungarian porcelain company Zsolnay, the minister shared some surprising news. After our lunch, he would announce that the Hungarian constitution would be amended. The court authority would no longer be able to transfer cases from one venue to another. It was an issue that I had been pressing him on for nearly three years and that the European Commission had consistently raised. Tim Betts shot a meaningful look at me, clearly pleased.

It was a wonderful lunch, with amity on both sides. János Martonyi was one of my favorite people in government, and despite all the bumps in the U.S.-Hungary relationship, the two of us had developed a genuine friendship. As I looked around the table at the smiling Hungarian and American faces, however, I wished that my time in Budapest had been entirely characterized by cooperation. Instead, it had been dominated by U.S. concerns over the direction of Hungarian democracy.

As if he was reading my mind, Martonyi leaned across the table and said, "You know, Ambassador—Eleni—I do believe that you helped us."

I knew that it was true. The embassy's engagement had been important—appropriate, constructive, and helpful. But I wondered what the future held. I would leave, but events would march on.

When lunch was over, the minister and I shook hands and warmly smiled at each other. The constitutional amendment encouraged me, but, as I reminded myself once more, Hungarian democracy was in the hands of Hungarians. They and only they would determine how Viktor Orbán's two-thirds revolution would turn out.

I had one more event to look forward to: my fourth and final Independence Day celebration at Embassy Budapest. The previous year, hoping to soothe the rising tensions between the United States and Hungary a little bit, we'd decided to lighten the mood with a Wild West theme. Guests were invited to wear jeans and cowboy attire instead of their customary suits, and everybody loved it. This year, Linda Mézes suggested a Hawaiian-themed party. After all, the Aloha State was President Obama's childhood home, and we could do great things with decorations. We spread the word that once again guests could leave their suits at home—this time, the dress code called for Hawaiian shirts. I wondered if tropical shirts would be hard to find in Budapest. But I soon learned that, oddly enough, they were one of the first things people could buy in the nineties, after the fall of the Iron Curtain. "Almost everyone has one somewhere in the back of their closet," a Hungarian official assured me.

Next, we had to arrange entertainment. Was it possible to find Hawaiian hula dancers? I entrusted the task to Linda, who had a gift for fulfilling seemingly impossible requests—she was the one, after all, who had found the opera singer to perform on short notice for Janet

Napolitano. With her usual skill, Linda tracked down a local hula dance group to entertain at the party. With blue Hawaiian cocktails flowing and everyone in their flowered shirts, the party was a great hit. Among our guests was Sándor Pintér, Hungary's interior minister and a longtime partner with the United States on law enforcement issues. He was a serious person, but when I put a flower lei around his neck, he burst into a wide smile. By the next day, the photo had gone viral around the country—the tag line was that it was the first time anyone had caught him smiling so happily.

That final embassy Fourth of July party was held on the property surrounding the residence rather than in the Táncsics Mihály compound. This had a symbolic purpose. By having the party at the house, I wanted to send the message that the historic Táncsics Mihály property would soon be back in the hands of the people of Hungary. A few weeks before, the Hungarian government, with our participation, held a "topping-out" ceremony for the annex building next to the Chancery. Early in my tour, I had managed to remove the roadblocks on both the Hungarian and U.S. sides that had nearly killed the project. Once that happened, progress was made quickly and efficiently. Though I would not be ambassador when the property swap deal was wrapped up, I was there to celebrate the completion of the work on the annex building all the way to the rooftop. It was a tremendous feeling. Early on, during the complex twists and turns of the swap project, I'd sometimes doubted whether I would be able to close the deal, as we used to say in real estate development. Yet it was, for all intents and purposes, done.

Protocol also required that the departing ambassador request a farewell call with the prime minister. But just like the first time my office had asked for a meeting with Viktor Orbán, we were not sure he would agree to it. Nothing with Orbán was ever easy, I'd learned, and that held true to the very end. Tim Betts came into my office one day to report, "He's invited you to come now, in an hour. And he wants a one-on-one."

It broke every rule of protocol in the book for the prime minister to offer a meeting this way and on such short notice. But I understood that it was classic Viktor Orbán to try to catch people off guard, and, in any case, I was determined to have a final sit-down with him.

Most of my meetings in Orbán's office had taken place at a long table filled with representatives of both our countries. This time, the two of us sat at a small round table in the middle of the cavernous room. I'd come with no agenda, no talking points, no instructions from Washington. I just wanted to make one last try at getting our message through to him.

I started our meeting by telling the prime minister how much my family and I had loved living in Hungary, how much we appreciated his country's history and culture, and how much we had enjoyed the wonderful things to do, both in Budapest and in the countryside.

Rather abruptly, Orbán cut in. "Have you ever read *The Unbearable Lightness of Being*?" I quickly switched gears and responded that, yes, I had. I'd read Milan Kundera's famous novel when I was in college and the Berlin Wall was coming down. In fact, Kundera had been my favorite writer in those days, and I'd read almost all of his novels.

Orbán continued. "We Hungarians suffer from the great heaviness of our history. You Americans suffer from the lightness of yours." He looked at me, waiting for a response.

Time suddenly slowed down, and my mind began to race, just as it had on that afternoon years before when I found myself crouched in a boar blind in a cold, strange landscape. Back then, I was new to Hungary and a little unsure of myself, but I trusted my instincts and experience. Now, more than three years later, I knew Viktor Orbán, and I knew that Kundera had been a voice for those who demanded freedom for Soviet satellite states like his own Czechoslovakia and Hungary. Kundera's iconic books helped the free world viscerally understand all that was wrong with autocratic, dictatorial government. Now I chose my words carefully. Maybe, just maybe, Viktor Orbán had given me an opening, a chance to pierce his thinking.

"Mr. Prime Minister, to Kundera, freedom meant the ability to live free from oppression—especially free from oppression by your own government. That's what democracy is all about."

His eyes narrowed and he waved his hand abruptly as if to beat away the comment. "All this talk about democracy is bullshit!" I drew back. By this point, I knew Orbán well enough to know that he probably didn't mean to say that democracy was bullshit, but that he rejected, and resented, my raising the subject with him again.

"We had an election, and the people gave me the power and the responsibility to lead this country," he said. "We had a lot of problems, and I'm doing my best to fix them. If people don't like what I do, they will have another election and they can vote for someone else."

I couldn't let that go unchallenged and tried again. "Mr. Prime Minister, in the United States we believe that government should be accountable to the people every single day, not just every four years."

"I am accountable to the people every day!" he insisted. "And if they don't like what I've done on any of those days, they can let me know on Election Day."

It was very clear where each of us stood on the topic. We'd had similar discussions before, and we weren't going to get anywhere this time either. At least, I thought, I had given it my best shot. We both rose, and he walked me to the door. Then he stopped me.

"I know how much you tried to learn about my country," Orbán said. "I know that you liked it here and you respect us. You are welcome back to Hungary any time."

I thanked the prime minister and left his office. I knew that I would return to Hungary in the future. But I would return as a citizen and never again as the ambassador extraordinary and plenipotentiary of the United States of America.

As for the United States, we weren't going anywhere. The new embassy annex would open the following year, and a new ambassador was scheduled to arrive even sooner. U.S.-Hungarian relations would march on. I had taken a baton from my predecessor. I would now hand it off to my successor, with the hope that relations would not just continue but somehow strengthen over time.

It was July 25, 2013, and my car was speeding along the highway, through miles of lush Hungarian farmland on the way to Austria. I would meet Markos and the boys in Greece, and then we would return together to San Francisco, to our family and friends and the city we loved. As the landscape swept past my window, my thoughts were tugged backward to my arrival in Budapest more than three-and-a-half years earlier and all that had happened along the way.

As I neared the Austrian border, leaving Hungary for the last time as ambassador, I realized that no other country could have given me the same experience. No other country could have given me the same mix of beauty, strangeness, excitement, frustration, challenges, and joy.

I would certainly miss my life as an American ambassador. But I'd always held close the knowledge that it was an extraordinary—and temporary—situation. I knew that I was returning to a life where no one would salute me each morning, where I would more likely be called "miss" than "ma'am." Where I would drive my own car and cook dinner for my growing boys.

But I felt ready to go back to that life, because I knew I had made the most out of every day of this extraordinary experience. I had strived to do my job well and to make sure that I lived up to the faith that President Obama and Secretary Clinton had placed in me by sending me to Hungary as our country's envoy. It had truly been the honor and the privilege of my life.

Although I had no idea what my future held, I knew that no matter how many decades passed, I would always be called Ambassador Kounalakis. I also knew that whatever I did with the rest of my life, I would continue to take every opportunity to advance the interests and the values of my country. I had been raised as a patriot. But my love of country had deepened in a way that I could never have imagined. I am completely convinced that the United States, with all of its faults, remains what Abraham Lincoln called "the last best hope of earth."

THE SECRETARY OF STATE
WASHINGTON

May 10, 2013

The Honorable
Eleni Tsakopoulos Kounalakis
American Ambassador
Budapest

Dear Madam Ambassador:

Thank you for your exceptional service as the Ambassador of the United States to Hungary. You have skillfully maintained the strong, mutually beneficial elements of our bilateral relationship with Hungary while effectively addressing our concerns over some of the sweeping changes the Hungarian government has implemented that undermine democratic institutions.

Your efforts convinced the Hungarian government to maintain its Provincial Reconstruction Team in Afghanistan until its mission was completed, won Hungary's agreement to take on new missions in Afghanistan, led to Hungary assuming status as our Protecting Power in Libya in 2011, and cemented a relationship with the Ministry of Interior that—during Hungary's EU presidency—was instrumental in concluding the U.S.-EU Passenger Name Record Agreement negotiations. Your personal involvement was critical in reviving a moribund property exchange agreement that will triple the size of the current Chancery—largely at the Hungarian government's expense.

You have been clear and candid about our concerns under the current government regarding the weakening of Hungary's democratic institutions and rising extremism in Hungary. The balance you struck in your tone, both publicly and privately with the Hungarian government, gave the U.S. government credibility on these issues and resulted in the Hungarian government making positive changes in areas such as the judiciary and proposed limits on media content.

Your leadership and commitment to public service have been exemplary, and I extend to you my best wishes for future success.

Sincerely,

John F. Kerry

# ACKNOWLEDGMENTS

There are many people who were instrumental in the writing and publishing of this book. Some of them are well known, while others may be less known but were equally important. I am grateful to them all for their support and assistance.

President Barack Obama provided me the honor and privilege of serving as his ambassador to Hungary. I am deeply grateful for the faith he placed in my abilities and for the opportunity to serve our nation. Secretary Hillary Rodham Clinton led the State Department during most of my tenure as ambassador. Her leadership as secretary of state made it possible for Embassy Budapest to carry out our duties with clarity and confidence. Democratic Leader Nancy Pelosi provided mentorship, encouragement, and advice for many years before my posting, throughout my time in Hungary, and to this day.

Writing this book required the assistance of several former colleagues who served with me at U.S. Embassy Budapest. Ambassador Jeffrey Levine, Timothy Betts, Paul O'Friel, and Colonel Robert Duggleby assisted greatly in the early stages of my writing—offering comments, checking facts, and reaffirming details. Linda Mézes and Máté Hegedűs at Embassy Budapest also contributed fact-checking assistance, comments, and the proper spelling of Hungarian names and places.

Consul General Jeffrey Lodinsky may reject being called a hero, but he was a hero to me even before the suicide bomb attack that nearly killed him in Afghanistan. I'm grateful to him for his service to our country, for his sacrifice, and for allowing me to tell his story. I thank them and many other former colleagues for their assistance not just in writing this memoir but for all they did during the years we worked together under challenging circumstances in Budapest.

The New Press has been an exceptional partner in the publication of this memoir. I am especially appreciative of the expertise and tireless work of Diane Wachtell, Ellen Adler, Jed Bickman, Sarah Fan, Sharon Swados, Maury Botton, Julie McCarroll, Raquel S. Avila, Chelsea Slosky Miller, Esi Hutchful, and Bev Rivero. I am also very grateful to the talented Ruth Hamel for her early assistance—as well as her sharp pencil, smart edits, and warm encouragement. Terry Phillips provided editing and much-needed support during my toughest writing period. Huma Abedin, Dave Eggers, David Streitfeld, Edward Loo, Tomicah Tillemann, Kati Marton, Ellen Hume, Annabel Barber, William Antholis, Amanda Jones, Gregory Maniatis, Judy Chu, Todd Werby, and Congressman John Sarbanes read all or parts of this book in its final stages and gave me advice, encouragement, and assistance. Professor István Rév of Central European University provided valuable insight for my summary of Hungarian history.

John Kerry served as secretary of state during my final months of service. I am grateful for his leadership and for the hard work of Anne Barbaro, Alden Fahy, and Behar Godani in the Department of State Office of Information Programs and Services. They worked tirelessly to advance this manuscript through the difficult and complex clearance process, and Anne Barbaro went beyond the call of duty, pushing for timely decisions and even providing helpful advice and edits. I would also like to acknowledge the many other U.S. government officers who worked on processing this manuscript for clearance, including officials at the State Department's Bureau of European and Eurasian Affairs and Regional Security Office, the U.S. Department of Defense, the U.S. Department of Justice, and officers currently serving at U.S. Embassy Budapest.

Many people appearing in this book provided important feedback during my writing process. Thank you to Secretary Hillary Rodham

Clinton, President William Jefferson Clinton, Democratic Leader Nancy Pelosi, U.S. Supreme Court Justice Anthony Kennedy, Secretary Janet Napolitano, Secretary Condoleezza Rice, Ambassador Marie Yovanovitch, Ambassador Karin Olofsdotter, Major Jason Seery, Stephanie Miley, Susie Buell, and Ambassador Tod Sedgwick. I am also grateful to Dennis Chang and Anja Manuel.

Many of the photographs in this book were provided courtesy of the State Department and taken by two talented former colleagues, Attila Neméth and Samaruddin Stewart. My friend the professional photographer Barbara Vaughn allowed me to use several photos that she took during her family's memorable visit to Budapest. I am also grateful to Sophie Cohen at the Cobalt Law firm for her expert legal advice during the publishing process. George Stamas at Kirkland Ellis has provided indispensable legal and personal advice. Chris Donnelly worked tirelessly to meet complex U.S. government reporting requirements during and after my service, and Tawny Por provided important administrative and accounting assistance.

Anyone writing a book knows how daunting a task it can be. The decision to start writing was made much easier by the early and enthusiastic encouragement of many friends, especially Christine Pelosi, Ayelet Waldman, Irene Pappas, Monique El-Faizy, Edie Lambert, Pasha Thornton, Costantza Constantakopoulos, Kathryn Lowell, Gina Papan, Mary Pat Bonner, Eleni Korani, Amy Conroy, Efi Papadopoulos, Marybeth Shimmon, Matina Kolokotronis, Nancy Ruiz, Izabella Zwack, and Grace O'Friel.

For nearly eighteen years before I became an ambassador, my father, Angelo Tsakopoulos, and I worked together side by side. He taught me important business tools and leadership skills, sometimes through coaching, sometimes by pushing me to try even when he knew I might stumble. I am enormously humbled by his life story. I am grateful for all he taught me and very, very proud to be his daughter. I also thank my four sisters, my mother, and my stepmother, who all helped me and provided support and encouragement during my years in Budapest.

Finally, I would not have this story to tell if it weren't for Markos Kounalakis. Markos opened a world of possibilities for me, encouraged me to aspire to become an American ambassador, and supported and assisted me each step of the way. Our sons, Antoneo and Evangelos, were unofficial ambassadors of our country and my own special junior officers. I am grateful for their unwavering support and for their dedicated service to our country.

# ABOUT THE AUTHOR

Ambassador Eleni Tsakopoulos Kounalakis served as the U.S. ambassador to Hungary from January 2010 until July 2013. She now chairs the California International Trade and Investment Advisory Council and is a senior adviser to the Albright Stonebridge Group. She lives with her husband, veteran journalist Markos Kounalakis, and their two sons in San Francisco.

# Publishing in the Public Interest

Thank you for reading this book published by The New Press. The New Press is a nonprofit, public interest publisher. New Press books and authors play a crucial role in sparking conversations about the key political and social issues of our day.

We hope you enjoyed this book and that you will stay in touch with The New Press. Here are a few ways to stay up to date with our books, events, and the issues we cover:

- Sign up at www.thenewpress.com/subscribe to receive updates on New Press authors and issues and to be notified about local events
- Like us on Facebook: www.facebook.com/newpressbooks
- Follow us on Twitter: www.twitter.com/thenewpress

Please consider buying New Press books for yourself; for friends and family; or to donate to schools, libraries, community centers, prison libraries, and other organizations involved with the issues our authors write about.

The New Press is a 501(c)(3) nonprofit organization. You can also support our work with a tax-deductible gift by visiting www.thenew press.com/donate.